CLUB COLOURS

CLUB COLOURS

An illustrated history of football clubs and their kits

THIS BOOK IS DEDICATED TO FRANK
WHO INTRODUCED ME TO THE DELIGHTS OF FOOTBALL

The author would also like to thank the following:-
Angie, Zoë and Blaise for their daily forbearance, the rest of his family and friends for their support.
Tony Williams, Geoffrey Peters, Barry Hugman, Ivan Ponting and Bernard Gallagher for practical and professional advice and further encouragement.
Rex Carr for his assistance in the production and David Scrace for inspiring him to illustrate again.

And last but not least, all the club secretaries and representatives who kindly replied to his requests for information, many of whom are obviously budding artists in their own right.

Acknowledgements
Publishing Director: Laura Bamford
Creative Director: Keith Martin
Cover design: Vivek Bhatia
Design Manager: Bryan Dunn
Editor: Adam Ward
Picture Research: Zoe Holtermann
Production: Bonnie Ashby

First published in Great Britain in 1998 by Hamlyn
an imprint of Octopus Publishing Group Ltd.,
Michelin House, 81 Fulham Road, London SW3 6RB.

ISBN 0 600 59542 0

Printed and bound in China

Photographic acknowledgements in Source Order

Bob Bickerton 9 Top Right
Colorsport 8 Centre Left
Empics 8-9 Centre

Jacket picture
Hulton Getty Picture Collection

INTRODUCTION

Either at home or in the pubs, fans young and old will always argue about the relative merits of players and teams. There will be heated arguments about dates, colours, goals, the successes and the failures.

This book contains a simple story about each of the clubs which have played in the Football League, their own glory days and the strips worn at the time. We trace the progress from the days when they wore caps and knickers to the present when sponsors and replica kits are the norm.

There have been unique sartorial contributions from most of the clubs as well as many major surprises from the past, when spots, sashes and halves were commonplace.

Check the story of the team's kit against a detailed record of each club's performances on a year-to-year basis, and see if your father was exaggerating when he compared his team with yours.

CONTENTS

KEY TO THE FOLLOWING CLUB RECORDS

LEAGUE

1	First Division
2	Second Division
3	Third Division
4	Fourth Division
3N	Third Division North
3S	Third Division South
Pr	Premier Division
N1	New First Division
N2	New Second Division
N3	New Third Division
C	Champions
P	Promoted
R	Relegated
(pl)	Via Play-offs
L	Failed to gain re-election

FA CUP

1,2	Round of Cup reached
qf	Quarter-finals
sf	Semi-finals
F	Finalists
W	Winners
q	Qualifying Rounds
p	Preliminary Rounds
e	Extra Qualifying Rounds
Sc	Scratched

Note: The years given on the club records pages refer to the second half of the season, e.g. 1977 refers to 1976/77.

PREVIOUS LEAGUES

AL	Athenian League
APL	Alliance Premier League
CL	Cheshire League
GL	Gola League
GMVC	GM Vauxhall Conference
IL	Isthmian League
LC	Lancashire Combination
ML	Midland League
NC	Northern Counties League
NE	North Eastern League
NP	Northern Premier League
SD	Scarborough & Dist League
SL	Southern League

THE COMMERCIAL ERA

As we approach the new millenium and witness the ever increasing commercialisation of football, it is difficult to imagine life before club superstores - a time when kit and supplementary clothing were not designed for the fans but the players themselves.

Now in England, as in many other parts of the world, even High Street shop windows are full of shirts not only of the local teams but of clubs many thousands of miles away!

But clubs have prized their individual identity - as displayed in their kits - for well over a century and today's retail bonanza has resulted from a gradual evolution of styles, colours and patterns through many fashion eras.

The following pages illustrate how the clubs have developed these very marketable images and why the fans associate successes and failures with the many variations.

Above: Robbie Fowler in a Liverpool away shirt - one definitely designed with the fan in mind.

Main picture: One of the many club superstores around the country.

TOPPER
UMBRO
SHARP
MANCHESTER UNITED
FOOTBALL CLUB
CREDITOR
THE HEART AND SOUL OF

DO YOU KNOW YOUR COLOURS?

Almost every schoolboy fan, young or middle-aged reckons he knows the colours of all the leading clubs of the land. It is not for nothing that clubs are nicknamed the Canaries, the Sky Blues, the Magpies or the Red Devils. In fact, it's hard to imagine Best, Charlton and Law and their predecessors playing in anything other than red. In that other great Lancastrian city, Liverpool, any mere suggestion of red or blue immediately identifies any fan's allegiance.

However, although football often values great traditions and most clubs have remained loyal to their adopted colours, many of today's famous teams began their existence sporting very different hues.

It is only when one delves into the detailed early histories of these clubs that it becomes clear why they adopted their original colours and also why these were eventually changed.

Illustrated left are 11 clubs, either currently in the top division or ones who have spent many years there. Without cheating, can you identify any of the familiar names?

To help, here is a list of the clubs involved, although in a different order:-

COVENTRY

EVERTON

LIVERPOOL

MANCHESTER UNITED

MIDDLESBROUGH

NEWCASTLE UNITED

NORWICH CITY

QUEEN'S PARK RANGERS

SUNDERLAND

WEST BROMWICH ALBION

WOLVERHAMPTON WANDERERS

image.
10 Liverpool: 1892-1893
The blue and white were leftovers from the Everton days. The now famous, traditional red was introduced to contrast with Everton.

11 Wolverhampton Wanderers: 1877-1879
The original St Lukes club wore red and white. After amalgamation with the local Wanderers club, they changed to old gold and black.

GUESS THE FAMOUS CLUBS

Answers

1 Sunderland: 1879-1885
The Wearmouth club originally sported an all blue strip which brought them no success. Red has often been associated with winners.

2 Newcastle United: 1893-1902
The red and white stripes belonged to the original Newcastle East End club. They changed because of too many colour clashes.

3 Coventry City: 1883-1891
Black or black and red were the colours of the Singer Cycle Factory. On becoming Coventry City they were altered to the traditional city colours.

4 West Bromwich Albion: 1883-1884
In the early days, the club wore a different bizarre strip every season. A sober blue and white was introduced to 'prevent wolf whistles'.

5 Queens Park Rangers; 1897-1926
QPR originally wore green and white to avoid clashing with local rivals Paddington. They turned to blue to help change the club's fortunes.

6 Middlesbrough: 1890-1894
The team wore blue and white to differ from breakaway Middlesbrough Ironopolis, then reverted to red on the latter's demise.

7 Everton: 1899-1903
The ruby red shirts were the last of a series of bizarre versions. Everton reverted to blue to reflect their professional status.

8 Norwich City: 1923-1927
The blue and white was a throwback to the very first strip.

The yellow and green returned to reflect the 'canary' image.

9 Manchester United: 1878-1893
The yellow and green belong to the earlier Newton Heath period. Eventually, the Manchester United club wanted a new, modern

BIZARRE EARLY STRIPS

With the recent tremendous technical advances in printing on woven materials, we have become accustomed to multi-patterned, rainbow coloured football shirts. However, until the last decade, prohibitive costs and conservative thinking restricted many possibilities, and most club jerseys were fairly bland and not very individual.

But in the early years of organised football, and again in the 1920s, many clubs were more concerned with either being true to the old school and church colours, or going to the other extremes of total originality in order to stand out against the crowd.

Before many of the existing Football League clubs had become preoccupied with status and the presentation of a professional image, they too had sported some of these exotic and often bizarre early strips. Some are featured here (right), but there are many others which will be recorded later in the club sections.

Often there was no deliberate club policy to wear specific colours or even to change them. West Bromwich and Everton, for example, in their early history wore whatever strip was available locally, often changing with every new season. The situations at Stoke City and Wrexham were very similar, with

TRANMERE 1889-1904

EVERTON 1881-1882

NORTHAMPTON 1897-1899

YORK CITY 1932-1936

WATFORD 1900-1909

LUTON TOWN 1885-1886

T BROMWICH
1881-1882

STOKE
1877-1878

CARDIFF CITY
1899-1900

COVENTRY CITY
1923-1925

LACKPOOL
1915-1916

BOLTON WANDERERS
1884-1885

BRISTOL ROVERS
1883-1885

vastly different outfits used as they changed every few years.

Some clubs chose to wear strips in unusual combinations because of a particular linkage with other organisations. York City once changed to chocolate and cream because of the support of many workers in the local Rowntree and Terry's factories. Coventry's first strip was black because, being the Singer bicycle factory side, they had to sport the company's colours. Featured here is a later Coventry uniform of red and green, the city's civic colours, worn when the club first took the City title. Even Northampton, having had a wonderful chocolate and blue strip, as shown, changed to claret and white, the county colours, in order to attract a wider audience.

Of course, there were some clubs who chose spectacular kits just for the hell of it. Tranmere, for example, changed from the established blue and white to maroon and orange, simply to 'dazzle their opponents'. Bristol Rovers introduced their later blue and white quarters also to impress their opponents and Bolton's red spots were certainly not designed to present a conservative image!

It's doubtful whether we will ever again see the likes of Luton's matching shirt and cap, or the sashes of Everton and Bristol Rovers, but if the recent revival fad continues, it's not so improbable to think of Cardiff in a chocolate and amber away kit.

ARSENAL

When one thinks of Arsenal's place in world football and their famous strip that has influenced so many around the globe, it's hard to imagine that their first set of red shirts came as a gift from Nottingham Forest. And yet, in 1886, when a few pennies scraped together by the workers of Dial Square in the Woolwich Foundry bought a ball, it was the midland club who gave the strip to remind some of the 'Arsenal' players of their previous connections with the Forest.

The club developed slowly from humble beginnings. The club's name changed from Dial Square to Royal Arsenal, Woolwich Arsenal, The Arsenal and finally in 1919 just Arsenal; and during the same period there were just as many grounds. It was as if the club were looking for an identity and a consistency. Apart from a short spell in the 1890s, when they wore one-inch red and blue stripes, the all-red shirts remained. First division status was attained, but by 1919 Arsenal had yet to set the world on fire. It took just two events to change that in 1926. They moved from their Plumstead backwater to Highbury and then persuaded Herbert Chapman, the architect of Huddersfield's supremacy, to join them as manager.

From the start of the 1930s, the club started to take off and became a dominant force, lifting the Cup in 1930 and the League in 1931. Chapman, however, was planning even more. For further efficiency on the field, the Yorkshire genius introduced white contrast sleeves and blue and white hooped stockings, so the Arsenal players could spot each other more easily. This, plus an assembly of British internationals, ensured that the Gunners added four more League titles and a FA Cup win in the next seven years. Sadly Chapman died early, but George Allison and Tom Whittaker ensured further successes after the War. However, from 1954 to 1969 Highbury suffered a barren period of frustration and disappointment.

It took the unlikely managerial appointment of Bertie Mee, previously the club's physiotherapist, to restore much of the glory. Working closely with Don Howe, he organised a highly efficient combination which followed a UEFA Cup win with a well-earned League and Cup double. The title was clinched on an emotional night at White Hart Lane against arch rivals, Spurs; then Liverpool were beaten at Wembley.

During those unrewarding 1960s, the club had toyed with all-red shirts again, but it was the now traditional white sleeves which had witnessed the modern revival. Even in the highly successful George Graham era, the Gunners took great care with kit presentation, including hints of that early blue, and set fashion styles (later including a little French chic!) both in Britain and around the football world.

The highly individual outfit of the mid-1930s, as envisaged by Herbert Chapman.

Arsenal (founded 1886) records and strips

Year	Division	Position	Cup round reached
1890			q
1891			1
1892			1

1886-1895

Year	Division	Position	Cup round reached
1893			1
1894	2	9	1
1895	2	8	1
1896	2	7	1

1895-1933

Year	Division	Position	Cup round reached
1897	2	10	q
1898	2	5	1
1899	2	7	1
1900	2	8	q
1901	2	7	2
1902	2	4	1
1903	2	3	1
1904	2	2P	2
1905	1	10	1
1906	1	12	sf
1907	1	7	sf
1908	1	14	1
1909	1	6	2
1910	1	18	2
1911	1	10	2
1912	1	10	1
1913	1	20R	2
1914	2	3	1

1933-1958

Year	Division	Position	Cup round reached
1915	2	5P	2
1920	1	11	2
1921	1	9	1
1922	1	17	qf
1923	1	11	1
1924	1	19	2
1925	1	20	1
1926	1	2	qf
1927	1	11	F
1928	1	10	sf
1929	1	9	qf
1930	1	14	W
1931	1	1C	4
1932	1	2	F
1933	1	1C	3
1934	1	1C	qf
1935	1	1C	qf
1936	1	6	W
1937	1	3	qf
1938	1	1C	5
1939	1	5	3
1946	1		3
1947	1	13	3
1948	1	1C	3
1949	1	5	4
1950	1	6	W
1951	1	5	5
1952	1	3	F
1953	1	1C	qf
1954	1	12	4
1955	1	9	4
1956	1	5	qf
1957	1	5	qf
1958	1	12	3

1958-1964

Year	Division	Position	Cup round reached
1959	1	3	5
1960	1	13	3
1961	1	11	3
1962	1	10	4

Year	Division	Position	Cup round reached
1963	1	7	5
1964	1	8	5
1965	1	13	4
1966	1	14	3
1967	1	7	5
1968	1	9	5
1969	1	4	5
1970	1	12	3
1971	1	1C	W
1972	1	5	F

1965-1967

Year	Division	Position	Cup round reached
1973	1	2	sf
1974	1	10	4
1975	1	16	qf
1976	1	17	3
1977	1	8	5
1978	1	5	F

1969-1982

Year	Division	Position	Cup round reached
1979	1	7	W
1980	1	4	F
1981	1	5	3
1982	1	5	3

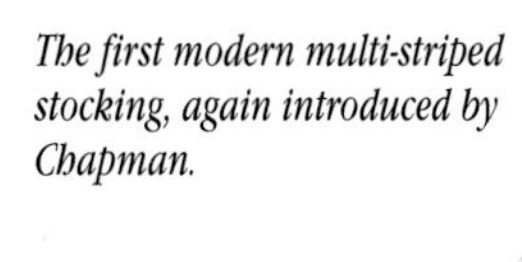

The first modern multi-striped stocking, again introduced by Chapman.

1987-1991

Year	Division	Position	Cup round reached
1983	1	10	sf
1984	1	6	3
1985	1	7	4
1986	1	7	5
1987	1	4	qf
1988	1	6	qf
1989	1	1C	3
1990	1	4	4
1991	1	1C	sf
1992	1	4	3
1993	Pr	10	W
1994	Pr	4	4
1995	Pr	12	5
1996	Pr	5	3
1997	Pr.	3	4
1998	Pr.	1C	W

1998

ASTON VILLA

When a group of young men met in the Manor of Aston district of Birmingham in 1874 to form their own football club, little did they realise the significance of their decisions. Aston Villa, a club to become famous for innovation and achievement, took the colours of deep red and blue from their old school. For a short period black was worn, and other combinations were tried before a claret and light blue combination was finally adopted. Such was Villa's early success and influence that many clubs, newly formed and striving for their own successes, adopted the Villa colours in the hope of emulating the Midlanders' feats. Burnley, West Ham, Crystal Palace, Scunthorpe and Walsall have all graced the Football League in their own claret and blue strips, and even today there are thousands of players similarly dressed at the weekend.

In the early years, shirts of all claret, blue and white hoops and chocolate and light blue halves were worn with success, but by the time of Villa's greatest achievements of the mid 1890s, the claret body with light blue sleeves had been introduced. Whether this version became associated with success or the Brummies were tired of change is uncertain, but from then until the last few years, it remained virtually unchanged.

Aston Villa's influence was great in the organising of competitions and of the clubs themselves. Famous Villans such as William McGregor, George Ramsey and Fred Rinder not only developed the FA Cup competition, but were also instrumental in establishing the Football League and laying the foundations of the modern professional football club. This early professionalism enabled Villa to win three FA Cups and five League titles by the turn of the century. Even their strips reflected a stylish appearance and attention to detail.

This style remained even when successes were not so frequent. During the 1920s the players wore a heavy-ribbed, knitted woollen jersey with a high polo-necked collar. It was a unique style, and although it looks a bit strange now, it could have sold thousands of replica kits in its day.

Even some of the change strips over the years were innovative. The white shirts and colour trims of the early period and the famous Cup-winning shirt of 1957 were to be influences on later shirt styling.

The 1957 FA Cup win proved to be a brief oasis in a long barren period for Villa, from the late 1920s to 1980. It was not until the arrival of Ron Saunders and the development of the side which was to win the League championship, followed by the European Cup, that Villa again began to resemble the club envisaged by McGregor, Ramsey and Rinder.

The strip itself had regained much of its stylish image and although, like most clubs', it continued to change from season to season, the imagination and originality that is Aston Villa remains strong.

The famous League and Cup double strip, featuring contrast sleeves and the ring collar.

Aston Villa (founded 1874) records and strips

Year	Division	Position	Cup round reached
1899	1	1C	1
1900	1	1C	qf
1901	1	15	sf
1902	1	8	1
1903	1	2	sf
1904	1	5	2
1905	1	4	W
1906	1	8	3

1874-1894

Year	Division and	position	Cup round reached
1880			3
1881			4
1882			4
1883			qf
1884			4
1885			3
1886			2
1887			W
1888			1
1889	1	2	qf
1890	1	8	2

Year	Division	Position	Cup round reached
1907	1	5	2
1908	1	2	3
1909	1	7	1
1910	1	1C	3
1911	1	2	2
1912	1	6	2
1913	1	2	W
1914	1	2	sf
1915	1	13	2
1920	1	9	W
1921	1	10	qf
1922	1	5	qf
1923	1	6	1

1894-1963

Year	Division	Position	Cup round reached
1891	1	9	2
1892	1	4	F
1893	1	4	1
1894	1	1C	qf
1895	1	3	W
1896	1	1C	1
1897	1	1C	W
1898	1	6	1

Year	Division	Position	Cup round reached
1924	1	6	F
1925	1	15	3
1926	1	6	5
1927	1	10	3
1928	1	8	5
1929	1	3	sf
1930	1	4	qf

Year	Division	Position	Cup round reached
1931	1	2	3
1932	1	5	4
1933	1	2	4
1934	1	13	sf
1935	1	13	3
1936	1	21R	3
1937	2	9	3
1938	2	1P	sf
1939	1	12	4
1946	1		qf
1947	1	8	3
1948	1	6	3
1949	1	10	4
1950	1	12	3
1951	1	15	4
1952	1	6	3
1953	1	11	qf
1954	1	13	3
1955	1	6	4

1970-1977

Year	Division	Position	Cup round reached
1956	1	20	4
1957	1	10	W
1958	1	14	3
1959	1	21R	sf
1960	2	1P	sf
1961	1	9	5
1962	1	7	qf
1963	1	15	4
1964	1	19	3

1982-83

1993-1995

Year	Division	Position	Cup round reached
1965	1	16	5
1966	1	16	3
1967	1	21R	4
1968	2	16	4
1969	2	18	5
1970	2	21R	3
1971	3	4	1
1972	3	1P	1

1998

Year	Division	Position	Cup round reached
1973	2	3	3
1974	2	14	5
1975	2	2P	5
1976	1	16	3
1977	1	4	qf
1978	1	8	3
1979	1	8	3
1980	1	7	qf
1981	1	1C	3
1982	1	11	5
1983	1	6	6
1984	1	10	3
1985	1	10	3
1986	1	16	4
1987	1	22R	3
1988	2	2P	4
1989	1	17	4
1990	1	2	qf
1991	1	17	3
1992	1	7	qf
1993	Pr	2	4
1994	Pr	10	4
1995	Pr	18	3
1996	Pr	4	sf
1997	Pr	5	4
1998	Pr	7	5

Yet another sartorial innovation. The woollen, heavy-ribbed jersey with the string-pull tie-up.

BARNET

To many football fans, Barnet FC have come to prominence only in recent years, but the north London club have had a long and rich history going back to their formation in 1888.

Barnet officials and members decided early that they wished to remain in the amateur game and in 1902 they became founder members of the Athenian League. They were lucky to be surrounded by equally talented and ambitious sides, in and around the capital. The competition obliged them to be one of the strongest in amateur circles, but it wasn't until about 1930 that the amber-and-black-striped men of Barnet began to dominate with players like the great Lester Finch. An England winger in 1933, he was still playing in 1945 when, clad in their now famous broad amber and black hoops, Barnet beat Bishop Auckland 3-2 to win the Amateur Cup for the only time. A second final in 1948 ended in defeat, 1-0 against Leytonstone, after which the club suffered a slump in fortune in the later 1950s. They finished bottom of the Athenian League in 1957, but coached by George Wheeler, one of their 1945 stars, they improved to reach their third final, sadly another defeat at the hands of mighty Crook Town. They were always a club at the head of fashion changes and this final saw the team sporting a candy-striped pattern made famous by Aston Villa in their own 1957 Wembley Cup Final win.

The 1960s were times of change. The pure amateur ideal at the top level had vanished and Barnet moved into the semi-professional world of the Southern League. Successes continued; in 1966 they were division one champions as they were again in 1977. National publicity came at this time with a handful of appearances by an ageing Jimmy Greaves, the ex-England goalscorer supreme looking somewhat out of place in the broad amber and black stripes which had returned at this time.

With the 1980s came simplification. Barnet lost their stripes and hoops and began to wear plain amber shirts and black shorts. Meanwhile, the top clubs of non-League football came together in first the Alliance Premier and later the GM Vauxhall Conference. The club's might grew with Barry Fry and Stan Flashman at the helm, and after being runners-up in three seasons out of four, Barnet were finally promoted to the Football League.

Sadly, despite early success and promotion, financial irregularities threaten to destroy all the previous good work.

A sight all Barnet fans had dreamed of; the amber shirts, ready for the Football League in 1991.

Barnet (founded 1888) records and strips

Division and position — Cup round reached

1883 to 1939 Olympian League, London League, Athenian League.

Year	Division and position	Cup round reached
1946	AL	1
1947	AL	2
1948	AL	q4
1949	AL	1

1888-1927

Year	Division and position	Cup round reached
1950	AL	q4
1951	AL	p
1952	AL	q1

1934-1953

1958-1960

Year	Division and position	Cup round reached
1953	AL	q1
1954	AL	p
1955	AL	1
1956	AL	q1
1957	AL	q1
1958	AL	p

1968

Year	Division and position	Cup round reached
1959	AL	q1
1960	AL	1
1961	AL	q2
1962	AL	1
1963	AL	q2
1964	AL	1
1965	AL	3
1966	SL	1
1967	SL	q4
1968	SL	1
1969	SL	1
1970	SL	2
1971	SL	3
1972	SL	2

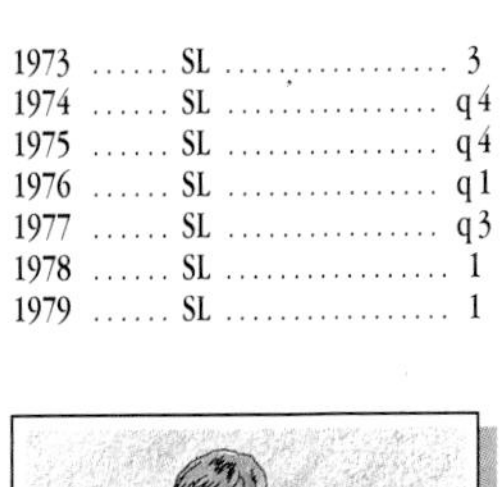

Year	Division and position	Cup round reached
1973	SL	3
1974	SL	q4
1975	SL	q4
1976	SL	q1
1977	SL	q3
1978	SL	1
1979	SL	1

1976

Year	Division and position	Cup round reached
1980	APL	q4
1981	APL	2
1982	APL	3
1983	APL	1
1984	APL	1
1985	GL	1
1986	GL	q4
1987	GMVC	q1

1988

1991

Year	Division	Position	Cup round reached
1988	GMVC		1
1989	GMVC		q3
1990	GMVC		1
1991	GMVC		3
1992	4	7	3
1993	N3	3P	1
1994	N2	24R	3
1995	N3	11	1
1996	N3	9	1
1997	N3	15	2
1998	N3	7	1

1998

The candy-striped shirts as worn during the club's Amateur Cup run in 1959.

BARNSLEY

The myths of 'Battling Barnsley', hewn from Yorkshire grit, fuelled by anecdotes from Michael Parkinson and pre-Industrial Revolution chronicles, have all suggested that the old football club did not belong to the mortal levels of today.

In truth, although the modern Barnsley is a very respected club experiencing previously unimagined League success, the few years before the First World War were times of unrepeated Cup glory.

A decade of being Barnsley St Peters, adorned in stripes of claret and blue, blue and white or chocolate and white, provided enough local success in south Yorkshire leagues to earn election to the Football League in 1898. Perhaps this new status persuaded the club officials to change their own presentation. The name was changed to Barnsley FC and the players now sported plain Nottingham Forest style shirts.

The new-style Barnsley continued to perform well, being noted for their battling performances, and from 1910 to the beginning of the War came their golden period. During that first year, when captained by a Mr Boyle, they lost to the mighty Newcastle United in a replayed FA Cup final. However, the disappointment of this first defeat was forgotten two years later when they actually won the Cup. The old never-say-die spirit enabled them to survive 12 games and another replayed final, and eventually overcome West Bromwich Albion. The only goal of the two games came in the last minute of extra time from hero Harry Tufnell.

Despite some minor successes in the early 1920s, the club never quite reached those giddy heights again. Through the 1930s, 1940s and 1950s (the decade in which Oakwell fans could watch the youthful Danny Blanchflower and Tommy Taylor), Barnsley remained a respectable second division side. There were three dips into the third division (north) but none lasted more than a couple of seasons. Those all-red shirts were equally consistent.

Strangely enough, when the club started playing around with their strip, their fortunes dipped accordingly, and the 1960s and 1970s witnessed several seasons in division four. Many famous old clubs were suffering and the future looked bleak, but in the 1980s, guided by Leeds United old boys Allan Clarke, Norman Hunter and Bobby Collins, Barnsley re-established themselves as second division stalwarts.

For a while, they have even allowed themselves the luxury of exotically patterned strips such as the famous 'star' kit of 1990, hoping they would shine as brightly as Messrs Boyle, Tufnell or even the character made famous by Michael Parkinson, dear old 'Skinner' Normanton.

Recently, Barnsley's star has been in the ascendancy. Talented young manager Danny Wilson took the Tykes into the Premier League for the 1997/98 season. The odds will always be against a long term presence there but 'Battling Barnsley' will continue to fight on.

The Cup-winning kit of 1912, when the red-clad 'Battling Barnsley' shook the football world.

Barnsley (founded 1887) records and strips

1875-1920

1976

1988-1989

1980-1985

1998

1945-1956

1921-1934

Year	Division	Position	Cup round reached
1895			1
1896			p
1897			1
1898			p
1899	2	11	1
1900	2	16	p
1901	2	15	p
1902	2	11	p
1903	2	8	2
1904	2	8	1
1905	2	7	1
1906	2	12	2
1907	2	8	q1
1908	2	16	1
1909	2	17	1
1910	2	9	F
1911	2	19	2
1912	2	6	W
1913	2	4	2
1914	2	5	1
1915	2	3	1
1920	2	12	2
1921	2	16	1
1922	2	3	3
1923	2	9	2
1924	2	11	1
1925	2	15	2
1926	2	18	1
1927	2	11	4
1928	2	14	3
1929	2	16	3
1930	2	17	3
1931	2	19	5
1932	2	21R	3
1933	N3	8	3
1934	N3	1P	1
1935	2	16	3
1936	2	20	qf
1937	2	14	3
1938	2	21R	4
1939	N3	1P	3
1946			5
1947	2	10	4
1948	2	12	3
1949	2	9	3
1950	2	13	3
1951	2	15	3
1952	2	20	4
1953	2	22R	4
1954	N3	2	2
1955	N3	1P	2
1956	2	18	4
1957	2	19	5
1958	2	14	3
1959	2	22R	3
1960	3	17	1
1961	3	8	qf
1962	3	20	2
1963	3	18	3
1964	3	20	5
1965	3	24R	2
1966	4	16	2
1967	4	16	3
1968	4	2P	1
1969	3	10	3
1970	3	7	3
1971	3	12	2
1972	3	22R	2
1973	4	14	1
1974	4	13	2
1975	4	15	1
1976	4	12	1
1977	4	6	2
1978	4	7	2
1979	4	4P	2
1980	3	11	2
1981	3	2P	5
1982	2	6	3
1983	2	10	4
1984	2	14	3
1985	2	11	6
1986	2	12	3
1987	2	11	5
1988	2	14	4
1989	2	7	5
1990	2	19	5
1991	2	8	3
1992	2	16	3
1993	N1	13	5
1994	N1	18	5
1995	N1	6	3
1996	N1	10	3
1997	N1	2P	4
1998	Pr.	19R	6

After many years of simple styling, the 1990 Barnsley 'star' kit was a radical and unique change.

BIRMINGHAM CITY

It seems strange that a club bearing the name of England's second city has never won either of the country's major trophies. Perhaps it is due to the fact that they were formed a year after neighbours Aston Villa, and the latter's dominance over the years has probably limited City's potential growth.

It was not as Birmingham City that the club first began in 1875, but as Small Heath Alliance, named after a local district in the city. Despite Villa's presence, the Heathens were elected into the League, and, following a decade of only moderate success, they adopted a new name in order to find a wider following. So Birmingham (City was not added until 1946) had to drop the old nickname of Heathens and just became the Blues.

Blue has been the colour ever since, with variations of white trimmings to suit the fashion demands. In the 1920s for example, when the club was becoming a regular member of the first division, a large white 'V' was added to the front of the shirts. Perhaps it was used to point centre-forward Joe Bradford towards goal!

In 1931 hopes were still high, but a Wembley appearance resulted in a narrow defeat by another set of neighbours, West Bromwich Albion. After that, the decade's promise seemed to drift away and just before the War the third of many relegations took them into the second division. More ups and downs occurred before a second FA Cup final in 1956, versus Manchester City. Perhaps the white shirts, made necessary by a colour clash, dampened the Blues' fire, but Birmingham couldn't really hold the Mancunians' talented forward line on the day.

Yet another decade of struggle saw the Blues return to division two, before two astute signings and a smart new strip seemed to offer a much brighter future. A youthful Trevor Francis teamed up with the dashing Bob Latchford, and City, in a striking outfit of blue with a broad white vertical panel, regularly appeared on the nation's screens as television coverage widened.

But again the momentum was lost as Francis and Latchford were sold and another relegation followed. In the 1980s promotion and relegation appeared as a regular seasonal feature, though the team continued to look smart. Red trimmings to the shirts seemed to work during one promotion year, but performances on the field remained as inconsistent as ever.

In 1989 the unthinkable happened and City were dropped into the third division. After a series of 'yo-yo' seasons, they were back in the second flight, but at St Andrews, the 'Blues' seemed synonymous with an attitude of despair rather than a call to attack!

By 1998, Trevor Francis had returned as manager, as too had the broad vertical white stripe, but still the City remain in Villa's shadow.

The highlight of the club's post-War history was the 1956 season, including the Cup final appearance versus Manchester City.

Birmingham City (founded 1875) records and strips

1875-1915

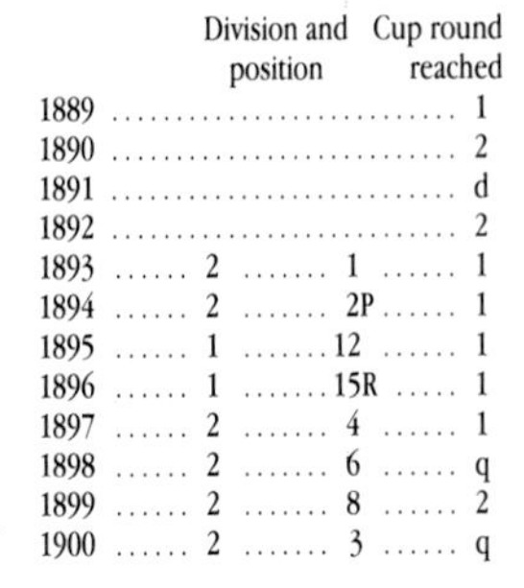

Year	Division and position		Cup round reached
1889			1
1890			2
1891			d
1892			2
1893	2	1	1
1894	2	2P	1
1895	1	12	1
1896	1	15R	1
1897	2	4	1
1898	2	6	q
1899	2	8	2
1900	2	3	q

1926-1929

Year	Division	Position	Cup round
1901	2	2P	3
1902	1	17R	p
1903	2	2P	1
1904	1	11	p
1905	1	7	1
1906	1	7	4
1907	1	9	1
1908	1	20R	1
1909	2	11	2
1910	2	20	1
1911	2	16	1
1912	2	12	1
1913	2	3	3

1937-1954

Year	Division	Position	Cup round
1914	2	14	3
1915	2	6	3
1920	2	5	3
1921	2	1P	1
1922	1	18	1
1923	1	17	1
1924	1	14	2
1925	1	8	3
1926	1	14	4
1927	1	17	4
1928	1	11	5
1929	1	15	4
1930	1	11	4

1969

Year	Division	Position	Cup round
1931	1	19	F
1932	1	9	4
1933	1	13	6
1934	1	20	5
1935	1	19	6
1936	1	12	3
1937	1	11	3
1938	1	18	3
1939	1	21R	5
1946			sf
1947	2	3	qf
1948	2	1P	3
1949	1	17	3
1950	1	22R	3
1951	2	4	sf
1952	2	3	4
1953	2	6	qf
1954	2	7	4
1955	2	1P	qf
1956	1	6	F
1957	1	12	sf
1958	1	12	3
1959	1	9	5

1973

Year	Division	Position	Cup round
1960	1	19	3
1961	1	19	5
1962	1	17	3
1963	1	20	3
1964	1	20	3
1965	1	22R	3
1966	2	10	4
1967	2	10	qf
1968	2	4	sf
1969	2	7	5
1970	2	18	3
1971	2	9	3

1981

Year	Division	Position	Cup round
1972	2	2P	sf
1973	1	10	3
1974	1	19	4
1975	1	17	sf
1976	1	19	3
1977	1	13	4
1978	1	11	3
1979	1	21R	3
1980	2	3P	5
1981	1	13	4
1982	1	16	3
1983	1	17	4
1984	1	20R	6
1985	2	2P	3
1986	1	21R	3
1987	2	19	4
1988	2	19	5
1989	2	23R	3
1990	3	7	3
1991	3	12	2
1992	3	2P	1
1993	N1	19	1
1994	N1	22R	3

Traditionally a simple blue and white kit, the 1980 version had a smart red and white shoulder trim.

1986

Year	Division	Position	Cup round
1995	N2	1P	3
1996	N1	15	3
1997	N1	10	5
1998	N1	7	5

1998

BLACKBURN ROVERS

Shouts of 'Up the Reds' or 'Come on the Blues' resound around the country every week, but such is the popularity of plain shirts that the descriptions could refer to many clubs. Only occasionally does one strip stand out to such a degree that the club is instantly recognised. The blue and white halves have distinguished Blackburn Rovers for well over a century. The club may have dabbled with quarters or blue trimmed with white during the first couple of years, but since they acquired a position of prominence in the 1880s, the halves have remained virtually unchanged.

And what prominence those years produced! Led by the great Jim Forrest and the Hargreaves brothers, Rovers won the FA Cup five times in eight seasons, a dominance never approached by any club since. Sadly for Blackburn, their momentum slackened and as the the new century unwound, Ewood Park was host to a strong first division side, but witnessed no great wins or honours.

However, just before the First World War came the second successful era for Rovers. There were two great League championship wins in 1912 and 1914, Cup semi-final appearances and every season they were in contention for the big prizes.

With the wartime break, Blackburn's new impetus was lost, and apart from the 1928 Cup win over Huddersfield, there were no further Cups. Perhaps it was because the halves were now royal blue and not the original paler version, but more likely it was the greater competition coming from Rovers' Lancashire rivals.

In 1936 they were relegated and despite one two-year spell at the top, it was not until 1960 that Rovers' fortunes took a turn for the better. A Wembley trip that year had followed an earlier promotion. Clayton, Douglas, Dobing and Co promised another great period, but the pressure from the big city teams proved too much. The club slipped not once, but twice, and a four-year spell in the third division seemed to indicate a similar story of gloom to those experienced by their Ribble Valley neighbours, Preston, Burnley and Accrington.

However, despite the usual limitations of a small-town catchment potential, the club proved resilient, and Rovers were promoted and survived well in the second division. This appeared to be Blackburn's niche in modern football, but the arrival of patron Jack Walker and manager Kenny Dalglish finally broke the recent promotion hoodoo.

After finishing runners-up to a great Manchester United side, the club finally won the League title after a gap of 81 years, and while Mr Walker's finances compensated for limited gate income, the blue and white halves would continue to represent not only individual attitudes but also football success.

The most feared sight in the 1880s, the blue and white halves during one of Rovers' many successful Cup runs.

Rovers (founded 1875) records and strips

1875-1892

Year	Division	Position	Cup round reached
1880			3
1881			2
1882			F
1883			2
1884			W
1885			W
1886			W
1887			2
1888			2
1889	1	4	sf
1890	1	3	W
1891	1	6	W
1892	1	9	2
1893	1	9	sf
1894	1	4	sf
1895	1	5	2
1896	1	8	1
1897	1	14	3
1898	1	15	1
1899	1	6	1
1900	1	4	2
1901	1	9	1
1902	1	4	1

1892-1914

1920-1938

Year	Division	Position	Cup round reached
1903	1	16	2
1904	1	15	3
1905	1	13	1
1906	1	9	1
1907	1	12	2
1908	1	14	1
1909	1	4	3
1910	1	3	3
1911	1	12	sf
1912	1	1C	sf
1913	1	5	qf
1914	1	1C	3

1952-1957

Year	Division	Position	Cup round reached
1915	1	3	1
1920	1	20	1
1921	1	11	1
1922	1	15	3
1923	1	14	2
1924	1	8	1
1925	1	16	sf
1926	1	12	4
1927	1	18	3
1928	1	12	W
1929	1	7	qf
1930	1	6	5
1931	1	10	5
1932	1	16	4
1933	1	15	4
1934	1	8	3
1935	1	15	5
1936	1	22R	5
1937	2	12	4
1938	2	16	3
1939	2	1P	qf
1946			3

In the early years there were many halved shirts, but only the Rovers have remained faithful to them throughout the 20th century.

Year	Division	Position	Cup round reached
1947	1	17	5
1948	1	22R	4
1949	2	14	3
1950	2	16	3
1951	2	6	3
1952	2	14	sf
1953	2	9	3
1954	2	3	4
1955	2	6	3
1956	2	4	5
1957	2	4	3
1958	2	2P	sf
1959	1	10	4
1960	1	17	F
1961	1	18	5
1962	1	16	qf
1963	1	11	3
1964	1	7	5
1965	1	10	3

1958-1962

Year	Division	Position	Cup round reached
1966	1	22R	qf
1967	2	4	3
1968	2	9	3
1969	2	19	5
1970	2	8	3
1971	2	21R	3
1972	3	10	1

1981

1994-1995

Year	Division	Position	Cup round reached
1973	3	3	2
1974	3	13	3
1975	3	1P	3
1976	2	15	3
1977	2	12	5
1978	2	5	4
1979	2	22R	4
1980	3	2P	5
1981	2	4	3
1982	2	10	3
1983	2	11	3

1998

Year	Division	Position	Cup round reached
1984	2	6	5
1985	2	5	5
1986	2	19	4
1987	2	12	3
1988	2	5	3
1989	2	5	5
1990	2	5	3
1991	2	19	3
1992	2	6P (pl)	4
1993	Pr	4	qf
1994	Pr	2	4
1995	Pr	1C	3
1996	Pr	7	3
1997	Pr.	13	4
1998	Pr.	6	5

BLACKPOOL

At times, it seems as if Blackpool FC existed only for the ten years from 1947 to 1957, when an ageing genius from the Potteries made a tangerine jersey famous. However, the club have had a long and reasonably successful history, and probably have appeared in more colours than any other major club.

After Blackpool were elected to the Football League in 1897, the progress was steady rather than spectacular. Yet, while consolidation seemed to be the aim on the pitch, the club's colours would vary from season to season. Blue and white stripes became all-red, followed by red and white halves, which then reverted again to all-red.

After the First World War, Blackpool regularly finished near the top of the second division, and finally achieved their ambition of promotion to the top flight in 1930. Even during this period the club could not decide which colours to wear. A wonderful rainbow shirt of red, yellow and blue stripes was followed by white shirts and blue shorts, before in 1924 the first of the tangerine shirts saw daylight. Sadly, despite a bagful of goals from Johnny Hampson, the first division spell lasted only three years.

The club then changed the strip yet again, and eventually it did the trick. In 1937, sporting a smart light and dark blue striped shirt, the Seasiders climbed back into the first division. Two years later, confidence in footballing success must have been high, as the tangerine shirts returned.

After the six-year gap caused by the War, it was in tangerine therefore that Blackpool pushed towards their greatest success. Manager Joe Smith pulled off some shrewd transfer moves, but the master stroke was in persuading Stanley Matthews to move to the seaside.

It was the beginning of a golden period. Matthews, with Mortensen, Mudie, Johnston and Farm just missed out in two FA Cup finals, and regularly went close in the League. By 1953 it looked as if time was running out for some of the 'oldies'. It seemed particularly so in that famous final, but, as it was Coronation Year and fairy tales came true at that time, the 'lads' won their medals. It was Blackpool's only major trophy, but the side was still a League force, and Jimmy Armfield and later Alan Ball played regularly for England.

However, in the late 1960s, when the maximum wage was lifted and financial pressures grew, the club's fortunes declined. Second, third and even fourth division experiences were sadly to become the norm.

In 1991, Blackpool climbed back out of the basement. Whether this limited success will lead to better things remains uncertain. Perhaps another change of colour would do the trick?

In the year of the Coronation, the conquest of Everest, Gordon Richards' Derby, the Matthews final completed the perfect fairy tale.

Blackpool (founded 1887) records and strips

Year	Division	Position	Cup round
1915	2	10	1
1920	2	4	2
1921	2	4	2
1922	2	19	1
1923	2	5	1
1924	2	4	2
1925	2	17	qf

Year	Division	Position	Cup round
1957	1	4	5
1958	1	7	3
1959	1	8	qf
1960	1	11	4
1961	1	20	3
1962	1	13	3
1963	1	13	3

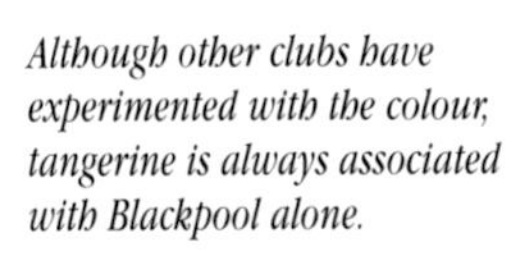
Although other clubs have experimented with the colour, tangerine is always associated with Blackpool alone.

1896-1914

1939-1956

1989

Year	Division and position		Cup round reached
1892			1
1893			1
1894			p
1895			p
1896			1
1897	2	8	1
1898	2	11	p
1899	2	16L	2
1900			p
1901	2	12	p
1902	2	12	p

Year	Division	Position	Cup round
1926	2	6	3
1927	2	9	3
1928	2	19	3
1929	2	8	3
1930	2	1P	4
1931	1	20	4
1932	1	20	3
1933	1	22R	5
1934	2	11	4
1935	2	4	3
1936	2	3	4
1937	2	2P	3
1938	1	12	4

Year	Division	Position	Cup round
1964	1	18	3
1965	1	17	3
1966	1	13	3
1967	1	22R	3
1968	2	3	4
1969	2	8	3
1970	2	2P	4
1971	1	22R	4
1972	2	6	3
1973	2	7	3
1974	2	5	3
1975	2	7	3
1976	2	10	4

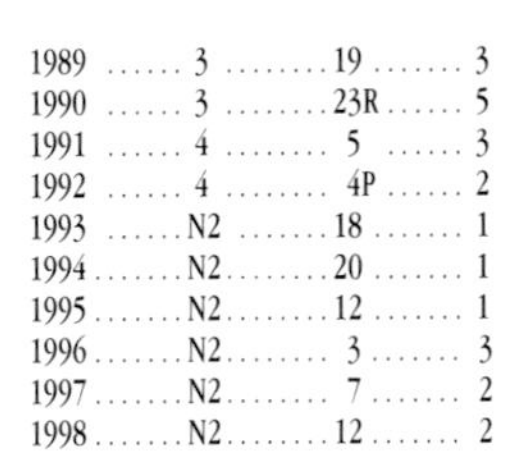

Year	Division	Position	Cup round
1989	3	19	3
1990	3	23R	5
1991	4	5	3
1992	4	4P	2
1993	N2	18	1
1994	N2	20	1
1995	N2	12	1
1996	N2	3	3
1997	N2	7	2
1998	N2	12	2

1915-1938

1962-1972

1998

Year	Division	Position	Cup round
1903	2	14	q
1904	2	15	p
1905	2	15	1
1906	2	14	3
1907	2	13	1
1908	2	15	1
1909	2	20	2
1910	2	12	1
1911	2	9	1
1912	2	14	2
1913	2	20	1
1914	2	16	1

Year	Division	Position	Cup round
1939	1	15	3
1946			4
1947	1	5	3
1948	1	9	F
1949	1	16	4
1950	1	7	qf
1951	1	3	F
1952	1	9	3
1953	1	7	W
1954	1	6	5
1955	1	19	3
1956	1	2	3

Year	Division	Position	Cup round
1977	2	5	3
1978	2	20R	3
1979	3	12	2
1980	3	18	1
1981	3	23R	2
1982	4	12	4
1983	4	21	2
1984	4	6	4
1985	4	2P	1
1986	3	12	2
1987	3	9	1
1988	3	10	4

BOLTON WANDERERS

In 1923, a white-shirted team won the FA Cup thanks to the efforts of a famous white horse, who helped clear the pitch, and during the next three decades those white shirts of Bolton Wanderers had many other successes, particularly at Wembley.

It is generally assumed that the club have always sported this strip, but in the wild and woolly days of the 1870s and 1880s things were very different. Red shirts with black shorts made up the first known uniform, followed by red and white quarters, which gave way to a salmon pink jersey, but in 1884 the players wore what were probably the most unusual shirts in British football history - white covered with red spots!

Perhaps the spots were to represent bloody wounds. Certainly the early days were full of dangers and uncertainties. Despite starting off as a church team, a row with the local vicar saw them groundless, then hooliganism at the new Burnden Park almost caused the club to be expelled from the FA, and in 1885 yet another row, this time over illegal payments, provoked another confrontation.

The last event encouraged the introduction of professionalism and Bolton Wanderers took full advantage, their strong side becoming one of the founder members of the Football League. By this time the famous white shirts had been acquired (from the former Turton club) and apart from the one exception of blue and white stripes in 1890, they have remained since.

Although Bolton soon became one of the stronger League sides, they have never won the League championship and it was in the FA Cup that fame came. A final defeat by Notts County in 1894 was followed ten years later by another by Manchester City.

The latter defeat was avenged in 1926, during the club's finest period. Three years earlier, the side inspired by David Jack and Joe Smith had won the inaugural Wembley final, and in 1929 a win over Portsmouth completed a wonderful decade.

A decline followed, including a short spell in the second division, but after the Second World War the 1950s saw another exciting time. Nat Lofthouse, who donned the white shirts of Bolton and England, shone both in the 1953 defeat and the win five years later when the Munich-depleted Manchester United team lost 2-0.

Sadly, as with many other smaller Lancashire towns, the 1960s and 1970s saw a gradual decline. Dwindling revenue meant unfair competition from the big city clubs and the Trotters failed to keep pace.

In 1987 they were relegated to division four, but since then astute management has improved the situation dramatically and by the mid-1990s promotion to the top flight plus a Coca Cola Cup final appearance had been achieved.

The initial success was short lived, but the hints of red on the latest kits might still spell danger for many clubs, and towards the end of the century Bolton were still battling with the best!

The white shirts of the famous 'White Horse Cup Final', the first to be held at Wembley.

Bolton (founded 1874) records and strips

1881-1890

1890-1962

	Division and position		Cup round reached
1882			2
1883			3
1884			4
1885			q
1886			3
1887			q
1888			q
1889	1	5	q
1890	1	9	sf
1891	1	5	1
1892	1	3	1
1893	1	5	1
1894	1	13	F
1895	1	10	qf
1896	1	4	sf
1897	1	8	2
1898	1	11	qf
1899	1	17R	1
1900	2	2P	1
1901	1	10	2
1902	1	12	2
1903	1	18R	1
1904	2	7	F
1905	2	2P	qf
1906	1	6	1
1907	1	6	3
1908	1	19R	3
1909	2	1P	1
1910	1	20R	1
1911	2	2P	1
1912	1	4	3
1913	1	8	1
1914	1	6	3
1915	1	17	sf
1920	1	6	1
1921	1	3	1
1922	1	6	2
1923	1	13	W
1924	1	4	2
1925	1	3	2
1926	1	8	W
1927	1	4	5
1928	1	7	4
1929	1	14	W
1930	1	15	3
1931	1	14	4
1932	1	17	3
1933	1	21R	1
1934	2	3	qf
1935	2	2P	sf
1936	1	13	3
1937	1	20	5
1938	1	7	3
1939	1	8	3
1946			sf
1947	1	18	4
1948	1	17	3
1949	1	14	3
1950	1	16	4
1951	1	8	4
1952	1	5	3
1953	1	14	F
1954	1	5	qf
1955	1	18	4
1956	1	8	4
1957	1	9	3
1958	1	15	W
1959	1	4	qf
1960	1	6	4
1961	1	18	4
1962	1	11	3
1963	1	18	3
1964	1	21R	4
1965	2	3	5
1966	2	9	4
1967	2	9	4
1968	2	12	3
1969	2	17	4
1970	2	16	3
1971	2	22R	3
1972	3	8	4
1973	3	1P	5
1974	2	11	4
1975	2	10	3
1976	2	4	5
1977	2	4	3
1978	2	1P	5
1979	1	17	3
1980	1	22R	5
1981	2	18	3
1982	2	19	4
1983	2	22R	3
1984	3	10	3
1985	3	17	1
1986	3	18	1
1987	3	21R	3
1988	4	3P	3
1989	3	10	2
1990	3	6	1
1991	3	4	4
1992	3	13	5
1993	N2	2P	5
1994	N1	14	qf
1995	N1	3P (pl)	3
1996	Pr	20R	4
1997	N1	1P	4
1998	Pr.	18R	3

1969-1971

1994-1995

1971-1976

1998

The only known spotted shirt ever worn by a senior club.

AFC BOURNEMOUTH

Some clubs are always chasing trophies, others have to survive periods of turmoil and threats to their very existence, but still others like Bournemouth seem to have played a century of football without experiencing these extremes.

Perhaps this is because of the genteel quality of Bournemouth itself, or because local football was never highly competitive. However, Boscombe FC, as they were formed in 1899, clad in red shirts and black shorts, soon dominated football in Dorset and western Hampshire. In 1914 professionals were engaged and the club's status grew to the point when they were elected to the third division (south) as Bournmouth and Boscombe Athletic in 1923.

Again, there were no dramas. After the early struggles, the club usually achieved a middle-the-table position, and it was only in the late 1930s that a challenge to the divisional leaders took place. It was an interesting period for Bournemouth. They changed their strip to red and white stripes, and in Welshman John Parris they had the first coloured player to appear in the home internationals.

After the Second World War, the club experienced great successes on the field. Dean Court saw three near misses in attempts at promotion to the second division. Clad in Arsenal-style shirts, the team of the 1950s continued to attract attention and, in 1957, Bournemouth reached the quarter-finals of the FA Cup. It provided the year's sensation as first Wolves, then Spurs were beaten and even the mighty Busby Babes had to struggle to overcome the Cherries. The United match attracted 28,799, bettering even the crowds of the exciting 1940s.

Of course it couldn't last. After the early 1960s, mediocrity set in and the club even dropped into the fourth division. Then, the appointment of John Bond as manager and the strike-force of Ted MacDougall and Phil Boyer lifted the club to within three points of the second division in 1972 and the new red and black stripes were often on television as Bournemouth challenged Aston Villa for the title.

Success is often costly in the lower divisions, and manager and stars left for bigger things. No great leader followed and again the side slipped to the lowest level.

Once more it took an ex-Hammer to shake the club out of the doldrums. Harry Redknapp even did the impossible by taking Bournemouth into the second division. The team, wearing a highly individual red and white strip, even flirted with the promotion places, aspiring to reach the ultimate level.

They didn't quite make it and sadly slipped back into the third, but in the mid-1990s they wore the same outfit as AC Milan – obviously the club still had aspirations.

The cherry and white shirts which brushed aside the Wolves and Spurs before worrying the mighty Busby Babes.

Bournemouth (founded 1899 records and strips

	Division and position		Cup round reached
1924	3S	21	
1925	3S	20	q
1926	3S	8	4
1927	3S	7	3
1928	3S	14	3
1929	3S	9	5
1930	3S	10	3
1931	3S	10	1

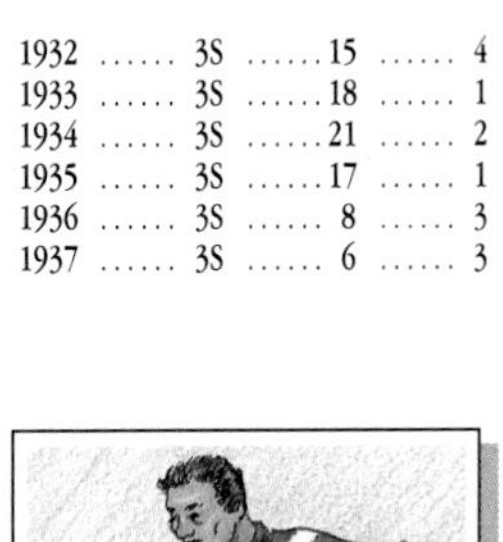

1901-1909

1932	3S	15	4
1933	3S	18	1
1934	3S	21	2
1935	3S	17	1
1936	3S	8	3
1937	3S	6	3

1936-1939

1938	3S	13	2
1939	3S	15	3
1946			1
1947	3S	7	3
1948	3S	2	3

1946-1955

1949	3S	3	3
1950	3S	12	4
1951	3S	9	2
1952	3S	14	1
1953	3S	9	1
1954	3S	19	2

1957-1962

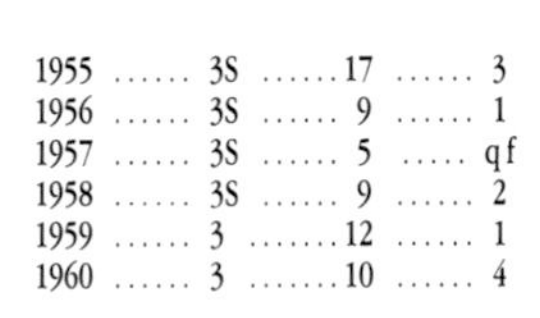

1955	3S	17	3
1956	3S	9	1
1957	3S	5	qf
1958	3S	9	2
1959	3	12	1
1960	3	10	4

1973

1961	3	19	3
1962	3	3	1
1963	3	5	1

1988

1964	3	4	1
1965	3	11	2
1966	3	18	3
1967	3	20	2
1968	3	12	3
1969	3	4	2
1970	3	21R	1
1971	4	2P	2
1972	3	3	3
1973	3	7	3
1974	3	11	3
1975	3	21R	2
1976	4	6	2

1991-1995

1977	4	13	1
1978	4	17	1
1979	4	18	2
1980	4	11	2
1981	4	13	2
1982	4	4P	3
1983	3	14	1
1984	3	17	4
1985	3	10	3
1986	3	15	3
1987	3	1P	2
1988	2	17	3
1989	2	12	5
1990	2	22R	3

1991	3	9	4
1992	3	8	4
1993	N2	17	3

1998

1994	N2	17	3
1995	N2	19	2
1996	N2	14	2
1997	N2	16	1
1998	N2	9	3

The imaginative white side-stripes of the '87 promotion jersey.

BRADFORD CITY

The story of Bradford City is not dissimilar to that of two other northern 'B's. Like Barnsley and Bury, the City achieved their greatest success just before the First World War and have spent the following 80 years struggling to emulate those feats.

Although a club had previously played regularly at Valley Parade, it was not until 1903 that Bradford City were officially formed. Clad in claret and amber hoops (the colours of Bradford Council livery) the club immediately gained the confidence of the Football League and were elected into the second division. That confidence was well rewarded, five years of determined effort ending in promotion to the first division in 1908.

These were exciting times in west Yorkshire and in 1911 the club not only finished fifth in the League but won the FA Cup. A single goal by O'Rourke brought the new trophy back to the city in which it had been made. By this time, the club sported an all-claret shirt with an amber yoke, a style evoked vividly in the many photographs remaining of that famous occasion.

However, as for many clubs at this time, the break for the War ended the momentum of success and the 1920s saw Bradford drop out of the top flight, never to return.

The introduction of striped shirts in the late 1920s provided no further inspiration and the team even dropped into the third division. Although promotion was achieved within a couple of years, just before the Second World War the club plunged into relegation again to commence a long dark period without any success.

In the early post-War years, the strip was always plain, usually claret trimmed with amber. Often the football on the pitch was even drabber and the 1960s were spent almost entirely in the fourth division. Even the introduction of an all-white outfit sporting two vertical panels of claret and amber failed to inspire further improvement.

By the beginning of the 1980s, the club looked in danger of following fellow Bradfordians, Park Avenue, out of the League altogether, but the arrival of Leeds old boy Trevor Cherry as manager saw a complete turn around at the club. Promotion in 1982 was followed by another to division two three years later. Although the terrible fire disaster prevented any major celebrations, City had finally recovered much of their pride and some of their glory.

A subsequent relegation proved only a temporary hiccup and in the late 1990s they were back in the second flight, reinforced by foreign stars, and in search for a second Cup success.

The claret and amber strip still famous in Bradford. The 1911 FA Cup win remains the only major trophy won by the west Yorkshire club.

Bradford City (founded 1903) records and strips

1908-1936

1974-1977

1991-1992

1998

Year	Division	Position	Cup round reached
1904	2	10	p
1905	2	8	p
1906	2	11	3
1907	2	5	3
1908	2	1P	1
1909	1	18	3
1910	1	7	2
1911	1	5	W
1912	1	11	qf
1913	1	13	1
1914	1	9	2
1915	1	10	qf
1920	1	15	qf
1921	1	15	2
1922	1	21R	2
1923	2	15	1
1924	2	18	1
1925	2	16	3
1926	2	16	3
1927	2	22R	3
1928	3N	6	2
1929	3N	1P	4
1930	2	18	5
1931	2	10	4
1932	2	7	3
1933	2	11	3
1934	2	6	3
1935	2	20	4
1936	2	12	5
1937	2	21R	3
1938	3N	14	3
1939	3N	3	1
1946			1
1947	3N	5	1
1948	3N	14	2
1949	3N	22	2
1950	3N	19	2
1951	3N	7	1
1952	3N	15	2
1953	3N	16	2
1954	3N	5	1
1955	3N	21	3
1956	3N	28	
1957	3N	9	1
1958	3N	3	3
1959	3	11	4
1960	3	19	5
1961	3	22R	2
1962	4	5	3
1963	4	23	3
1964	4	5	1
1965	4	19	1
1966	4	23	1
1967	4	11	1
1968	4	5	2
1969	4	4P	1
1970	3	10	3
1971	3	19	2
1972	3	24R	1
1973	4	16	4
1974	4	8	4
1975	4	10	1
1976	4	17	qf
1977	4	4P	1
1978	3	22R	1
1979	4	15	2
1980	4	5	3
1981	4	14	1
1982	4	2P	1
1983	3	12	3
1984	3	7	1
1985	3	2P	3
1986	2	13	3
1987	2	10	4
1988	2	4	5
1989	2	14	4
1990	2	23R	3
1991	3	8	1
1992	3	16	2
1993	N2	10	2
1994	N2	7	1
1995	N2	14	1
1996	N2	`6P(pl)	3
1997	N1	21	5
1998	N1	13	3

1950-1958

1963-1964

1984-1987

The famous amber yoke of the Cup-winning jersey.

BRENTFORD

Although Brentford did not enter the Football League until 1920, a junior version of the club had been competing in west London since 1889. Whether it was the team's dramatic blue and yellow stripes, or a shout of support from the local Borough Road teachers college, but since those early days, the club has always been known as the Bees.

For the next 30 years, Brentford began to prosper and develop and in 1920 became founder members of the division three (south). For the first season, the players were still clad in blue and yellow, but at this stage, probably looking for greater success, the club changed from the stripes to all-white shirts.

The new strip took a while to gain effect. The 1920s were times of struggle, but a second change, this time to red and white stripes, seemed to be an inspirational move and the next decade saw Brentford's finest period. Promotion in 1933 was quickly followed by another two years later and the Bees were in division one! Nor was the team out of its depth. With stars like John Holliday and Idris Hopkins, they finished fifth, sixth and sixth again. Sadly, the War stopped a great run of success and the 1940s and 1950s saw a drop in fortunes and divisions.

Such was the despair that for a short time the club reintroduced the old colours. The yellow shirts with blue collar and cuffs were very unusual at the time, but did nothing to inspire the players. Following fan pressure and the lack of success , the red and white stripes returned, but still failed to change the downward trend. Many years were spent in the fourth division and those glorious times just before and just after the War, when nearly 40,000 saw an FA Cup tie at Griffin Park, seemed light years away.

In the 1980s, hard work and a professional approach from excellent young managers such as Steve Perryman and Phil Holder began to turn the club's fortunes around.

The team regularly finished in the top half of the third division and it was not a great surprise to the football world when the Bees finally won promotion to the second flight in 1992.

Their first year back proved just too difficult and they could not survive, but it was hoped the atmosphere of those heady pre-War years would yet return to west London, even though in the summer of 1998, relegation and possible buy-outs had left much uncertainty.

In the late 1930s the red and white stripes of Brentford were as feared as those of long-time giants Sunderland and Sheffield United.

Brentford (founded 1889) records and strips

	Division and position		Cup round reached
1920			1
1921	3	21	1
1922	3S	9	1
1923	3S	14	p
1924	3S	17	p
1925	3S	21	p
1926	3S	18	2
1927	3S	11	5
1928	3S	12	3

1889-1922

1929	3S	13	2
1930	3S	2	1
1931	3S	3	4
1932	3S	5	4

1923-1928

1933	3S	1P	1
1934	2	4	3
1935	2	1P	3
1936	1	5	3
1937	1	6	4
1938	1	6	qf
1939	1	18	3

1929-1956

1946			qf
1947	1	21R	4
1948	2	15	4
1949	2	18	qf
1950	2	9	3
1951	2	9	4
1952	2	10	4
1953	2	17	3
1954	2	21R	3
1955	3S	11	4
1956	3S	6	2
1957	3S	8	2
1958	3S	2	1
1959	3	3	4

1961-1962

1965-1972

1960	3	6	2
1961	3	17	1
1962	3	23R	3
1963	4	1P	1
1964	3	16	4
1965	3	5	3
1966	3	23R	2
1967	4	9	3
1968	4	14	1

1988-1989

1969	4	11	2
1970	4	5	1
1971	4	14	5
1972	4	3P	1
1973	3	22R	1
1974	4	19	1
1975	4	8	2
1976	4	18	3
1977	4	15	2
1978	4	4P	2
1979	3	10	1

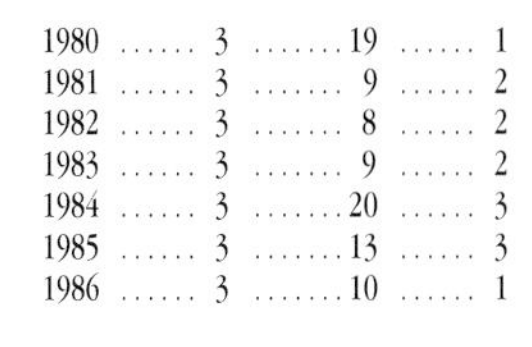

1980	3	19	1
1981	3	9	2
1982	3	8	2
1983	3	9	2
1984	3	20	3
1985	3	13	3
1986	3	10	1

1992

1987	3	11	2
1988	3	12	1
1989	3	7	qf
1990	3	13	1
1991	3	6	3
1992	3	1P	2
1993	N1	22R	3
1994	N2	16	2
1995	N2	2	1
1996	N2	15	4
1997	N2	4	1
1998	N2	21R	1

1998

The early yellow and blue striped jersey was a marked contrast to the later traditional red and white.

BRIGHTON AND HOVE ALBION

Like Bournemouth, Brighton have always had to struggle to arouse great interest in football. The easy going seaside atmosphere always seemed to provide too many distractions.

It was the public school influence of the local Brighton College which first stimulated regional interest, the school itself grooming several England internationals. Even the club's first colours of red, white and blue had all the appearances of contemporary school strips.

Early interest was often dampened when spectators had to watch matches exposed to all the elements, but eventually Sussex football began to flourish and the club itself achieved great success in the Southern League. In 1911, now wearing blue and white stripes, Brighton and Hove Albion as they had become, played the mighty Aston Villa in the Charity Shield. To qualify for this distinction the club had been Southern League champions and it was following a second championship in 1921 that they were elected to the Football League.

The Seagulls had a great record in the third division (south) for over 30 years without winning anything. Regularly they finished in the top six, but promotion was not achieved until 1958. The club must have doubted the desirability of promotion when they lost their first game 9-0 to Middlesbrough, a certain Brian Clough scoring five times! The team's form did improve, but after four years in the second division there followed consecutive drops to the fourth, and the future looked decidedly bleak.

During this time, the club sported blue shirts with white sleeves before returning to stripes and the latter style did witness another short visit to division two. But it was not until 1977 that Brighton's glory days finally arrived. Two promotions in three years saw yet another small club break into division one, and in 1979 the Seagulls began a four-year stay in the top flight. They never had the resources or support to challenge the big boys, but all the same, the Sussex club enjoyed the experience.

In fact, even in their relegation year, Brighton almost achieved the impossible in reaching their first FA Cup final. Only a last minute save by the Manchester United goalkeeper from Gordon Smith took the match to a replay, which the Seagulls lost 4-0.

During those heady days, the club wore blue shirts with white trimmings. Since then the early red has returned in trims and styles have changed every year. By the early 1990s Brighton were famous only for their striped shirts and shorts, and later the club seemed to have lost its way altogether.

In this all-blue kit, the Seagulls almost achieved the 'impossible' of beating Manchester United in the 1983 FA Cup Final.

Brighton (founded 1901) records and strips

	Division and position		Cup round reached
1906			2
1907			1
1908			2

1901-1924

1909			1
1910			1
1911			2
1912			1
1913			2
1914			3
1915			2
1920			p
1921	3	18	2
1922	3S	19	2
1923	3S	4	2

1924-1933

1950-1952

1924	3S	5	3
1925	3S	8	2
1926	3S	5	1
1927	3S	4	3
1928	3S	4	2
1929	3S	15	1
1930	3S	5	5
1931	3S	4	4
1932	3S	8	3
1933	3S	12	5
1934	3S	10	4

1961-1969

1935	3S	9	3
1936	3S	7	3
1937	3S	3	1
1938	3S	5	3
1939	3S	3	1
1946			5
1947	3S	17	1
1948	3S	22	3
1949	3S	6	1
1950	3S	8	1
1951	3S	13	4
1952	3S	5	1
1953	3S	7	3
1954	3S	2	2
1955	3S	6	3

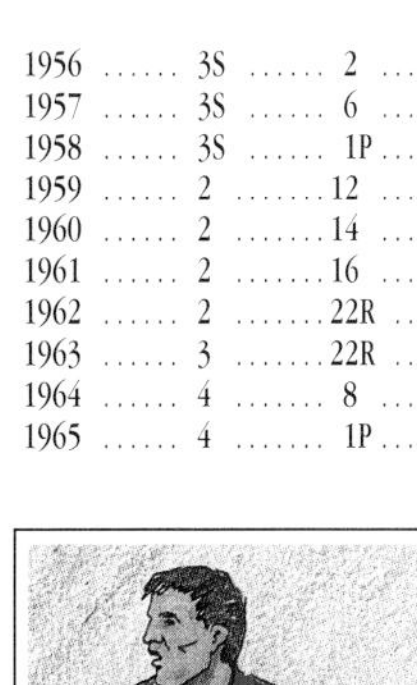

1956	3S	2	2
1957	3S	6	1
1958	3S	1P	2
1959	2	12	3
1960	2	14	5
1961	2	16	4
1962	2	22R	3
1963	3	22R	1
1964	4	8	1
1965	4	1P	1

1970-1976

1966	3	15	2
1967	3	19	4
1968	3	10	2
1969	3	12	2
1970	3	5	2
1971	3	14	3
1972	3	2P	2
1973	2	22R	3
1974	3	19	1
1975	3	19	3
1976	3	4	3
1977	3	2P	1
1978	2	4	4
1979	2	2P	3
1980	1	15	4
1981	1	19	3

1981-1983

1991-1992

1982	1	13	4
1983	1	22R	F
1984	2	9	5
1985	2	6	4
1986	2	11	6
1987	2	22R	3
1988	3	2P	4
1989	2	19	3
1990	2	18	4
1991	2	6	4
1992	2	23R	4
1993	N2	9	4

1998

1994	N2	14	1
1995	N2	16	1
1996	N2	23R	2
1997	N3	23	1
1998	N3	23	1

The famous (or infamous) striped shirt and shorts strip of 1991 was only slightly better received than the much derided away kit.

BRISTOL CITY

Bristol City must be regarded as one of the 'almost' clubs of the Football League. There is a large catchment area with huge potential support, a fine stadium which once held over 43,000 people and only neighbours Bristol Rovers within miles. However, despite occasional periods of semi-success, the Robins have never fully realised their potential.

As Bristol South End, and clad in red shirts and navy blue shorts, they were one of five semi-professional organisations in Bristol in the 1890s and it was only when they amalgamated with Bedminster did they become known as Bristol City. The players now wore red shirts and white shorts, a combination almost unchanged for the following 100 years.

Financial resources were slim in the early years, but the appointment of Sam Hollis as manager plus a excellent publicity campaign saw much success on the field and eventual election to the Football League in 1901. These were exciting days in south Bristol. Promotion to division one was followed by a runners-up spot in 1907 and two years later the Robins reached their only FA Cup Final. A single goal by Manchester United denied Billy Wedlock and his team. It was an obvious blow, and probably was the beginning of a slow but steady decline.

Apart from another fine Cup run in 1920, ended only in the semi-finals by the emerging Huddersfield superteam, the years between the wars saw City spend most of their time in the depths of the third division. Even great loyal support resulting in many 30,000-plus gates failed to achieve more than a few seasons back in division two.

During the 1950s, the prolific goal-scoring of England's John Atyeo provided lots of excitement but no trophies, whilst from 1966, sporting an all-red strip, City began a whole decade of second division obscurity.

At the end of this time, it appeared that the club was finally going to live up to its big city status. Alan Dicks moulded a team good enough to return to the top flight after an absence of over 60 years, and for four seasons the team held its own. However, another shortage of cash saw a dramatic dive to division four in consecutive seasons. It didn't go unnoticed that the introduction of black (either on shorts or numbers) had a negative effect on results.

The removal of the black, and a return to the traditional red and white, plus a steady and sensible period of rebuilding, coincided with another climb back to the second flight. That ought to be the club's rightful place. But do City have the resources and will to stay there?

Alan Dick's first division side sported a traditionally simple red and white kit.

Bristol City (founded 1894) records and strips

Year	Division and position		Cup round reached
1899			1
1900			2
1901			q
1902	2	6	4q
1903	2	4	2
1904	2	4	1
1905	2	4	2
1906	2	1P	1
1907	1	2	2
1908	1	10	1
1909	1	8	F
1910	1	16	2
1911	1	19R	1
1912	2	13	1
1913	2	16	1
1914	2	8	1
1915	2	13	2
1920	2	8	sf
1921	2	3	1
1922	2	22R	1
1923	3S	1P	2
1924	2	22R	3
1925	3S	3	2
1926	3S	4	3
1927	3S	1P	2
1928	2	12	3
1929	2	20	3
1930	2	20	3
1931	2	16	3
1932	2	22R	4
1933	3S	15	2
1934	3S	19	3
1935	3S	15	5
1936	3S	13	1
1937	3S	16	1
1938	3S	2	2
1939	3S	8	q1
1946			4
1947	3S	3	2
1948	3S	7	2
1949	3S	16	3
1950	3S	15	1
1951	3S	10	5
1952	3S	15	2
1953	3S	5	1
1954	3S	3	3
1955	3S	1P	1
1956	2	11	3
1957	2	13	5
1958	2	17	5
1959	2	10	4
1960	2	22R	3
1961	3	14	4
1962	3	6	3
1963	3	14	3
1964	3	5	4
1965	3	2P	3
1966	2	5	3
1967	2	15	5
1968	2	19	5
1969	2	16	3
1970	2	14	3
1971	2	19	3
1972	2	8	3
1973	2	5	4
1974	2	16	qf
1975	2	5	3
1976	2	2P	3
1977	1	18	3
1978	1	17	3
1979	1	13	4
1980	1	20R	3
1981	2	21R	5
1982	3	23R	4
1983	4	14	1
1984	4	4P	3
1985	3	5	2
1986	3	9	2
1987	3	6	3
1988	3	5	2
1989	3	11	3
1990	3	2P	5
1991	2	9	3
1992	2	17	5
1993	N1	15	3
1994	N1	13	5
1995	N1	23R	4
1996	N2	13	1
1997	N2	5	3
1998	N2	2P	2

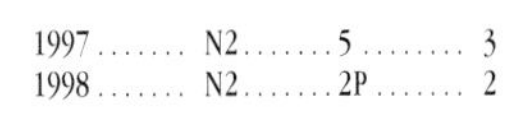

One of City's few alternatives to a plain shirt was the double pin-stripe version of 1988.

1894-1897

1936-1939

1968

1988

1897-1927

1946-1957

1975-1978

1998

BRISTOL ROVERS

Whilst neighbours City have remained loyal to their red shirts throughout their history, Bristol Rovers have appeared in almost every colour combination imaginable! As the Black Arabs, their players sported black shirts with a yellow sash, as Eastville Rovers blue and white hoops were the vogue, and on becoming Bristol Rovers in 1898 there was another change to black and white stripes. At least this combination was to last for over 20 years, but following local success and the election to division three after the First World War, yet another strip was introduced.

The club had been nicknamed the Pirates for several seasons, and now their new white shirts were adorned with a black skull-and-crossbones badge. All the club's outfits had been well considered and had some great significance. The original strip had been adopted from the neighbouring rugby team; the blue hoops were the racing colours of the Duke of Badminton, one of the club's great supporters; and the black and white stripes had been worn with remarkable success by the clubs from further north.

Although by 1930 the team had achieved no success on the field, the sartorial adventures continued. Plain blue was introduced but this still failed to inspire any major League or Cup achievements. However, the following season Rovers' flamboyant manager, Albert Prince-Cox, decided his players should sport blue and white quartered shirts. He claimed the players would look bigger and more robust. Whether this was true or not was difficult to decide. There certainly was a slight improvement, but it was not until the 1950s that the Pirates really began to impress the football world.

Still clad in their now famous quarters, and led by the great goal scorers Alfie Biggs and Geoff Bradford (the club's only England international), Rovers regularly pushed for promotion to division one, and for a while they were certainly the city's premier club.

However, by 1962 the perennial desire to alter the strip returned. First there were blue pinstripes, which became wider, and eventually the whole shirt was blue again. Sadly, the lack of success was also repeated with several seasons spent in the third division.

Perhaps Mr Prince-Cox was proved correct again when the quarters returned in 1973. Promotion to the second division was immediate and although there were subsequent relegations and a cash shortage, the Rovers battled on – a club with larger-than-life characters, struggles and colours.

The most successful Pirates sported the quarters in the late 1950s.

Bristol Rovers (founded 1883) records and strips

Year	Division	Position	Cup round
1951	3S	6	6
1952	3S	7	4
1953	3S	1P	3
1954	2	9	3
1955	2	9	4
1956	2	6	4
1957	2	9	4
1958	2	10	6
1959	2	6	3

1883-1931

	Division and position		Cup round reached
1921	3	10	1
1922	3S	14	q
1923	3S	13	q
1924	3S	9	q
1925	3S	17	1
1926	3S	19	1
1927	3S	10	3
1928	3S	19	2
1929	3S	19	2
1930	3S	20	3
1931	3S	15	4

Year	Division	Position	Cup round
1960	2	9	4
1961	2	17	3
1962	2	21R	3
1963	3	19	1
1964	3	12	4
1965	3	6	3
1966	3	16	1
1967	3	5	3
1968	3	15	3
1969	3	16	5
1970	3	3	2
1971	3	6	2
1972	3	6	3

1931-1957

1962-1963

Year	Division	Position	Cup round
1932	3S	18	2
1933	3S	9	3
1934	3S	7	2
1935	3S	8	3
1936	3S	17	3
1937	3S	15	3
1938	3S	15	1
1939	3S	22	2
1946			2
1947	3S	14	1
1948	3S	20	4
1949	3S	5	1
1950	3S	9	1

Year	Division	Position	Cup round
1973	3	5	1
1974	3	2P	3
1975	2	19	4
1976	2	18	3
1977	2	15	3
1978	2	18	5
1979	2	16	5
1980	2	19	3
1981	2	22R	4
1982	3	15	1
1983	3	7	2
1984	3	5	2

1963-1966

1973-1992

Year	Division	Position	Cup round
1985	3	6	3
1986	3	16	4
1987	3	19	1
1988	3	8	3

Year	Division	Position	Cup round
1992	2	13	4
1993	N1	24R	3
1994	N2	8	1
1995	N2	4	3

1966-1969

1998

Year	Division	Position	Cup round
1989	3	5	2
1990	3	1P	1
1991	2	13	3

Year	Division	Position	Cup round
1996	N2	10	1
1997	N2	17	1
1998	N2	5	3

Although not introduced until the 1930s, the quarters are synonymous with the Rovers.

BURNLEY

In the 1960s, Burnley had become one of the leading clubs in the land, with a team of internationals and a famous nickname of the Clarets. Eighty years earlier, when the club was founded by some YMCA boys, all that was to be achieved must have seemed an impossible dream.

Many of the neighbouring Ribble Valley clubs were then well established and teams from Accrington, Darwen and Nelson regularly gave the then Burnley Rovers lads, who wore dark blue, a good thrashing. However, lessons were learnt, the club becoming just Burnley and despite early financial problems, the team now clad in bright green jerseys continued to progress.

By the time the Football League was founded, Burnley were considered good enough to be elected, although after early moderate successes, they began the 20th century in the second division, apparently going nowhere.

In 1911 an old lady told the players green was unlucky, and so, seeing that Aston Villa had the most successful image of all, the club adopted the Midlanders', famous claret and blue strip.

We all know it takes more than good luck to become winners, but within two years of the change, Burnley were back in the first division and had won the FA Cup! Great things were now envisaged by the fans, and even though the First World War intervened, in 1921 the Clarets became League champions. The team, shaped around the great half-back line of Halley, Boyle and Watson and the outstanding goalkeeper William Watson, had also been runners-up the previous season and their 30 games without defeat seemed to suggest many years ahead at the very top. Strangely these successes were never really repeated and the 1930s were spent entirely in the second division.

After the Second World War, promotion was accompanied by a second FA Cup final. The opposition that day, Charlton, found compensation for their own previous year's defeat, but later in the 1950s another successful Burnley side was put together. An exciting championship was won in 1960, followed by another Wembley loss, this time to the great Spurs side.

Sadly, history repeated itself as international stars such as McIlroy, Adamson, Connelly and Pointer aged, or in some cases were sold off to balance the books, and the club began a terrible period of decline, ending up in the fourth division.

Even when the strip was either streamlined or highlighted with patterns, it failed to inspire the players. In fact, it was only after the calamity of nearly losing League status in 1987 and the great response from the fans, that the club finally seemed to wake up. After that, a decent side was assembled and a place in the new Football League division one was achieved. Although relegation followed soon after, the Turf Moor faithful had found some renewed hope.

Other than the 1920 vintage, the Clarets of Jimmy McIlroy and company had no peers in Turf Moor history.

Burnley (founded 1882) records and strips

1882-1911

Year	Division and position		Cup round reached
1889	1	9	2
1890	1	11	1
1891	1	8	2
1892	1	7	2
1893	1	6	2
1894	1	5	1
1895	1	9	1
1896	1	10	2
1897	1	16R	1
1898	2	1P	3
1899	1	3	1

1912-1929

Year	Division	Position	Cup round
1900	1	17R	1
1901	2	3	2
1902	2	9	1
1903	2	18	q
1904	2	5	q
1905	2	11	q
1906	2	9	1
1907	2	7	1
1908	2	7	1
1909	2	14	qf
1910	2	14	2
1911	2	8	qf

1930-1956

Year	Division	Position	Cup round
1912	2	3	1
1913	2	2P	sf
1914	1	12	W
1915	1	4	3
1920	1	2	2
1921	1	1C	3
1922	1	3	1
1923	1	15	1
1924	1	17	sf
1925	1	19	1
1926	1	20	3

1956-1962

Year	Division	Position	Cup round
1927	1	5	5
1928	1	18	3
1929	1	19	4
1930	1	21R	3
1931	2	8	4
1932	2	19	3
1933	2	19	qf
1934	2	13	3
1935	2	12	sf

The early green jerseys, eventually discarded because the colour was considered unlucky.

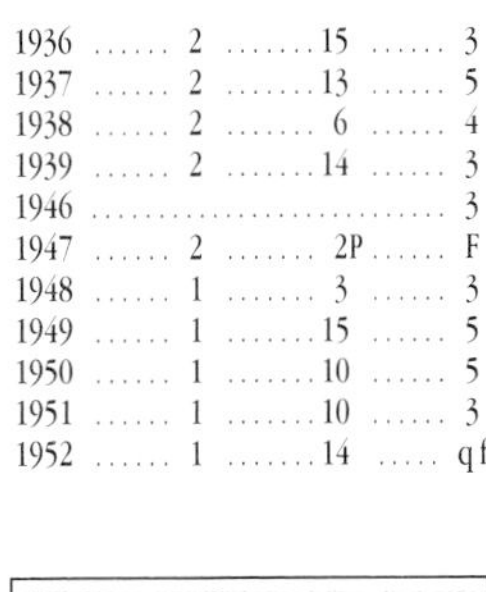

Year	Division	Position	Cup round
1936	2	15	3
1937	2	13	5
1938	2	6	4
1939	2	14	3
1946			3
1947	2	2P	F
1948	1	3	3
1949	1	15	5
1950	1	10	5
1951	1	10	3
1952	1	14	qf

1968-1975

Year	Division	Position	Cup round
1953	1	6	5
1954	1	7	4
1955	1	10	3
1956	1	7	4
1957	1	7	qf
1958	1	6	4
1959	1	7	qf
1960	1	1C	qf
1961	1	4	sf
1962	1	2	F
1963	1	3	4
1964	1	9	qf
1965	1	12	5
1966	1	3	4
1967	1	14	3

1976-1981

1991

Year	Division	Position	Cup round
1968	1	13	3
1969	1	14	4
1970	1	14	4
1971	1	21R	3
1972	2	7	3
1973	2	1P	3
1974	1	6	sf
1975	1	10	3
1976	1	21R	3
1977	2	16	4
1978	2	11	4
1979	2	13	5
1980	2	21R	4
1981	3	8	2
1982	3	1P	4
1983	2	21R	6

1998

Year	Division	Position	Cup round
1984	3	12	3
1985	3	21R	3
1986	4	14	2
1987	4	22	1
1988	4	10	1
1989	4	16	1
1990	4	16	1
1991	4	6	3
1992	4	1P	3
1993	N2	13	3
1994	N2	6P(pl)	3
1995	N1	22R	4
1996	N2	17	1
1997	N2	9	2
1998	N2	20	1

BURY

Bury share much in common with Lancashire neighbours Preston; great early successes, a long, slow and gentle decline, plus a traditional uniform of white shirts and dark blue shorts which has hardly changed over 100 years of football.

It is not clear why white was chosen for the shirts; perhaps it was as a symbol of purity as the club was formed from the amalgamation of two local church sides. Soon the new team had acquired a tenancy at Gigg Lane on the Earl of Derby's estate and this ground became an example of continuity and stability until today.

As with many of the clubs of the day, local successes eventually led to entry to the Football League. Instant promotion to the first division was the foundation for greater success in the FA Cup competition. A 4-0 win in the 1900 final over Southampton was a great achievement in itself, but three years later a 6-0 victory against Derby County still remains the highest final victory ever.

The Shakers, a nickname which resulted from the 'We'll give them a good shaking' threat from the club's chairman before a match against a celebrated rival club, certainly created fear in all Cup opponents during this period, but Bury never really threatened to win the League championship. After the First World War, they slipped back to the second division for a while, only to return in 1925, when for four seasons the club enjoyed its best results.

However, from then on the story was a familiar one for a small Lancashire club. The big city teams became more successful and survival became the chief ambition for the Shakers. The 1940s and 1950s were a struggle and in 1958 relegation to the third division was unavoidable. Even in the 1960s when Bury discovered great young talent such as Colin Bell and fought their way back to division two, it was difficult to take on the big clubs. Spacious Gigg Lane seemed empty with crowds of less than 4,000 and the talent had to be sold.

For the last 25 years, Bury have yo-yoed between the bottom two divisions, occasionally putting a good team together only to run out of cash just before success could be consolidated. The white-shirted heroes of the past such as Johnny Settle, Charles Sager and Jack Plant would be particularly welcomed today.

Or at least that would have been the case until 1997. Under Stan Ternant's management the Shakers had shot up to the new first division. Did they have the resources to stay there on a regular basis?

The simple outfit worn by the double FA Cup winners at the turn of the century.

Bury (founded 1885) records and strips

1885-1914

Year	Division	Position	Cup round reached
1895	2	1P	2
1896	1	11	qf
1897	1	9	2
1898	1	14	1
1899	1	10	2
1900	1	12	W
1901	1	5	2
1902	1	7	qf
1903	1	8	W
1904	1	12	2
1905	1	17	2
1906	1	17	1
1907	1	16	3
1908	1	7	2
1909	1	17	2
1910	1	13	2
1911	1	18	1
1912	1	20R	2
1913	2	11	2
1914	2	10	2
1915	2	11	2
1920	2	5	2
1921	2	11	1
1922	2	11	1
1923	2	6	3
1924	2	2P	1
1925	1	5	1
1926	1	4	4
1927	1	19	3
1928	1	5	4
1929	1	21R	5
1930	2	5	3
1931	2	13	4
1932	2	5	qf
1933	2	4	4
1934	2	12	4
1935	2	10	3
1936	2	14	4
1937	2	3	4
1938	2	10	4
1939	2	16	3
1946			4
1947	2	17	3
1948	2	20	3
1949	2	12	3
1950	2	18	4
1951	2	20	3
1952	2	17	3
1953	2	20	4
1954	2	17	3
1955	2	13	3
1956	2	16	3
1957	2	21R	3
1958	3N	4	2
1959	3	10	3
1960	3	7	3
1961	3	1P	1
1962	2	18	3
1963	2	8	4
1964	2	18	4
1965	2	16	3
1966	2	19	3
1967	2	22R	4
1968	3	2P	3
1969	2	21R	3
1970	3	19	1
1971	3	22R	2
1972	4	8	3
1973	4	13	1
1974	4	4P	1
1975	3	14	4
1976	3	13	4
1977	3	7	2
1978	3	15	1
1979	3	19	3
1980	3	21R	5
1981	4	12	3
1982	4	9	2
1983	4	5	1
1984	4	14	2
1985	4	4P	1
1986	3	20	2
1987	3	18	1
1988	3	14	1
1989	3	13	2
1990	3	5	1
1991	3	7	1
1992	3	21R	1
1993	N3	7	3
1994	N3	13	1
1995	N3	4	3
1996	N3	3P	1
1997	N2	1P	1
1998	N1	17	3

1920-1929

1949-1956

1964-1971

1975-1979

1980-1982

1992-1993

1998

For many years after the Second World War, Bury were the only club to wear a single hoop at the top of their stockings.

CAMBRIDGE UNITED

In a city with more interest in academia and almost every sport other than football, it was not surprising that Abbey United were not founded until 1919. Besides, the university town had already a successful club in Cambridge City.

However, whereas the City preferred the rarefied atmosphere of the amateur world, Abbey went for the semi-professional arena of the Southern League. In the striking amber and black stripes, the club continued to prosper without indicating any great ambitions to obtain League status.

After the Second World War, and stimulated by further extensions to League membership, the powers at Abbey decided to take the name of their home city to offer an image of greater credibility. A series of successes in the Southern League prompted several applications for Football League membership. Finally, at the expense of ailing Bradford Park Avenue, and ironically, their near neighbours Cambridge City, they finally made it in 1970.

Although in early post-War years United had sported quartered shirts and then plain amber with a large black 'V', to celebrate their new status they decided to wear an all-white strip with amber and black trim. However, after the first two undistinguished seasons the amber shirts returned and promotion followed immediately!

Sadly, the team faced instant relegation, and the incoming manager, a young Ron Atkinson, decided to revert to the original stripes, which seemed to help inspire his team to great heights. After two successive promotions, the Abbey Road fans were treated to footballing delights undreamed of in the town. John Doherty then took over as manager and continued the good work. However, once Doherty had moved on , and the stars such as George Reilly and Alan Biley had left, the fall was as dramatic as the earlier rise had been. In 1984, for example, Cambridge deprived Crewe of their least cherished record by going 31 games without a win.

A vibrant all-yellow strip failed to brighten the gloom that had descended over the Abbey Stadium and it was not until John Beck took over in the 1990 season that a whole new glorious era in the club's history dawned.

That season, the United side sneaked into the play-offs, and at Wembley won the first ever 'final' match. The following season, the play-offs were avoided by taking the third division championship and the club was back in the dizzy heights of the second flight.

For a while, it almost seemed possible to go even higher, United's direct style proving difficult for most opponents. Unfortunately, the final promotion was just missed, and eventually John Beck also left. By the late 1990s a real fight for survival was on, as Cambridge, despite a mighty attempt to stop a repeat of the earlier decline, found themselves back in soccer's basement.

Cambridge United 1992. The team went so close to gaining promotion to the first division.

Cambridge (founded 1919) records and strips

1919-1962

	Division and position	Cup round reached
1919 to 1939 Southern League		
1946	SL	q1
1947	SL	
1948	SL	p
1949	SL	q1
1950	SL	q1
1951	SL	q1
1952	SL	q1
1953	SL	q3
1954	SL	2
1955	SL	1
1956	SL	p
1957	SL	q1
1958	SL	q2
1959	SL	q2
1960	SL	q3
1961	SL	q4
1962	SL	q4
1963	SL	1
1964	SL	1
1965	SL	1
1966	SL	q4
1967	SL	q2
1968	SL	q4
1969	SL	q1
1970	SL	q4
1971	4	20	2
1972	4	10	2
1973	4	3P	1
1974	3	21R	3
1975	4	6	3
1976	4	13	1
1977	4	1P	1
1978	3	2P	2
1979	2	12	3
1980	2	8	4
1981	2	13	3
1982	2	14	3

1968-1970

1970-1971

1978

1991-1992

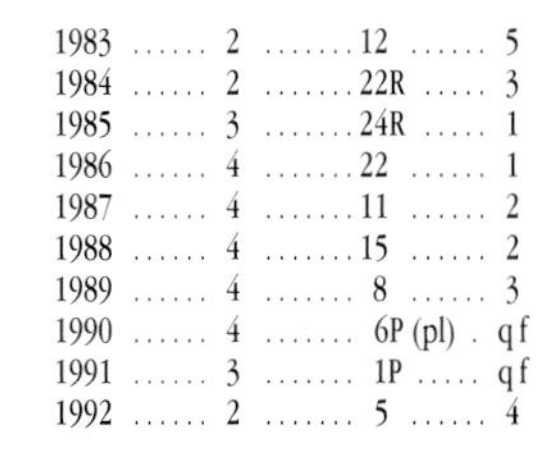

1983	2	12	5
1984	2	22R	3
1985	3	24R	1
1986	4	22	1
1987	4	11	2
1988	4	15	2
1989	4	8	3
1990	4	6P (pl)	qf
1991	3	1P	qf
1992	2	5	4
1993	2	23R	3
1994	N2	10	2
1995	N2	20R	3
1996	N3	16	1
1997	N3	10	2
1998	N3	16	1

1983

1998

The bold black chevron of the 1960s teams eventually gave way to plain shirts.

CARDIFF CITY

Despite some of the early successes of clubs such as Aberdare and Merthyr Town, soccer in South Wales has always had to struggle against the fierce competition of rugby union. Therefore it is not surprising that the capital city did not boast a senior club until the turn of the century.

Born out of the Riverside club, who sported the wonderful colours of chocolate and amber quarters, with chocolate shorts, the club had many venues and team changes until 1908. Then, following the Borough of Cardiff obtaining City status in 1905 the present title was adopted.

By this time, the early colourful ensemble had been changed to royal blue shirts and white shorts, and it was in this combination and the newly acquired Ninian Park stadium that the club was elected to the Football League in 1920.

Their success was immediate and spectacular. Promotion was achieved in the first season, and in 1924 the League championship was missed only on goal average. A year later, the Bluebirds lost by a single goal to Sheffield United in their first FA Cup final; then, in 1927, Cardiff made history by becoming the only club to take the Cup outside England. The driving force of Fred Keenor was inspirational for a while, but the 1930s witnessed a rapid decline and rivals Swansea became the dominant force in South Wales.

The war break helped the club to regroup, and immediate promotion in 1947 was followed by another five years later and for a while the glory days returned. Marauding forwards Trevor Ford and Gerry Hitchens threatened first division defences and Welsh hopes were high for a while.

Since then the top division status has been lost, but the great Cup tradition has continued. Stars such as John Toshack and sometimes just efficient teamwork have provided great successes in the Welsh Cup, which has been a passport to exciting times in Europe. A semi-final versus SV Hamburg and a single-goal defeat at the hands of mighty Real Madrid were highlights of a series of thrilling European campaigns.

Even in the 1980s and 1990s, when many seasons were spent in the depths of the fourth division, the Welsh Cup still offered the possibility of further European glory. In 1927, it was the red shirts of Arsenal who suffered at the hands of the Bluebirds - in the 1990s, it might have been the reds of Benfica, Roma or Bayern Munich!

In an historical FA Cup final, the 1927 Bluebirds took the trophy out of England for the only time.

Cardiff City (founded 1899) records and strips

Year	Division	Position	Cup round reached
1920			3
1921	2	2P	sf
1922	1	4	qf
1923	1	9	3
1924	1	2	qf
1925	1	11	F
1926	1	16	4
1927	1	14	W
1928	1	6	5
1929	1	22R	3
1930	2	8	4
1931	2	22R	3
1932	3S	9	3
1933	3S	19	1
1934	3S	22	2
1935	3S	19	1
1936	3S	20	1
1937	3S	18	3
1938	3S	10	3
1939	3S	13	4
1946			3
1947	3S	1P	3
1948	2	5	3
1949	2	4	5
1950	2	10	5
1951	2	3	3
1952	2	2P	3
1953	1	12	3

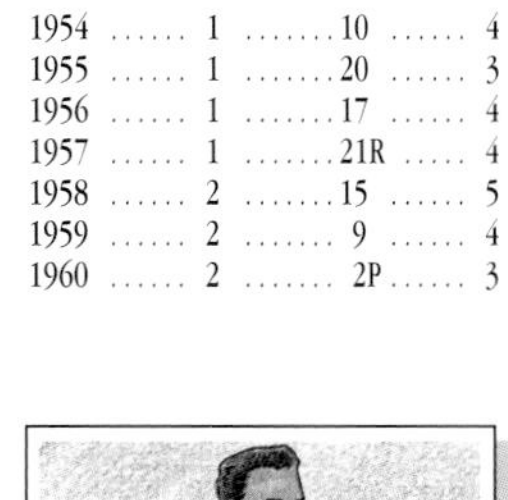

Year	Division	Position	Cup round reached
1954	1	10	4
1955	1	20	3
1956	1	17	4
1957	1	21R	4
1958	2	15	5
1959	2	9	4
1960	2	2P	3

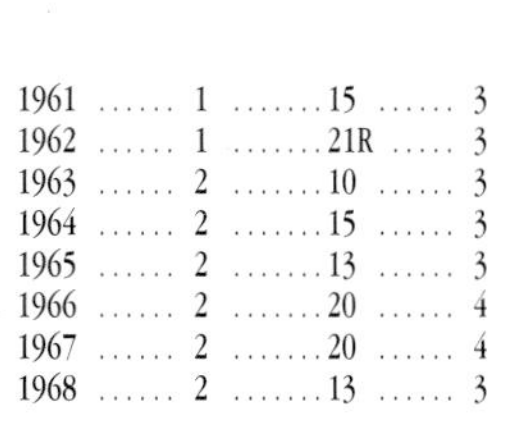

Year	Division	Position	Cup round reached
1961	1	15	3
1962	1	21R	3
1963	2	10	3
1964	2	15	3
1965	2	13	3
1966	2	20	4
1967	2	20	4
1968	2	13	3
1969	2	5	3
1970	2	7	3
1971	2	3	4
1972	2	19	5
1973	2	20	4
1974	2	17	3
1975	2	21R	3
1976	3	2P	3
1977	2	18	4
1978	2	19	5
1979	2	9	3
1980	2	15	3
1981	2	19	3
1982	2	20R	3
1983	3	2P	2
1984	2	15	3
1985	2	21R	3
1986	3	22R	1
1987	4	13	4
1988	4	2P	1
1989	3	16	3
1990	3	21R	3
1991	4	13	1
1992	4	9	1
1993	4	1P	1
1994	N2	19	5
1995	N2	22R	1
1996	N3	22	2
1997	N3	7	2
1998	N3	21	4

1899-1900

1921-1935

1936-1953

1957-1964

1968-1972

1975-1980

1983-1987

1998

In the pre-Adidas era around 1960, Cardiff were the only club to have three rings at the top of their stockings.

CARLISLE UNITED

In the remote border regions of northern Cumbria, several clubs fought for supremacy at the turn of the century. Finally, two of the more successful ones, Shaddongate and Red Rose, amalgamated to form Carlisle United, a club strong enough to take on the might of the rest of the country.

The new club chose blue for its colours either as striped or plain shirts, and as they progressed through northern regional leagues, Carlisle acquired a reputation for being difficult to beat, particularly as they could count on the services of talented Scots from over the border. Because the club was so geographically isolated and had to travel far even in northern league circles, it was felt that membership of the national competition could only be beneficial - but it was not until 1929 that election was achieved. Those pre-Second World War years produced only comfortable survival and it was not until the early 1950s under the player/management of Ivor Broadis, the great England schemer, that United began to realise that there was more to life than survival. For a while there was no great progress, and the club even dropped into the fourth division. Then one of the 1951 team, Alan Ashman, systematically built up a workmanlike side which eventually achieved more than even the club's greatest fans had dreamed possible. A team built around experienced professionals such as Chris Balderstone and Bobby Owen advanced to the second flight and then, in 1974, squeezed into the last promotion place to put the club in the first division.

The first table of the 1974/75 season showed Carlisle at the top of the League. Of course it could not last and eventually United finished at the bottom and were relegated. However, the team had fought well and looked smart throughout the campaign. The traditional blue shirts now included a broad white central stripe trimmed with red, still a unique design and, of course well remembered in the many photographs taken at the time.

Almost every time a small club has reached the top, a rapid decline has followed and Carlisle slipped gradually to the League basement again. However, the officials and fans now knew the possibility of success, even for the smaller clubs, was never far away. For a club whose blue shirts had been proudly worn by the likes of Peter Beardsley and Stan Bowles, and managed by such brilliant motivators as Bill Shankly and Bob Stokoe, another climb to greater things was always possible. In the late 1990s, despite inconsistencies in the league, someone like chairman Michael Knighton *might* be just the man to inspire one.

In 1974, Carlisle United were once top of division one. In this smart strip, they looked the part.

Carlisle United (founded 1903) records and strips

1904-1924

Year	Division	Position	Cup round reached
1929	3N	8	2
1930	3N	15	3
1931	3N	8	3
1932	3N	18	2
1933	3N	19	2
1934	3N	13	2
1935	3N	22	1
1936	3N	13	1
1937	3N	10	3
1938	3N	12	1
1939	3N	19	1
1946			2
1947	3N	16	3

1934-1939

1946-1955

Year	Division	Position	Cup round reached
1948	3N	9	1
1949	3N	15	1
1950	3N	9	3
1951	3N	3	3
1952	3N	7	1
1953	3N	9	1
1954	3N	13	1
1955	3N	20	2

1970-1974

Year	Division	Position	Cup round reached
1956	3N	21	1
1957	3N	15	3
1958	3N	16	2
1959	4	10	2
1960	4	19	1
1961	4	19	2
1962	4	4P	3
1963	3	23R	3
1964	4	2P	5
1965	3	1P	1
1966	2	14	4
1967	2	3	4
1968	2	10	4
1969	2	12	3
1970	2	12	5
1971	2	4	4
1972	2	10	3

This red-trimmed white panel was never repeated in any other League kit.

1975-1976

Year	Division	Position	Cup round reached
1973	2	18	5
1974	2	3P	4
1975	1	22R	qf
1976	2	19	3
1977	2	20R	4
1978	3	13	3
1979	3	6	3
1980	3	6	4
1981	3	19	4

1980

Year	Division	Position	Cup round reached
1982	3	2P	3
1983	2	14	3
1984	2	7	3
1985	2	16	4
1986	2	20R	4
1987	3	22R	1
1988	4	23	1

1994-1995

Year	Division	Position	Cup round reached
1989	4	12	2
1990	4	8	2
1991	4	20	1
1992	4	22	1
1993	N3	18	1
1994	N3	7	3

1998

Year	Division	Position	Cup round reached
1995	N3	1P	3
1996	N2	21R	1
1997	N3	3P	4
1998	N2	23R	1

CHARLTON ATHLETIC

For a spell either side of the Second World War, Charlton Athletic became members of football's elite, situated near the top of the first division and appearing in Wembley finals. The club's beginnings, however, would not have suggested such heights.

Founded in 1906 by some local lads, they enjoyed only modest success for the next 15 years, their bright red shirts appearing only in south eastern regional leagues.

In 1920 the situation changed dramatically. Professionals were brought in and the following year the club was elected into the third division (south). However, this big step produced very little success on the field and the only occasion of note during the 1920s was a proposed amalgamation with Catford Southend. For a while, Charlton sported the light and dark blue stripes of the other club but the link, which was purely for financial benefit, was eventually ended and Charlton returned to the Valley, wearing red shirts again.

It was the appointment of Jimmy Seed as manager in the 1930s which enabled the club to make a breakthrough into the big time. Two consecutive promotion seasons were followed by three more in which Charlton finished in the top four in division one. Excitement was high and in 1938 over 75,000 people crammed into the great natural bowl at the Valley. The Second World War put the success on ice for six years, and although on resumption league results were never as good, two Wembley finals provided wonderful memories, especially in 1947 when Chris Duffy's goal defeated Burnley. Few would forget the winger's celebration run after his superb late strike.

However, it was the red-headed goalkeeper Sam Bartram who become the club's biggest hero. Rated the greatest English keeper not to have played for his country, Sam played a record number of games for the Valients. After he and Jimmy Seed left, the club's fortunes never reached the same heights again.

A long spell in the second division was only highlighted by the 1969 season, when Charlton were pipped for promotion by south London neighbours Crystal Palace. Even a smart white shirt with a red yoke had failed to inspire, and eventually there were two spells in the third division.

In recent years, adversity has united staff and fans; the supporters' reaction to the move from the Valley and the efforts of manager Lenny Lawrence provided sufficient momentum to rise again to first division status. Even subsequent relegation did not dampen the tremendous spirit in the club, especially after the Valients returned to the Valley in 1992, and the fans were rewarded with promotion to the top flight via a thrilling play-off victory in 1998.

Certainly, if manager Alan Curbishley can hold on to his bright young starlets, Charlton could still make an impact at the top level.

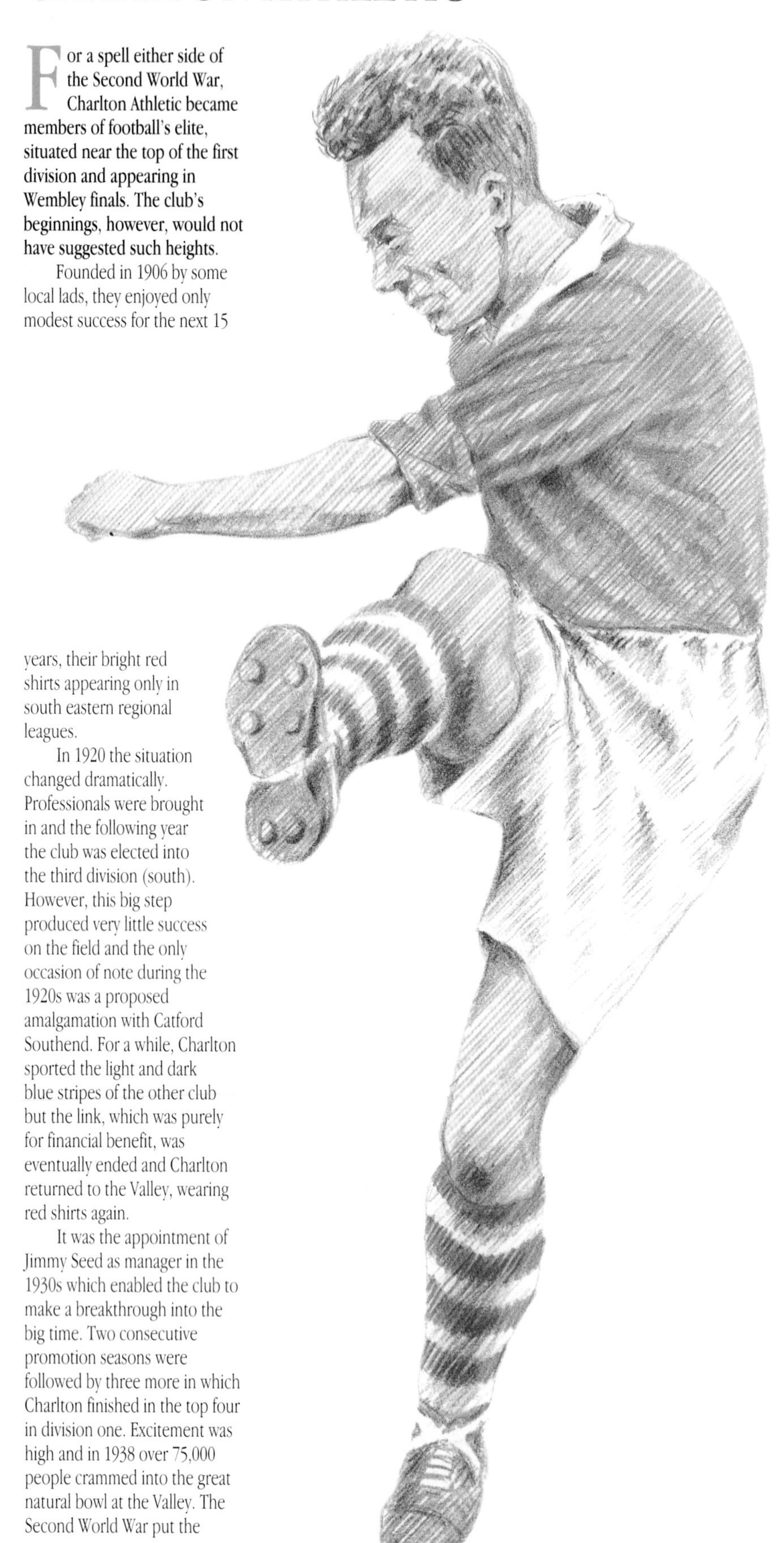

During the immediate post-Second World War period this Charlton strip was prominent in the great Cup campaigns.

Charlton (founded 1905) records and strips

1905-1923

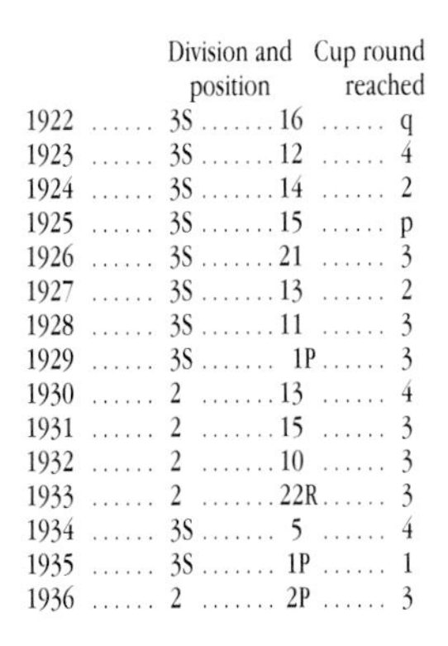

	Division and position		Cup round reached
1922	3S	16	q
1923	3S	12	4
1924	3S	14	2
1925	3S	15	p
1926	3S	21	3
1927	3S	13	2
1928	3S	11	3
1929	3S	1P	3
1930	2	13	4
1931	2	15	3
1932	2	10	3
1933	2	22R	3
1934	3S	5	4
1935	3S	1P	1
1936	2	2P	3

1923-1924

1936-1939

1937	1	2	3
1938	1	4	5
1939	1	3	3
1946			F
1947	1	19	W
1948	1	13	5
1949	1	9	3
1950	1	20	4
1951	1	17	3
1952	1	10	3

1946-1958

1953	1	5	3
1954	1	9	3
1955	1	15	3
1956	1	14	5
1957	1	22R	3
1958	2	3	4

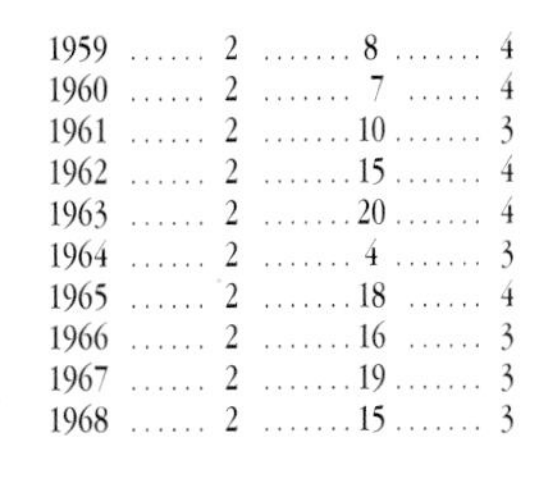

1959	2	8	4
1960	2	7	4
1961	2	10	3
1962	2	15	4
1963	2	20	4
1964	2	4	3
1965	2	18	4
1966	2	16	3
1967	2	19	3
1968	2	15	3

1964-1966

1969	2	3	4
1970	2	20	4
1971	2	20	3
1972	2	21R	3
1973	3	11	3
1974	3	14	1
1975	3	3P	2

1974-1977

1988-1991

1976	2	9	5
1977	2	7	3
1978	2	17	3
1979	2	19	4
1980	2	22R	3
1981	3	3P	5
1982	2	13	3
1983	2	17	3
1984	2	13	4
1985	2	17	3
1986	2	2P	3

1998

1987	1	19	3
1988	1	17	3
1989	1	14	5
1990	1	19R	4
1991	2	16	3
1992	2	7	4
1993	N1	12	3
1994	N1	11	qf
1995	N1	15	3
1996	N1	6	5
1997	N1	15	3
1998	N1	4(P)pl	4

In the mid 1960s a new technique in shirt manufacturing enabled Charlton to wear this red-yoked white shirt.

CHELSEA

Chelsea are in many ways a unique force. They did not compete before their election to the Football League in 1905. Chairman Gus Mears created a club in order to play at his newly acquired Stamford Bridge stadium; he chose Lord Chelsea's colours to play in, applied for League membership, got it, and the club's history began.

At the time everyone expected the club to crash. but promotion was quickly won and, apart from one slight hiccup, they stayed in the top division until 1924. An FA Cup final defeat in 1915 was merely a foretaste of the frustrating 'nearly' history in football's oldest senior competition.

The huge stadium was often used to host Cup finals and in later years nearly 83,000 people came to watch a local derby against Arsenal.

Chelsea always enjoyed the support of local west Londoners and celebrities alike. Proximity to the West End enabled many a famous face to turn up for the big match, and it was this association, plus the fact that during the 1920s and 1930s the team never lived up to its potential, that the Pensioners were never really taken seriously.

Things changed in 1952 with the appointment of Ted Drake, who discarded the old 'star' system and instead assembled a workmanlike team, which three seasons later won the first division championship, the club's first trophy. In the next few years, the manager introduced many young players who became known as 'Drake's Ducklings'. Those were exciting times, as the young Jimmy Greaves regularly got three or four goals a game.

Unfortunately the bubble burst as Greaves went to Milan and others failed to make the grade. Following the slump and temporary relegation, it was left to Tommy Doherty, then Dave Sexton to raise the playing standards again; and how well they succeeded. Sporting a very smart all-blue shirt and shorts outfit, the team regularly challenged for the League. But it was in the Cup where the chief successes came.

A sad defeat in 1967 by London rivals Spurs was followed by a dramatic replay victory over mighty Leeds United. Twelve months later another famous team clad in all-white, Real Madrid, were defeated in the final of the European Cup Winners' Cup and Chelsea were certainly in the big time.

However, the old Chelsea jokes returned with inconsistencies on the pitch. The arrival of Ken Bates as chairman gave the club new vitality, and although an unhealthy number of managers came and went over the next ten years, the Pensioners were firmly back in the top flight. Modern thinking and a readiness to seek the best players from abroad supported their quest to become the capital's premier club once more.

Under the guidance of Ruud Gullit and his successor Gianluca Vialli, the club won the FA Cup, the Coca-Cola (League) Cup and the European Cup Winners' Cup within a year. As the millennium approached, the new cosmopolitan Chelsea had established themselves amongst the Premiership's elite

In this strikingly simple kit, Osgood and company won the FA Cup and the European Cup Winners' Cup.

Chelsea (founded 1905) records and strips

1905-1914

	Division and position		Cup round reached
1906	2	3	3
1907	2	2P	1
1908	1	13	2
1909	1	11	2
1910	1	19R	2
1911	2	3	sf
1912	2	2P	2
1913	1	18	2
1914	1	18	1
1915	1	19	F
1920	1	2	sf
1921	1	18	qf
1922	1	9	1
1923	1	19	2
1924	1	21R	1
1925	2	5	1
1926	2	3	4
1927	2	4	qf
1928	2	3	3
1929	2	9	5
1930	2	2P	3
1931	1	12	qf
1932	1	12	sf
1933	1	18	3
1934	1	19	5
1935	1	12	3

1915-1929

1936-1958

1936	1	8	5
1937	1	13	4
1938	1	10	3
1939	1	20	qf
1946			5
1947	1	15	4
1948	1	18	4
1949	1	13	5
1950	1	13	sf
1951	1	20	5
1952	1	19	sf
1953	1	19	5

1959-1963

1954	1	8	3
1955	1	1	5
1956	1	16	5
1957	1	12	4
1958	1	11	4
1959	1	14	4
1960	1	18	4
1961	1	12	3
1962	1	22R	3
1963	2	2P	5
1964	1	5	4
1965	1	3	sf
1966	1	5	sf
1967	1	9	F
1968	1	6	qf

1969	1	6	qf
1970	1	3	W
1971	1	6	4
1972	1	7	5
1973	1	12	6
1974	1	17	3
1975	1	21R	4
1976	2	11	6
1977	2	2P	3
1978	1	16	5

1964-1975

1979	1	22R	3
1980	2	4	3
1981	2	12	3
1982	2	12	qf
1983	2	18	4
1984	2	1P	3
1985	1	6	4
1986	1	6	4

1987

Just before Jimmy Greaves left for Milan, Chelsea wore this at the time unique, two-coloured ring top to their stockings.

1993-1995

1987	1	14	4
1988	1	18R	4
1989	2	1P	3
1990	1	5	4
1991	1	11	3

1998

1992	1	14	qf
1993	Pr	11	3
1994	Pr	14	F
1995	Pr	11	4
1996	Pr	11	sf
1997	Pr.	6	W
1998	Pr.	4	3

CHESTER CITY

Although Chester were not founded until 1884, football had been played in the town for many centuries before, particularly on the Roodee on Shrove Tuesday. Perhaps it was because of this long association with the game that the senior local football club took many years to raise their sights to achieving national league status.

In the homely Sealand Road stadium, the team clad in black and white stripes, continued to battle away in the Cheshire League. Probably it was the relative success of the other Cheshire sides in the third division (north) which inspired the club to seek greater competition, because finally in 1932 Chester were elected to the Football League.

By this time, the strip had been changed to blue and white stripes, and for nearly two decades this combination seemed to suit Chester. They regularly finished in the top three or four, sadly always just failing to achieve promotion.

After the Second World War, fortunes changed and the Cheshire club struggled like its county rivals. By the early 1960s drastic measures were required - and taken. The team turned out in green shirts trimmed with gold collars and cuffs, and white shorts; young talent was blooded, and the great Ron Davies terrorised division four defences before being snapped up by Luton.

However, the talent dried up, the blue and white returned and for a decade a fourth division mid-table finish was all the club had to look forward to. But in the mid 1970s a fine side was put together and in 1975 not only was promotion achieved but Chester reached the League Cup semi-finals, only to lose by the odd goal to the eventual winners Aston Villa.

Three years later, a fifth position in division three revived memories of those great days of the 1930s. Just four points separated this team from promotion to the second division. It was during this period towards the late 1970s that Ian Rush delighted the Sealand Road faithful. Everyone knows of his transfer to Liverpool, but who is to say what might have been if he had stayed just a little longer.

Since those days little of great significance was to happen on the pitch, mid-table anonymity broken only by relegations and subsequent promotion. However, Chester's change of status meant adding 'City' to the title of the club in 1983.

Also, in the meantime, Sealand Road was sold and the team played at Macclesfield Town's ground, until the new custom-built Deva Stadium was finished in 1992, allowing Chester to look forward to many more centuries of football.

In 1978, Chester's blue and white stripes were feared in division three.

Chester (founded 1884) records and strips

	Division and	position	Cup round reached
1932	3N	3	2
1933	3N	4	4
1934	3N	10	2
1935	3N	3	3
1936	3N	2	2
1937	3N	3	4
1938	3N	9	3
1939	3N	6	4
1946			3
1947	3N	3	4
1948	3N	20	4
1949	3N	18	2
1950	3N	12	2
1951	3N	13	1
1952	3N	19	3
1953	3N	20	1
1954	3N	24	1
1955	3N	24	1
1956	3N	17	1
1957	3N	21	1
1958	3N	21	2
1959	4	3	2
1960	4	20	2
1961	4	24	1
1962	4	23	2
1963	4	21	1
1964	4	12	2
1965	4	8	3
1966	4	7	3
1967	4	19	1
1968	4	22	2
1969	4	14	2
1970	4	11	4
1971	4	5	3
1972	4	20	1
1973	4	15	1
1974	4	7	3
1975	4	4P	1
1976	3	17	2
1977	3	13	5
1978	3	5	2
1979	3	16	2
1980	3	9	5
1981	3	18	1
1982	3	24R	1
1983	4	13	1
1984	4	24	1
1985	4	16	1
1986	4	2P	1
1987	3	15	4
1988	3	15	1
1989	3	8	2
1990	3	16	2
1991	3	19	3
1992	3	18	2
1993	N2	24R	1
1994	N3	2P	3
1995	N2	23R	2
1996	N3	8	1
1997	N3	6	2
1998	N3	14	2

1889-1930

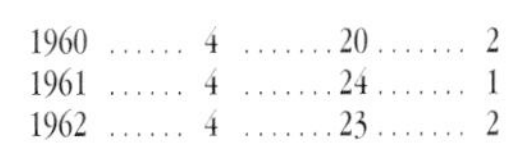

1961-1962

1976-1977

1993-1994

1967-1971

1986

1998

1932-1957

Although only a temporary colour switch, this green and gold helped to launch Ron Davies to stardom.

CHESTERFIELD

Chesterfield's location between Sheffield and Derby has been responsible for both their early beginnings and the general lack of success in over a century of football activity. In 1866 they were already taking on the might of the nearby big cities without ever having a real chance of achieving permanent success. The first teams sported a patriotic strip of white shirts with a Union flag emblazoned across the front, but by 1870 the records show that 'blue and white jerseys and white trowsers' were the official dress and this has remained ever since.

Having gone through the traditional process of growth, Chesterfield were elected into the Foootball League in 1900. The initial 'success' of mid-table security soon gave way to several seasons at the bottom of division two and in 1909 the club went back to the Midland League. However, with the expansion of the Football League in 1921, the 'Spirites' returned to the senior competition this time to the third division (north).

The club proved to be one of the strongest at this level and after a decade of relative success, it was no surprise that Chesterfield were promoted in 1936. The Spirites were well capable of holding their own, and crowds of 30,000 turned up at the big games at the Recreation Ground.

After the War, in the wonderful 1947 season promotion to the first division was only just missed. The club, now wearing all-blue shirts, confidently finished above Spurs, Newcastle and other famous names. But consistent success at this level demands financial back-up and the pressure from bigger clubs in the area eventually proved too strong.

The club's fortunes did not collapse, but there was a gradual decline. From being a strong third division side, the Spirites became one of the many clubs to hover between the bottom two divisions. Lack of resources meant a constant selling of top players to balance the books.

One such player was Gordon Banks, who like another ex-Chesterfield 'keeper, Sam Hardy, went on to play for England. Strangely, Bob Wilson, the Scottish goalie, was also born in the town.

During the last decade Chesterfield have survived well. But in order to overcome the problem of losing support to the local big clubs, a new crop of talent was always needed, players who would stay long enough to create another exciting period. By the mid-1990s it looked promising, and in 1997 John Duncan took the Spirites into the FA Cup semi-finals and were only minutes away from an appearance in the final itself.

The first division still remains tantalisingly elusive but not unattainable.

The all-blue shirts of 1947, when Chesterfield almost became a first division club.

Chesterfield (founded 1866) records and strips

	Division and position		Cup round reached
1900	2	7	p
1901	2	14	1

1866

1902	2	16	p
1903	2	6	p
1904	2	11	p
1905	2	5	p
1906	2	18	2
1907	2	18	1
1908	2	19	2
1909	2	19L	1
1910			1
1911			p
1912			p
1913			1
1914			1
1915			p
1920			p
1921			p
1922	3N	13	p
1923	3N	4	p
1924	3N	3	p
1925	3N	7	p
1926	3N	4	3
1927	3N	7	3
1928	3N	16	1

1910

1929	3N	11	3
1930	3N	4	3
1931	3N	1P	2
1932	2	17	4
1933	2	21R	5
1934	3N	2	3
1935	3N	10	3
1936	3N	1P	2
1937	2	15	3
1938	2	11	5
1939	2	6	3
1946			3
1947	2	4	4
1948	2	16	3
1949	2	6	3
1950	2	14	5

1939

1951	2	21R	3
1952	3N	13	2
1953	3N	12	2
1954	3N	6	4
1955	3N	6	1
1956	3N	6	2
1957	3N	6	3
1958	3N	8	1
1959	3	16	3
1960	3	18	1
1961	3	24R	3
1962	4	19	2
1963	4	15	2
1964	4	16	3
1965	4	12	3
1966	4	20	1
1967	4	15	1
1968	4	7	3
1969	4	20	3
1970	4	1P	1
1971	3	5	2
1972	3	13	3
1973	3	16	2

1950

1973

1974	3	5	1
1975	3	15	3
1976	3	15	1
1977	3	18	2

1981

1978	3	9	2
1979	3	20	1
1980	3	4	1
1981	3	5	3
1982	3	11	2
1983	3	24R	1
1984	4	13	2
1985	4	1P	2
1986	3	17	1
1987	3	17	1
1988	3	18	1
1989	3	22R	1

In the very early years, the Spirites wore this patriotic jersey to impress opponents.

1990	4	7	2
1991	4	18	2
1992	4	13	1
1993	N3	12	1
1994	N3	8	1
1995	N3	3P(pl)	1

1995

1996	N2	7	2
1997	N2	10	sf
1998	N2	10	2

1998

COLCHESTER UNITED

Abandoning their customary stripes, Colchester found lasting Cup fame in 1971.

Colchester, like Chester, is one of the oldest towns in Britain and also has a long history of football-type games. In the 1920s and early 1930s, the local military establishments regularly used to play against FA XIs. However, it was not until the remarkably advanced date of 1937 that the present senior club was formed, making it the 'baby' of present League clubs. Colchester joined the Southern League and enjoyed early success there and in the FA Cup.

Normally such a young club would have found the six-year lay-off caused by the Second World War difficult to cope with, but in 1948 the Oystermen caused a sensation by reaching the fifth round of the FA Cup. First division Huddersfield, then second division Bradford PA were brushed aside before United went down to the eventual runners-up Blackpool. The club had become news!

Manager Ted Fenton's men, proudly sporting their blue and white stripes, were still in the public eye in 1950 when the League was to be expanded, and so within seven seasons of being formed United were in division three (south).

Probably promotion had been achieved a little too quickly, as those first few years were a great struggle. However, results slowly improved and in 1957 further promotion to the second division was missed by a single point. But consistency was still missing and the next decade saw a yo-yoing between divisions three and four. The Oystermen's fans were still waiting for some more Cup glory.

In 1971 they were more than rewarded. A wonderful FA Cup campaign was highlighted by an amazing 3-2 win over Leeds United, the then first division leaders. This was followed by a further unforeseen success in the Watney Cup, then a popular competition. Colchester had battled through to the final to meet first division West Bromwich Albion. It was an exciting final, ending in a 4-4 draw, with the Oystermen eventually succeeding 4-3 on penalties.

The town celebrated and for a while the fourth division must have seemed quite unbearable. The club even played around with the strip, sometimes wearing all-blue, sometimes plain white shirts, but on the pitch nothing more was really achieved.

Eventually Colchester found themselves drifting down the table and in 1990 the unthinkable happened when they were relegated into the GM Vauxhall Conference. It could have been the end then, but they showed character and after two traumatic years, fought their way back into the Football League. The blue and white stripes continued to battle in the compact Layer Road ground, and promotion was won via the play-offs at the end of the 1997/98 season.

Colchester (founded 1937) records and strips

1937-1956

Division and position — Cup round reached

1937 to 1939 Southern League.

Year	Division	Position	Cup round reached
1946	SL		p
1947	SL		1
1948	SL		5
1949	SL		1
1950	SL		p
1951	3S	16	1
1952	3S	10	3
1953	3S	22	3
1954	3S	23	1
1955	3S	24	1

1966

1971

Year	Division	Position	Cup round reached
1956	3S	12	1
1957	3S	3	1
1958	3S	12	1
1959	3	5	4

1973

Year	Division	Position	Cup round reached
1960	3	9	1
1961	3	23R	2
1962	4	2P	1
1963	3	12	1
1964	3	17	2
1965	3	23R	2
1966	4	4P	1
1967	3	13	2
1968	3	22R	2
1969	4	6	2
1970	4	10	1
1971	4	6	qf
1972	4	11	1
1973	4	22	2
1974	4	3P	1

Year	Division	Position	Cup round reached
1975	3	11	2
1976	3	22R	1
1977	4	3P	4
1978	3	8	2

1979-1981

Year	Division	Position	Cup round reached
1979	3	7	5
1980	3	5	3
1981	3	22R	3
1982	4	6	3

1983

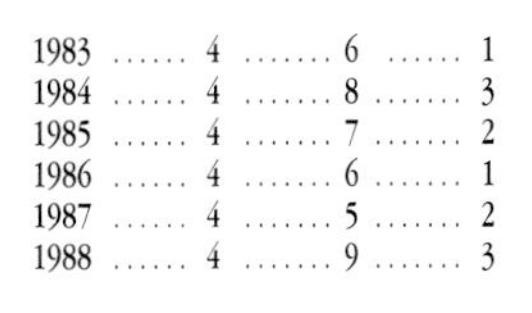

Year	Division	Position	Cup round reached
1983	4	6	1
1984	4	8	3
1985	4	7	2
1986	4	6	1
1987	4	5	2
1988	4	9	3

1990-1992

Year	Division	Position	Cup round reached
1989	4	22	4
1990	4	24R	2
1991	GMVC		2
1992	GMVC		1
1993	N3	10	1
1994	N3	17	1
1995	N3	10	3
1996	N3	7	1
1997	N3	8	1
1998	N3	4P(pl)	2

1998

An unusual pinstripe version of the traditional shirts.

COVENTRY CITY

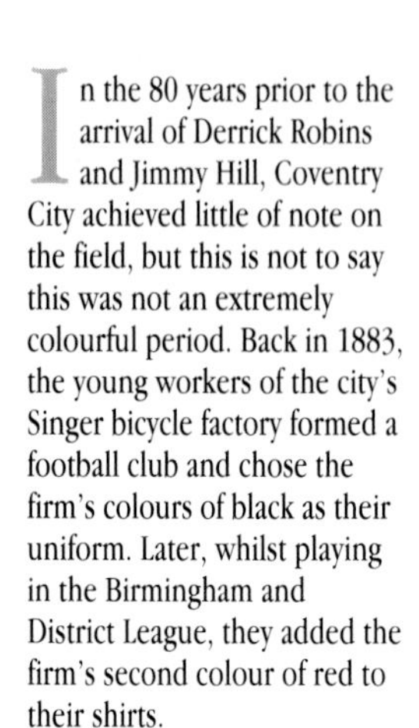

In the 80 years prior to the arrival of Derrick Robins and Jimmy Hill, Coventry City achieved little of note on the field, but this is not to say this was not an extremely colourful period. Back in 1883, the young workers of the city's Singer bicycle factory formed a football club and chose the firm's colours of black as their uniform. Later, whilst playing in the Birmingham and District League, they added the firm's second colour of red to their shirts.

Local success fuelled ambitions and the club's name was changed from Singer FC to Coventry City in 1898 in an attempt to take on the major clubs. The city's traditional colours of light and dark blue were now introduced, first in halved form, then as dark blue jerseys with light blue sleeves. However, it was not until 1920 that Coventry City finally entered the Football League. At first they struggled, and even another change of colours, this time to the civic colours of red and green, failed to improve results. In fact, in this strip, the club was relegated and although there was a return to the light blue and white stripes of 1913, the third division was their home until 1936.

For their first season back in division two, yet another new shirt, which consisted of royal blue shirts with a broad white centre stripe and sleeves, was adopted to symbolise new hope. This outfit remained for nearly 30 years, even though the club's fortunes faded again. By 1962, Coventry had only just escaped from division four and were still looking for inspiration. This, of course, arrived in the form of Messrs Robins and Hill.

A revolutionary all-sky blue strip symbolised not only hope but a whole series of supporter and community innovations. The club attracted great attention and publicity, and better players than ever before wanted to be part of it. Rapid promotion to the first division followed and although Coventry have never dominated at this level - in fact they have often struggled - they have an obvious firm foundation and capacity to stay at the top.

Of course, the temptation to fiddle around with the strip remains. Many variations have been tried, including the famous matching shirt and shorts stripes, but it was a return to the early sky blue and white stripes which inspired the club's greatest moment. Old boy George Curtis and popular extrovert John Sillett took their side to Wembley where they won an exciting FA Cup final against Spurs in 1987.

No further honours followed, but Coventry regularly continued to survive in the Premier Division sporting many smart variations of sky blue, including yet another combination with dark blue in a promising 1997/98 season.

Coventry's golden day, winning the 1987 Cup final, in a return to their old sky blue and white stripes.

Coventry (founded 1883) records and strips

Year	Division	Position	Cup round
1936	3S	1P	1
1937	2	8	5
1938	2	4	3
1939	2	4	3
1946			3
1947	2	8	4
1948	2	10	4
1949	2	16	3

1883-1912

Year	Division and position		Cup round reached
1908			1
1909			q
1910			qf
1911			3
1912			2
1913			1
1914			4q
1915			6q
1920	2	20	1
1921	2	21	6q
1922	2	20	2
1923	2	18	5q
1924	2	19	1
1925	2	22R	1
1926	3N	16	1
1927	3S	15	2
1928	3S	20	1
1929	3S	11	1
1930	3S	6	3
1931	3S	14	2
1932	3S	12	1
1933	3S	6	2
1934	3S	2	2
1935	3S	3	3

Year	Division	Position	Cup round
1950	2	12	3
1951	2	7	3
1952	2	21R	4
1953	3S	6	3
1954	3S	14	1
1955	3S	9	3
1956	3S	8	1
1957	3S	16	1
1958	3S	19	2
1959	4	2P	2
1960	3	5	1
1961	3	15	3
1962	3	14	2
1963	3	4	qf
1964	3	1P	2
1965	2	10	3
1966	2	3	5
1967	2	1P	3
1968	1	20	4
1969	1	20	4
1970	1	6	3
1971	1	10	3
1972	1	18	4
1973	1	18	6
1974	1	16	5
1975	1	14	4

1913-1961

1962-1972

Year	Division	Position	Cup round
1976	1	14	4
1977	1	19	4
1978	1	7	3
1979	1	10	3
1980	1	15	4
1981	1	16	5
1982	1	14	qf
1983	1	19	4

1976-1981

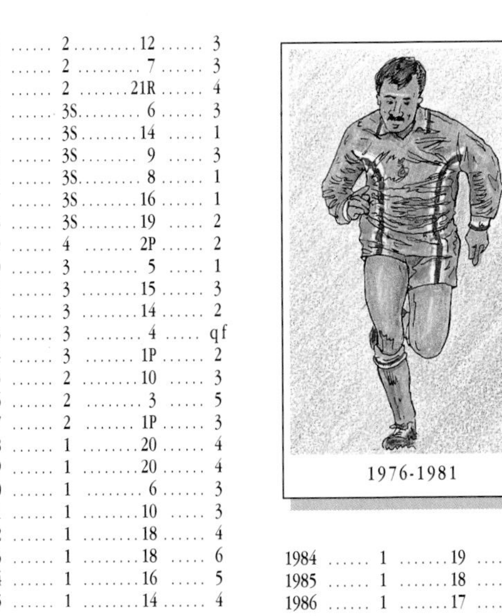

Year	Division	Position	Cup round
1984	1	19	4
1985	1	18	4
1986	1	17	3

1986-1987

1987-1988

Year	Division	Position	Cup round
1987	1	10	W
1988	1	10	4
1989	1	7	3
1990	1	12	3
1991	1	16	4
1992	1	19	3
1993	Pr	15	3
1994	Pr	11	3

1998

Year	Division	Position	Cup round
1995	Pr	16	4
1996	Pr	16	4
1997	Pr.	17	5
1998	Pr.	11	6

The famous striped kit, where the motif was continued through the shirt and shorts.

CREWE ALEXANDRA

Over the years, Crewe has been the butt of many jokes about the railway and its football team. Indeed as you approach the town by train, the giant floodlights are not in the adjoining football ground but in the railway marshalling yards. And it was a group of railway workers who met in a local pub, The Alexandra, in 1877 and formed their first club.

The north-west of England was one of the hotbeds of football and the red shirts of the Alex were soon elected into the second division of the League. However, a reluctance to adopt professionalism cost the club dear and in 1896 they failed to be re-elected. This was the beginning of a quarter of a century in the wilderness.

Those early days had been eventful. The club, having lost to Swifts in the FA Cup, objected that the latter's crossbar was too low. The FA agreed and a replay was ordered. The Swifts refused to replay and Crewe proceeded to the semi-finals, their best ever run. The incident, however, resulted in a change to the rules and no such post-match objection was tolerated again.

In 1921 Crewe were back in the League as original members of the third division (north) and between the Wars usually finished in a respectable mid-table position. The red became 'scarlet', and the club even won the Welsh Cup on two occasions, and in William Lewis, Crewe had a regular Welsh international.
The same level was maintained for the first ten years after the Second World War, but from the mid-1950s the Alex dropped into a terrible playing decline. The team regularly finished bottom of the League, once went 30 matches without a win (three years without an away win), and in 1960 were humiliated 13-2 at Spurs in a Cup replay. Strangely enough, in the first match at Crewe, Bill Brown, the Spurs' goalkeeper had saved his team with a brilliant last-minute stop on the line.

The next year a revitalised team beat Chelsea at Stamford Bridge and the improvement continued until, in 1963, promotion was achieved. Fine players such as Frank Lord and Ron Smith were sold and the Alex were soon relegated, but they had begun to believe in themselves. A second promotion took place in 1968 but this was followed again by instant relegation and another long period of gloom and despair, which did not lift until the arrival of manager Dario Gradi in 1983.

The club had avoided financial and administrative disasters, but did not have any positive footballing approach. Gradi soon changed this, creating his own 'school of excellence'. Young talent was attracted and the red shirts were proudly worn by future England stars such as David Platt, Geoff Thomas and Rob Jones.

Another promotion was gained and after two seasons sadly lost, but while the Gradi approach remained the club's reputation was good and by the mid-1990s the Alex had risen to undreamed of heights.

After a gap of over 100 years Crewe were back in the second flight. Limited resources and long term realism still couldn't dampen the delights of being with Manchester City, Wolves, Nottingham Forest et al.

This stylish kit witnessed the most successful period in the Alex's modern history.

Crewe (founded 1877) records and strips

1877-1914

1938-1957

1967-1971

This unusual half-sleeved shirt was worn by the promotion side in 1990.

1994-1995

1963-1965

1920-1937

1988-1990

1998

Year	Division	Position	Cup round reached
1886			3
1887			p
1888			sf
1889			1
1890			p
1891			1
1892			1
1893	2	10	p
1894	2	12	p
1895	2	16	p
1896	2	16L	1
1897			p
1898			p
1899			p
1900			p
1901			p
1902			p
1903			p
1904			p
1905			p
1906			1
1907			1
1908			p
1909			p
1910			p
1911			2
1912			1
1913			p
1914			p
1915			p
1920			p
1921			p
1922	3N	6	p
1923	3N	6	p
1924	3N	20	p
1925	3N	15	p
1926	3N	11	2
1927	3N	15	3
1928	3N	17	4
1929	3N	9	4
1930	3N	11	2
1931	3N	18	2
1932	3N	8	1
1933	3N	10	2
1934	3N	14	1
1935	3N	13	1
1936	3N	6	3
1937	3N	20	3
1938	3N	8	2
1939	3N	8	2
1946			1
1947	3N	8	1
1948	3N	10	4
1949	3N	12	3
1950	3N	7	2
1951	3N	9	2
1952	3N	16	1
1953	3N	10	1
1954	3N	16	2
1955	3N	22	1
1956	3N	24	1
1957	3N	24	1
1958	3N	24	1
1959	4	18	1
1960	4	14	4
1961	4	9	4
1962	4	10	2
1963	4	3P	2
1964	3	22R	1
1965	4	10	1
1966	4	14	4
1967	4	5	3
1968	4	4P	1
1969	3	23R	2
1970	4	15	1
1971	4	15	2
1972	4	24	1
1973	4	21	3
1974	4	21	1
1975	4	18	1
1976	4	16	1
1977	4	12	1
1978	4	15	2
1979	4	24	2
1980	4	23	1
1981	4	18	1
1982	4	24	2
1983	4	23	1
1984	4	17	1
1985	4	10	1
1986	4	12	1
1987	4	17	1
1988	4	17	1
1989	4	3P	3
1990	3	12	3
1991	3	22R	5
1992	N3	6	3
1993	N3	6	4
1994	N3	3P	3
1995	N2	3	2
1996	N2	5	4
1997	N2	6P(pl)	3
1998	N1	11	3

CRYSTAL PALACE

Football had been played on the site of the Crystal Palace since early times and indeed a club by that name, wearing blue and white, was a founder member of the FA in 1863. Many FA Cup finals were played there and in 1905 it was decided to form a separate club to use the ground regularly.

The new club, wearing at first white shirts with red and blue hoops, then cardinal red and blue stripes, eventually left the Palace site to settle at Selhurst Park, and by 1921 had gained sufficient status to be elected into the Football League. By now the team wore claret and light blue shirts, obviously in an attempt to emulate the great Aston Villa successes. There was immediate progress with promotion in the first season, but after four terms of struggle the club slumped back into the third division. In the years before the Second World War the Palace were always one of the top teams in the division without ever managing that final breakthrough.

After the Second World War, it was sad to see a club with great resources, a huge stadium and much potential languishing in the lower levels. However, in the early 1960s, clad in innovative white shirts with claret and light blue hoops, Palace began a great revival. With star players such as Johnny Byrne and Vic Rouse, there were promotions to division three, then division two, and in an exciting end to the 1968/69 season the Glaziers finally entered the top flight.

Sadly, the team was not really up to it and another unusual outfit of claret with light blue pinstripes appeared on television when, it seemed, only for their entertainment value in conceding big scores. The inevitable happened and Palace dropped back to the third division. Obviously the club needed a radical reappraisal. Accordingly, a successful youth policy was developed under Terry Venables and the whole attitude at Selhurst became more professional. The fragile image of the Glaziers was replaced by the aggressive upward image of the Eagles.

Soon the new-look Palace, now clad in all-white trimmed with the early red and blue colours, fought their way back to the first division. After Venables had left, there was another dip into the second division, but another forward-looking manager, Steve Coppell, revived the momentum and the Eagles returned to the top.

By now, the outfit was all red and blue. The stay among the elite proved longer this time and a Cup final appearance was achieved. The chief problem appeared to be in inspiring the catchment area of south London to support their local talent in the same way fans in the north of the capital respond to their clubs. Even though the Eagles have dived three times since, if the huge Selhurst bowl could be regularly filled, there are grounds for genuine optimism that, eventually they might fly higher than before.

Initially the return of Coppell and the presence of a few Italians suggested as much, but Palace have so far failed to establish themselves in the Premiership.

The return of the early colours of red and blue stripes eventually saw the Palace reach their first FA Cup final.

Crystal Palace (founded 1905) records and strips

	Division and position		Cup round reached
1921	3	1P	2
1922	2	14	2
1923	2	16	1
1924	2	15	3
1925	2	21R	2
1926	3S	13	5
1927	3S	6	1
1928	3S	5	2
1929	3S	2	5
1930	3S	9	3
1931	3S	2	4
1932	3S	4	2
1933	3S	5	1
1934	3S	12	4
1935	3S	5	1
1936	3S	6	2
1937	3S	14	1
1938	3S	7	3
1939	3S	2	1
1946			3
1947	3S	18	3
1948	3S	13	3
1949	3S	22	1
1950	3S	7	1
1951	3S	24	1
1952	3S	19	1
1953	3S	13	2
1954	3S	22	1
1955	3S	20	2
1956	3S	23	1
1957	3S	20	3
1958	3S	14	3
1959	4	7	3
1960	4	8	3
1961	4	2P	2
1962	3	15	3
1963	3	11	2
1964	3	2P	2
1965	2	7	qf
1966	2	11	3
1967	2	7	3
1968	2	11	3
1969	2	2P	3
1970	1	20	5
1971	1	18	3
1972	1	20	3
1973	1	21R	4
1974	2	20R	3
1975	3	5	2
1976	3	5	sf
1977	3	3P	3
1978	2	9	3
1979	2	1P	5
1980	1	13	3
1981	1	22R	3
1982	2	15	qf
1983	2	15	5
1984	2	18	4
1985	2	15	3
1986	2	5	3
1987	2	6	4
1988	2	6	3
1989	2	3P	3
1990	1	15	F
1991	1	3	3
1992	1	10	3
1993	Pr	20R	3
1994	N1	1P	3
1995	Pr	19R	sf
1996	N1	3	3
1997	N1	6P(pl)	3
1998	Pr.	20R	5

1905-1937

1968-1971

1978-1982

This striking claret and light blue chestband impressed everyone in the early days of the fourth division.

1946-1958

1958-1962

1989-1993

1998

DARLINGTON

Darlington appears to be one of the many clubs with a long history of relatively little happening, broken only by isolated pockets of excitement. Indeed there was a Darlington club wearing blue and white stripes, playing in the north-east, as far back as 1865, but it was not until 1883 that the present club was founded on modern lines. In those early days, the players were purely amateur, and Darlington were one of the original entrants into the FA Amateur Cup.

Just before the First World War the club acquired professional status and in 1921 became founder members of the third division (north), clad in black and white hoops, colours which have remained until today.

Darlington were immediately a success. After four seasons at the top, the Quakers were promoted to division two. Sadly, the jump in status proved too much too soon, and after two years Darlington were back in the third division. As many clubs discovered before the founding of the four-divisional system, getting out of the regional third divisions with only one promotion place was so difficult as to be a disincentive to try. Therefore the club, with just two exceptions, hovered in the bottom section for the next 40 years without any major highlights. The second of these near misses in 1949, offered some hope at the time, but the competition from the local big clubs prevented any consolidation and continuation of success.

Since the introduction of the fourth division in 1958, it's interesting that the only two temporary highlights, in the promotion years of 1966 and 1985, were achieved when the players wore unusual variations in shirt patterns. In 1966 they wore white shirts with three black chestbands and in 1985 all-white with black chevrons on the shoulders and sleeves.

It took a situation of near disaster to add spice to recent history. The shock of demotion to the GM Vauxhall Conference demanded a concentrated effort from management, players and fans alike, and in two glorious years the Quakers won the championships of both the Conference and the fourth division.

The subsequent relegation perhaps illustrated that the north-east had not room for a fourth big club, and like neighbours Hartlepool, Darlington would remain forever humble. But once more clad in either striking black and white hooped shirts or thin hooped chestbands, the team would try to defy all the odds.

Darlington's hoops proudly took on the big clubs of the second division in the 1920s.

Darlington (founded 1883) records and strips

1883-1935

1959-1963

1976

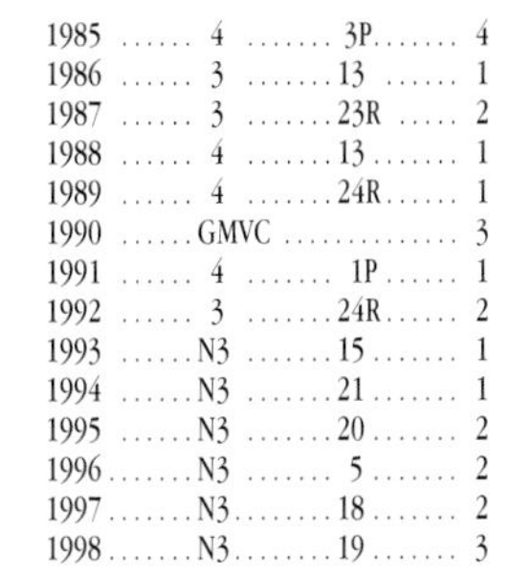

Year	Division	Position	Cup round reached
1911			3
1912			2
1913			p
1914			p
1915			1
1920			2
1921			1
1922	3N	2	1
1923	3N	9	p
1924	3N	6	1
1925	3N	1P	1
1926	2	15	2
1927	2	21R	4
1928	3N	7	3
1929	3N	19	3
1930	3N	3	1
1931	3N	11	1
1932	3N	11	3
1933	3N	22	4
1934	3N	16	1
1935	3N	5	2
1936	3N	12	3
1937	3N	22	4
1938	3N	19	1
1939	3N	18	2
1946			2
1947	3N	17	2
1948	3N	16	1
1949	3N	4	3
1950	3N	17	1
1951	3N	18	1
1952	3N	23	1
1953	3N	21	1
1954	3N	21	1
1955	3N	15	3
1956	3N	15	2
1957	3N	18	2
1958	3N	20	5
1959	4	16	3
1960	4	15	2
1961	4	7	2
1962	4	13	1
1963	4	12	1
1964	4	19	1
1965	4	17	3
1966	4	2P	2
1967	3	22R	2
1968	4	16	1
1969	4	5	2
1970	4	22	1
1971	4	12	2
1972	4	19	2
1973	4	24	1
1974	4	20	1
1975	4	21	2
1976	4	20	1
1977	4	11	3
1978	4	19	1
1979	4	21	3
1980	4	22	2
1981	4	8	1
1982	4	13	1
1983	4	17	1
1984	4	16	4
1985	4	3P	4
1986	3	13	1
1987	3	23R	2
1988	4	13	1
1989	4	24R	1
1990	GMVC		3
1991	4	1P	1
1992	3	24R	2
1993	N3	15	1
1994	N3	21	1
1995	N3	20	2
1996	N3	5	2
1997	N3	18	2
1998	N3	19	3

1985

1966-1968

The striking compromise between the Real Madrid all-white and the traditional hoops, as worn in the 1960s.

1936-1957

1991

1998

DERBY COUNTY

The history of Derby County is a colourful one in all senses of the word. The original club was an offshoot of the County Cricket Club and its first set of colours were borrowed from the latter. The chocolate and amber halved jerseys and pale blue shorts remain a unique combination to this day.

Derby County became an instant success. They were one of the founder members of the Football League and during the next two decades went close to being champions several times. It was this success which prompted a change of colours first to dark blue and red, then a few years later white shirts and black shorts, the football club no longer wishing to be associated with a cricketing organisation. The same near-success was repeated in the FA Cup. Apart from several semi-final appearances, the Rams also reached three finals, only to lose them all. The third defeat, 6-0 to Bury, seemed only to add fuel to the legend of a gypsy's curse that Derby would never win the Cup.

Indeed in both Cup and League, despite having a galaxy of stars between the the two World Wars, County never quite became a dominant club, always just missing out even in the more successful seasons.

Immediately after the Second World War, all seemed to have changed. A talented forward line including Raich Carter and Peter Doherty inspired a great FA Cup final win over Charlton, finally laying that gypsy's curse. More famous names were bought, but inexplicably in the mid-1950s, the club dropped into the third division following two successive relegations. Within two seasons they were back in the second, but only a moderate force.

In 1969 Brian Clough arrived, changed the club's strip to echo that of the England team and demanded his players to perform to that level. He certainly assembled a talented squad. Promotion was followed three years later by the Ram's first ever League title. These were great times; the following year a European Cup final place was just missed, and even when Clough moved on he left a team good enough to take a second tltle in 1975. This side, managed by Dave Mackay, gave belief that success would last forever.

Unfortunately, by the time of the club's centenary in 1984 everything had gone wrong. Derby had overspent, players had to be sold, the team were playing in the third division, and a winding-up order had been served. The Maxwell family intervened at the last minute and Arthur Cox eventually built a team to return to the first division. The black shorts returned, but the cash was still short and some of the new stars had to go. In the 1990s the club were back, battling away, in the second flight, before finally returning again to the top. Hopefully it probably wouldn't be long before the colourful times returned. Jim Smith and a few exotic stars certainly had brightened up the town and its new stadium.

Brian Clough's Derby looked like the England team and often played like it.

Derby (founded 1884) records and strips

1884-1895

Year	Division	Position	Cup round reached
1885			1
1886			3
1887			2
1888			2
1889	1	10	2
1890	1	7	1
1891	1	11	2
1892	1	10	1
1893	1	13	1
1894	1	3	qf
1895	1	15	1
1896	1	2	sf
1897	1	3	sf
1898	1	10	F
1899	1	9	F
1900	1	6	1
1901	1	12	1
1902	1	6	sf
1903	1	9	F
1904	1	14	sf
1905	1	11	1
1906	1	15	2

1895-1905

1905-1956

Year	Division	Position	Cup round reached
1907	1	19R	3
1908	2	6	1
1909	2	5	sf
1910	2	4	2
1911	2	6	qf
1912	2	1P	2
1913	1	7	1
1914	1	20R	1
1915	2	1P	1
1920	1	18	1
1921	1	21R	2
1922	2	12	1

1958-1962

Year	Division	Position	Cup round reached
1923	2	14	sf
1924	2	3	2
1925	2	3	1
1926	2	2P	4
1927	1	12	4
1928	1	4	4
1929	1	6	4
1930	1	2	4
1931	1	6	3
1932	1	15	5
1933	1	7	sf
1934	1	4	5
1935	1	6	5
1936	1	2	qf
1937	1	4	5
1938	1	13	3
1939	1	6	3
1946			W
1947	1	14	5
1948	1	4	sf

Year	Division	Position	Cup round reached
1949	1	3	qf
1950	1	11	qf
1951	1	11	4
1952	1	17	3
1953	1	22R	3
1954	2	18	3
1955	2	22R	3

1968-1970

Year	Division	Position	Cup round reached
1956	3N	2	2
1957	3N	1P	2
1958	2	16	3
1959	2	7	3
1960	2	18	3

1971-1973

Year	Division	Position	Cup round reached
1961	2	12	3
1962	2	16	4
1963	2	18	4
1964	2	13	3
1965	2	9	3
1966	2	8	3
1967	2	17	3
1968	2	18	3
1969	2	1P	3
1970	1	4	5
1971	1	9	5
1972	1	1C	5
1973	1	7	6
1974	1	3	4
1975	1	1C	5
1976	1	4	sf
1977	1	15	qf
1978	1	12	5

1985-86

Year	Division	Position	Cup round reached
1979	1	19	3
1980	1	21R	3
1981	2	6	3
1982	2	16	3
1983	2	13	5
1984	2	20R	6
1985	3	7	1
1986	3	3P	3
1987	2	1P	3
1988	1	15	3
1989	1	5	4
1990	1	16	3

1998

Year	Division	Position	Cup round reached
1991	1	20R	3
1992	2	3	4
1993	N1	8	qf
1994	N1	6	3
1995	N1	9	3
1996	N1	2P	3
1997	Pr.	12	6
1998	Pr.	9	4

Believe it or not the team which finished third in the first division in 1894 wore this wonderful strip.

DONCASTER ROVERS

Although founded as long ago as 1879, Doncaster Rovers are another club to have suffered limited success because of the 'unfair' competition from the big city clubs. The area of south Yorkshire, Notts and Derbyshire has for a long time reached saturation point in the attraction of support. Against this background, the men of Belle Vue have often struggled and yet there have been odd moments of glory.

In those early days the club looked a colourful outfit with their striking blue jerseys with a gold St Andrew's cross, playing in local leagues for a while until eventually joining the Midland League. Ambitious to achieve Football League status and now wearing red and white stripes, Rovers applied for election several times before joining the second division in 1902. However, they were out of their depth and returned to the Midland League. In 1904 the situation was repeated, and this time the Midland League was Doncaster's lot for 20 years.

Eventually, after the First World War, when the club was reformed into a much more professional outfit, a permanent place in the Football League was secured. Rovers were steady if not spectacular performers, and in the mid-1930s, now wearing hoops, they even managed two seasons in the second division. Yet another one-year spell followed after the Second World War but the club could still not hold on to a place in the higher levels of League football.

In 1950, led by the brilliant Irishman Peter Doherty, Rovers returned to division two and stayed there. Many young stars were attracted to the club, amongst them Harry Gregg and the unlucky Alick Jeffrey, whose early injury ended a promising career.

With the going of Doherty, Gregg and Jeffrey, a weakened staff underwent two successive relegation seasons and looked set for a future in the fourth division. The lack of playing talent was offset by many unique sartorial experiments, involving either plain red or white, with contrasting trims on the necks or bodies of the jerseys.

In the last 30 years, there have been several promotions but the challenge of even the third division seemed to be beyond the club's capabilities. Managers such as Billy Bremner, Dave MacKay and Laurie McMenemy could not achieve continued success, and the only hope in the fight for survival, seemed to be the return of the red and white hooped shirts, the image of the glorious Doherty days.

In 1998, Rovers' luck finally ran out. They were relegated from the Football League and faced a struggle to survive.

Inspired by Peter Doherty, the hooped Rovers survived well in the second division.

Doncaster (founded 1879) records and strips

Year	Division and position		Cup round reached
1933	3N	6	3
1934	3N	5	1
1935	3N	1P	1
1936	2	18	3
1937	2	22R	3
1938	3N	2	3
1939	3N	2	4
1946			1
1947	3N	1P	3

1879-1909

Year	Division and position		Cup round reached
1902	2	7	p
1903	2	16	p
1905	2	18L	q
1924	3N	9	q

Year	Division and position		Cup round reached
1948	2	21R	3
1949	3N	3	1
1950	3N	1P	4
1951	2	11	3
1952	2	16	5
1953	2	13	3

1910-1962

Year	Division and position		Cup round reached
1925	3N	18	1
1926	3N	10	2
1927	3N	8	2
1928	3N	4	1
1929	3N	5	1
1930	3N	14	4
1931	3N	15	2
1932	3N	15	2

Year	Division and position		Cup round reached
1954	2	12	5
1955	2	18	5
1956	2	17	5
1957	2	14	3
1958	2	22R	3
1959	3	22R	3
1960	4	17	3
1961	4	11	1

1967-1971

Year	Division and position		Cup round reached
1962	4	21	1
1963	4	16	2
1964	4	14	3
1965	4	9	3
1966	4	1P	1
1967	3	23R	1
1968	4	10	3
1969	4	1P	3
1970	3	11	2
1971	3	23R	1
1972	4	12	1
1973	4	17	3
1974	4	22	3
1975	4	17	2
1976	4	10	1
1977	4	8	1

1973

Year	Division and position		Cup round reached
1978	4	12	1
1979	4	22	2
1980	4	12	2
1981	4	3P	3
1982	3	19	2
1983	3	23R	1
1984	4	2P	1

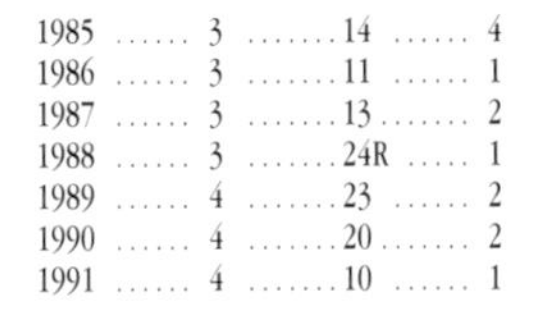

Year	Division and position		Cup round reached
1985	3	14	4
1986	3	11	1
1987	3	13	2
1988	3	24R	1
1989	4	23	2
1990	4	20	2
1991	4	10	1

1988

Year	Division and position		Cup round reached
1992	4	21	1
1993	N3	16	1
1994	N3	15	1
1995	N3	9	1
1996	N3	13	1
1997	N3	19	1
1998	N3	24R	1

1998

The 1960 double-collar style was unique in its modern form.

Despite the club's long history of successes, the Everton of the late 1980s still stands out as a great side.

EVERTON

Liverpool, red; Everton, blue. It's easy, everyone knows that. Everton stars throughout the century have always sported a royal blue shirt, but in those early years after the club's foundation in 1878 things were very different.

St Domingo, the original club, did wear blue and white stripes, but as players from other clubs were attracted to the newly named Everton FC, and often wore their old kit, it was decided to have a new uniform altogether. Black shirts with red sashes were the striking result, but within the next few years players also turned out in salmon pink and even ruby red! Finally in 1901 the Toffeemen decided upon royal blue shirts and white shorts - the rest is history.

However, even before the arrival of the blue shirts Everton had already become one of the country's major clubs. After being founder members of the Football League, they won one League championship and reached two FA Cup finals before the turn of the century and Everton went on to taste success in virtually every decade.

By the mid-1920s there was another championship, two Cup finals (one victorious) and several near misses in both competitions. The arrival of Bill 'Dixie' Dean heralded a truly golden period of success. In the championship year of 1928, Dean set a new League scoring record of 60 goals, one which will probably last forever. And, although a leaky defence caused the freak relegation in 1930, the arrivals of Joe Mercer, Cliff Britton, Tommy Lawton and Tommy Jones meant the following decade realised even more trophies.

After the Second World War they experienced their leanest period. There were many near misses in the Cup, but a second drop to division two followed by many seasons in the wrong half of division one were not what the Goodison faithful expected. Happily, there were two more wonderful eras to come.

The first materialised in the 1960s when manager Harry Catterick assembled a fine footballing side starring Alan Ball, Colin Harvey and Howard Kendall. Consistently brilliant League form and exciting Cup runs seemed to suggest a never-ending dominance of the English game.

Somehow the consistency vanished and it was not until Howard Kendall returned as manager in 1981 that trophy-winning form also reappeared. Every year, it seemed, Everton were either winners or runners-up in a major competition, including the club's first European trophy (the Cup Winners' Cup) in 1985.

During this period, several variations were made to the blue shirts, but the colour remained unchanged as did the challenge for trophies. It was probably the only way to survive in their city.

Everton (founded 1878) records and strips

Year	Division and position		Cup round reached
1887			1
1888			2
1889	1	8	q
1890	1	2	2
1891	1	1C	1
1892	1	5	1
1893	1	3	F
1894	1	6	1
1895	1	2	qf
1896	1	3	qf
1897	1	7	F
1898	1	4	sf
1899	1	4	2
1900	1	11	1
1901	1	7	2
1902	1	2	1
1903	1	12	qf
1904	1	3	1
1905	1	2	sf
1906	1	11	W
1907	1	3	F
1908	1	11	qf
1909	1	2	2
1910	1	10	sf
1911	1	4	3
1912	1	2	qf
1913	1	11	qf
1914	1	15	1
1915	1	1C	sf
1920	1	16	1
1921	1	7	qf
1922	1	20	1
1923	1	5	1
1924	1	7	2
1925	1	17	3
1926	1	11	3
1927	1	20	4
1928	1	1C	4
1929	1	18	3
1930	1	22R	4
1931	2	1P	sf
1932	1	1C	3
1933	1	11	W
1934	1	14	3
1935	1	8	qf
1936	1	16	3
1937	1	17	5
1938	1	14	4
1939	1	1C	qf
1946			3
1947	1	10	4
1948	1	14	5
1949	1	18	4
1950	1	18	sf
1951	1	22R	3
1952	2	7	3
1953	2	16	sf
1954	2	2P	5
1955	1	11	4
1956	1	15	qf
1957	1	15	5
1958	1	16	4
1959	1	16	5
1960	1	15	3
1961	1	5	3
1962	1	4	5
1963	1	1C	5
1964	1	3	5
1965	1	4	4
1966	1	11	W
1967	1	6	qf
1968	1	5	F
1969	1	3	sf
1970	1	1C	3
1971	1	14	sf
1972	1	15	5
1973	1	17	4
1974	1	7	4
1975	1	4	5
1976	1	11	3
1977	1	9	sf
1978	1	3	4
1979	1	4	3
1980	1	19	sf
1981	1	15	qf
1982	1	8	3
1983	1	7	3
1984	1	7	W
1985	1	1C	F
1986	1	2	F
1987	1	1C	5
1988	1	4	5
1989	1	8	F
1990	1	6	5
1991	1	9	qf
1992	1	12	4
1993	Pr	13	3
1994	Pr	17	3
1995	Pr	15	W
1996	Pr	6	4
1997	Pr.	15	4
1998	Pr.	17	3

1878-1914

1928-1938

1959-1962

1964-1967

1983-1985

1986-1989

1998

Everton shirts are normally nearly all-blue, and this deep-yoked version was the only one of its kind.

EXETER CITY

Devon is one of the more beautiful parts of England, but its geographical isolation and great interest in the rugby code has meant that soccer has always had to struggle. In Exeter, a football club had been in existence for many years, but it was not until 1904 that the current club was formed and maybe it was the same insular character of the region which influenced the City to sport the same green and white shirts as local 'giants' Plymouth Argyle.

Certainly there was no instant success and the players, deciding that green was unlucky, influenced the change to red and white stripes in 1910. However, unlike at Burnley where the same anti-green decision had been made, there was no huge change in fortunes. The team did reasonably well in the Southern League, but it was not until the enlargement of the Football League in 1920 that the Grecians first played in the third division.

Again, only moderate success was achieved. The club's finances were never too healthy and rare local talents, such as Cliff Bastin and Dick Pym, were soon transferred to Arsenal and Bolton Wanderers respectively. But somehow in the early 1930s, enough footballing quality remained at the club to create two of Exeter's greatest occasions. In the 1931 season the team rocked the football world by knocking out Derby County, Bury and Leeds before losing to the mighty Sunderland side in a sixth round FA Cup replay. Exeter were obviously stirred with ambitious inspiration, for two years later only the fast emerging Brentford denied them promotion to the second division.

But good things don't last without resources, and a slump in form resulted in re-elections and a humble League position for decades to come. Indeed, the only significant changes came in the playing strip. The red and white remained, but hoops, stripes, white sleeves, plain red and plain white have constantly been swapped around in an attempt to inspire further successes.

Occasionally there were highlights, such as a short spell in the third division in the mid-1960s, followed by a longer one in the early 1980s. The latter even included a second great Cup run in which only the eventual winners Tottenham Hotspur halted the Grecians, again in the quarter-finals. However, once more the demands of the third division proved too great and relegation followed. Over the years it became obvious that only creative and inspirational management could overcome the limited resources of such an isolated club. In 1990, happily, such an occasion arose. Leeds old boy Terry Cooper led the team to the divisional title by ten clear points, thrilling the club's supporters by remaining undefeated at St James' Park. But the bubble burst when Cooper was snatched away and a small squad decimated by injuries could not sustain the effort. As the 1990s progressed, City were again waiting for the next time.

The successful Exeter team of the early 1980s wore stripes, the most common of the club's red and white permutations.

Exeter (founded 1904) records and strips

1904-1910

	Division and position		Cup round reached
1909			2
1910			5
1911			1
1912			4
1913			4
1914			2
1915			1
1920			6
1921	3S	19	1
1922	3S	21	5
1923	3S	20	5
1924	3S	16	2
1925	3S	7	1
1926	3S	20	1
1927	3S	12	3
1928	3S	8	4

1910-1939

1946-1953

1929	3S	21	3
1930	3S	16	1
1931	3S	13	6
1932	3S	7	3
1933	3S	2	1
1934	3S	9	1
1935	3S	11	2
1936	3S	22	1
1937	3S	21	5
1938	3S	17	2
1939	3S	14	1
1946			2
1947	3S	15	1
1948	3S	11	1

1957-1962

1949	3S	12	3
1950	3S	16	4
1951	3S	14	4
1952	3S	23	2
1953	3S	17	1
1954	3S	9	1
1955	3S	22	1
1956	3S	16	3
1957	3S	21	1

1962-1965

1958	3S	24	1
1959	4	5	1
1960	4	9	3
1961	4	21	1
1962	4	18	1
1963	4	17	1
1964	4	4P	2
1965	3	17	2
1966	3	22R	1
1967	4	14	1
1968	4	20	2
1969	4	17	3

1966-68 & 1977-79

1970	4	18	2
1971	4	9	1
1972	4	15	2
1973	4	8	1
1974	4	10	1
1975	4	9	1
1976	4	7	1
1977	4	2P	1
1978	3	17	3
1979	3	9	2
1980	3	8	1
1981	3	11	qf

1982	3	18	1
1983	3	19	1
1984	3	24R	1
1985	4	18	1
1986	4	21	3
1987	4	14	1
1988	4	22	1
1989	4	13	1
1990	4	1P	3
1991	3	16	1
1992	3	20	3
1993	N2	19	1
1994	N2	22R	3

1990-1992

1995	N3	24	2
1996	N3	14	1
1997	N3	22	2
1998	N3	15	1

1998

Before deciding it was unlucky, the early Exeter players wore green and white like Devon neighbours Plymouth Argyle.

FULHAM

Just as Exeter City have had to overcome the problems of geographical isolation, then Fulham have had to contend with just the opposite. For over a century, they have been one of the smaller, more homely clubs in the capital, and the dumping of big rivals, Chelsea, on their doorstep took much of their potential support.

Founded as St Andrews, a church team, in 1879 in a uniform of white shirts and black shorts, the club soon found a base at Craven Cottage; so ground and colours have remained the same ever since.

In 1898 the name was changed to Fulham and success on the field improved to such a degree that in 1908 the Lilywhites were elected to division two of the Football League. These were exciting times in south-west London as Fulham reached the semi-final of the FA Cup before going down to mighty Newcastle United.

The next 20 years were steady rather than spectacular, but a gradual decline culminated in relegation in 1928. It took four years to return but 43 goals by Frank Newton saw the club back as champions with a team more than capable of holding their own. Indeed, in 1936 another semi-final Cup run included a wonderful win over Chelsea, before Sheffield United proved too strong.

After the Second World War came the Cottagers' greatest and most colourful period. In 1949, amongst scenes of tremendous excitement, Fulham were promoted to division one, but despite great efforts the team was not up to it and three years later came relegation. This was not the end of the good times, though. Under the colourful chairmanship of comedian Tommy Trinder, Craven Cottage saw some wonderful football from Johnny Haynes, Bedford Jezzard, Bobby Robson, Tosh Chamberlain and Jimmy Hill. By 1960 they were back in the top flight and although it was always a struggle, players like George Cohen, Tony Macedo and Alan Mullery kept the Cup spirit alive with two more semi-final appearances.

At the end of the 1960s, the pace was just too hot, and second division days returned. Again there was no gloom yet; Bobby Moore, swapping his England white for that of the Cottagers, led Fulham to the 1975 FA Cup final, against West Ham of all clubs. Sadly for Bobby and the lads, they lost 2-0.

Since then, no-one has quite managed to recreate such eventful times. Seasons have been split between the second and third divisions, and Fulham were just one of London's other clubs. Craven Cottage was the house where 'The last days of Pompeii' was written and the uncertainty hanging over the ground often suggested another vanished culture. However, old boys like Jimmy Hill did much to help the club to survive, perhaps in the hope of adding another successful chapter to the Fulham story.

Eventually, after dropping into the bottom division, a saviour in the form of multi-millionaire Mohamed Al Fayed whose money persuaded Kevin Keegan and, for a time, Ray Wilkins back into the hurly burly of League management. The world waits.

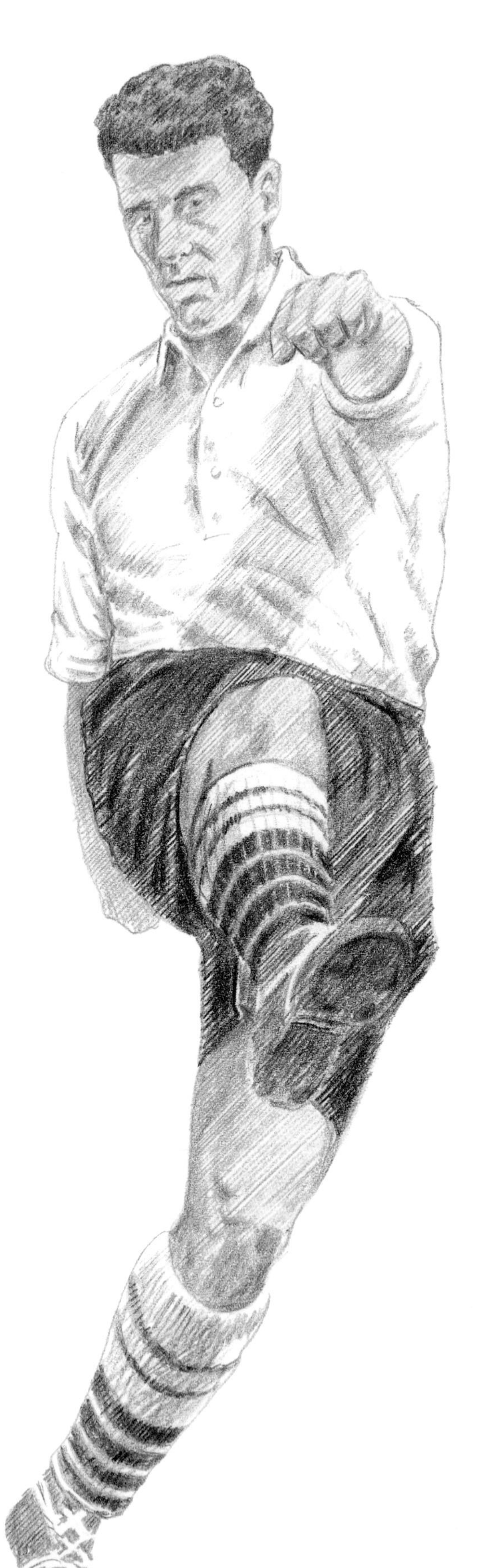

The strip worn by Johnny Haynes and company in the 1950s, when the club sparred with the best.

Fulham (founded 1879) records and strips

	Division and position		Cup round reached
1904			1
1905			qf
1906			2
1907			2

1879-1928

1908	2	4	sf
1909	2	10	2
1910	2	7	2
1911	2	10	1
1912	2	8	qf
1913	2	9	1
1914	2	11	1

1929-1939

1915	2	12	2
1920	2	6	1
1921	2	9	3
1922	2	7	2
1923	2	10	1
1924	2	20	2
1925	2	12	2
1926	2	19	qf
1927	2	18	4

1948-1955

1928	2	21R	3
1929	3S	5	2
1930	3S	7	4
1931	3S	9	3
1932	3S	1P	3
1933	2	3	3
1934	2	16	3
1935	2	7	3
1936	2	9	sf
1937	2	11	3
1938	2	8	3
1939	2	12	4

1956-1960

1946			3
1947	2	15	3
1948	2	11	qf
1949	2	1P	3
1950	1	17	3
1951	1	18	qf
1952	1	22R	3
1953	2	8	3
1954	2	8	4
1955	2	14	3
1956	2	9	4
1957	2	11	4
1958	2	5	sf
1959	2	2P	4
1960	1	10	4
1961	1	17	3
1962	1	20	sf
1963	1	16	3
1964	1	15	4
1965	1	20	3
1966	1	20	3

1964-1969

1967	1	19	4
1968	1	22R	4
1969	2	22R	4
1970	3	4	1
1971	3	2P	1
1972	2	20	4
1973	2	9	3
1974	2	13	4
1975	2	9	F
1976	2	12	3
1977	2	17	3
1978	2	10	3

1974-1977

1979	2	10	4
1980	2	20R	3
1981	3	13	4
1982	3	3P	2
1983	2	4	4
1984	2	11	3
1985	2	9	3
1986	2	22R	3
1987	3	18	3
1988	3	9	1
1989	3	4	1

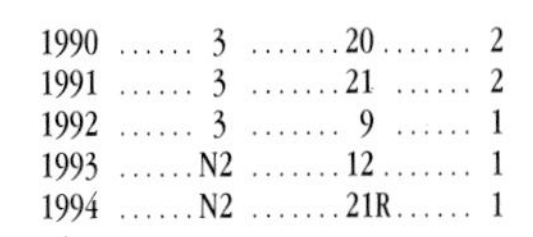

1990	3	20	2
1991	3	21	2
1992	3	9	1
1993	N2	12	1
1994	N2	21R	1

1988-1989

1995	N3	8	2
1996	N3	17	3
1997	N3	2P	1
1998	N2	6	3

1998

Yet another unique stocking style, with contrasting pinstripe hoops in each section.

GILLINGHAM

Before the First World War it was stated that Kent would never produce a major football club without sufficient population to maintain a first-rate team. The Medway towns should have provided one such opportunity, but somehow the area's team has never scaled great heights.

New Brompton, as Gillingham were first called, grew out of a desire to emulate or better the earlier exploits of neighbouring clubs, the Royal Engineers and Chatham. The black and white stripes chosen as club colours illustrated a desire to copy the success of Notts County and Newcastle United.

The energies of the chairman, Alderman J Barnes, helped to overcome early crises, usually financial, and regular successes in FA Cup matches provided Gilingham with sufficient good publicity to eventually reach Football League status by 1920

However, the team continually struggled on the field, with re-election an almost annual problem. By 1928 they had become desperate enough to hope that a change of colours might provide a change of fortune; but the new blue shirts and white shorts altered nothing in playing standards. Only three times before 1938 did the Gills finish in the top half of the division, and yet another application for re-election in that year saw the club drop out of the League and go into liquidation.

The club re-formed the following year but it was not until after the Second World War, when the third division expanded, that the club came back. Results even then were poor and Gillingham became one of the founder members of the fourth division. Perhaps this status enabled the club to become less overawed by the task in hand. In 1964 they proudly topped the division and consolidated well at the higher level. In fact, for nearly 30 years only a short spell back in the basement broke a fairly successful level of achievement.

In 1979 the Gills were just a point off promotion to Division Two. Surprisingly, such success often precedes a decline, but their record during the 1980s was impressive. For several seasons a top-six placing was achieved, usually accompanied by FA Cup runs to the third or fourth round. The colours were still blue and white, but presented in smart patterned versions, including the zig-zag chest hoop at the end of the decade.

Sadly, after relegation in 1989 the 1990s witnessed a return to the bad old days. Relegation to the basement saw a second great threat to the club's existence. Financial and playing crises had them tottering on the brink of extinction, but in 1996, now sporting the addition of the old New Brompton colours to the familar blue, promotion was again achieved.

After a good start in the new second division, it is hoped that Medway support will see them improve even further.

In the late 1980s, this smart strip was worn by the successful Gills.

Gillingham (founded 1893) records and strips

1893-1928

1947-1957

1972-1974

1996-97

1929-1939

1958-1963

1985-1987

1998

Year	Division and position		Cup round reached
1899			1
1900			p
1901			p
1902			p
1903			p
1904			p
1905			p
1906			1
1907			2
1908			2
1909			p
1910			p
1911			1
1912			p
1913			1
1914			2
1915			1
1920			1
1921	3	22	p
1922	3S	18	1
1923	3S	16	p
1924	3S	15	1
1925	3S	13	p
1926	3S	10	2
1927	3S	20	2
1928	3S	16	3
1929	3S	22	1
1930	3S	21	1
1931	3S	16	2
1932	3S	21	1
1933	3S	7	2
1934	3S	17	2
1935	3S	20	1
1936	3S	16	2
1937	3S	11	2
1938	3S	22L	1
1939			q
1946			q
1947			3
1948			3
1949			q
1950			2
1951	3S	22	2
1952	3S	22	2
1953	3S	20	2
1954	3S	10	1
1955	3S	4	2
1956	3S	10	1
1957	3S	22	2
1958	3S	22	3
1959	4	11	1
1960	4	7	3
1961	4	15	3
1962	4	20	1
1963	4	5	3
1964	4	1P	1
1965	3	7	2
1966	3	6	1
1967	3	11	2
1968	3	11	1
1969	3	20	2
1970	3	20	5
1971	3	24R	1
1972	4	13	3
1973	4	9	1
1974	4	2P	1
1975	3	10	1
1976	3	14	2
1977	3	12	1
1978	3	7	2
1979	3	4	1
1980	3	16	1
1981	3	15	2
1982	3	6	4
1983	3	13	2
1984	3	8	4
1985	3	4	4
1986	3	5	3
1987	3	5	3
1988	3	13	3
1989	3	23R	1
1990	4	14	1
1991	4	15	1
1992	4	11	1
1993	N3	21	3
1994	N3	16	2
1995	N3	19	3
1996	N3	2P	3
1997	N2	11	3
1998	N2	8	1

The zig-zag hoops of 1990 were unique in the Football League. The Gills also sported a reversed white version.

GRIMSBY TOWN

This is a club with a colourful history, great contrasts in fortunes, many changes in playing strips and even a quirky situation of playing in another town.

The first club, founded in 1878 and playing in neighbouring Cleethorpes, called themselves Grimsby Pelham after the family name of local landowners. Their initial outfit of blue and white hoops was probably derived from this source too. The colours remained when the title 'Town' replaced 'Pelham' the following year, but later, after successful runs in the FA Cup had enabled the club to join the Football League, a bold strip of carmine and light blue halves was the vogue.

In this strip promotion to the first division was earned, but after relegation two years later , a desire for an improvement in fortunes saw the introduction of salmon pink shirts. Yet another change – white shirts with a red-yoked collar – followed, but by 1910 the club decided enough was enough and settled for the now recognisable black and white stripes. Strangely enough, the first season in this new strip coincided with failure to gain re-election and the loss of League status for a year, but the club bounced back and struggled on.

In 1924 black shorts were introduced along with the famous red stockings and this change worked. A third division championship was followed by another promotion season three years later and, but for a two-year hiccup, the Mariners were a proud first division outfit up to the outbreak of the Second World War. Two semi-finals appearances and a tenth place in the League made heroes such as Jackie Bestall and Pat Glover household names.

But Grimsby's history is one of contrasts; from being a first division club in 1948, they experienced the humiliation of application for re-election seven years later. Come 1956, they were divisional champions again, but by the 1960s another collapse had taken place as well as another change of outfit. The white shirts trimmed with black, and red shorts, a permutation of the old colours, had been adopted to improve results. Promotion followed straight away.

Since then, after another dive, the stripes returned as did further ups and downs. Lawrie McMenemy turned a poor team into a promotion-winning side, then left for higher things. George Kerr took the club from fourth to second divisions in consecutive seasons; others sadly led the return trip.

Of course that was not the end of the story and Alan Buckley inspired another dramatic rise back to the second division. Eventually they dropped down again, but came straight back via the play-off system .... they get their money's worth at Grimsby. Everything is either black or white .... or carmine or salmon pink!

In 1939 Grimsby were tenth in the first division and reached the semi-finals of the FA Cup.

Grimsby (founded 1878) records and strips

1878-1909

1960-1962

1992-1993

1910-1924

1924-1957

1973-1976

1998

Year	Division and position		Cup round reached
1893	2	4	2
1894	2	5	1
1895	2	5	p
1896	2	3	2
1897	2	3	1
1898	2	12	1
1899	2	10	1
1900	2	6	1
1901	2	1P	p
1902	1	15	1
1903	1	17R	2
1904	2	6	1
1905	2	13	1
1906	2	8	1
1907	2	11	1
1908	2	18	qf
1909	2	13	1
1910	2	19L	1
1911			3
1912	2	9	p
1913	2	7	1
1914	2	15	1
1915	2	17	1
1920	2	22L	1
1921	3	13	2
1922	3N	3	1
1923	3N	14	p
1924	3N	11	1
1925	3N	12	p
1926	3N	1P	3
1927	2	17	3
1928	2	11	3
1929	2	2P	3
1930	1	18	3
1931	1	13	5
1932	1	21R	5
1933	2	13	4
1934	2	1P	4
1935	1	5	3
1936	1	17	sf
1937	1	11	5
1938	1	20	3
1939	1	10	sf
1946			3
1947	1	16	4
1948	1	22R	3
1949	2	11	4
1950	2	11	4
1951	2	22R	3
1952	3N	2	2
1953	3N	5	3
1954	3N	17	3
1955	3N	23	3
1956	3N	1P	3
1957	2	16	3
1958	2	13	3
1959	2	21R	4
1960	3	4	2
1961	3	6	1
1962	3	2P	1
1963	2	19	3
1964	2	21R	3
1965	3	10	2
1966	3	11	4
1967	3	17	1
1968	3	21R	1
1969	4	23	1
1970	4	16	1
1971	4	19	1
1972	4	1P	1
1973	3	9	4
1974	3	6	3
1975	3	16	2
1976	3	18	1
1977	3	23R	2
1978	4	6	3
1979	4	2P	1
1980	3	1P	3
1981	2	7	3
1982	2	17	5
1983	2	19	4
1984	2	5	3
1985	2	10	4
1986	2	15	3
1987	2	21R	3
1988	3	22R	2
1989	4	9	5
1990	4	2P	3
1991	3	3P	1
1992	2	19	1
1993	N1	9	5
1994	N1	16	4
1995	N1	10	3
1996	N1	17	5
1997	N1	22R	3
1998	N2	3P (pl)	4

A dramatic streamlining of the black and white shirts saw this strangely under-used collar style.

HALIFAX TOWN

When you have a permanent battle against the elements, the competition of other major sports, lack of cash and dwindling support, then survival itself becomes a significant success.

Sited on the edge of the rain soaked Pennines, but in the middle of Rugby League and Union strongholds, it was surprising that an Association club of any standing was established at all.

The club, formed in 1911 following tireless efforts of Dr Muir and Jock McClelland, adopted the blue and white colours used by both rugby codes in the town. Perhaps it was the influence of League neighbours, Huddersfield Town, that influenced the striped shirt format, and a desire to emulate their League successes saw Halifax eventually enter the third division (north) in 1921.

By this stage, The Town played at The Shay, a ground with great potential, but despite a couple of exciting seasons in 1926 and 1927, the club was constantly struggling against increasing financial burdens. Huddersfield Town were at their peak and attracted crowds from all around that part of Yorkshire.

During the 1930s, Halifax began to sport all blue shirts, probably to distinguish them from their neighbours and in 1935 had a rare moment of glory when they just just missed promotion to division two.

The club had much to celebrate in 1971, their best ever season.

Former England and Sheffield United star Fred Tunstall was the inspiration that season, but further successes were not to follow. In fact, in the first six seasons immediately after the Second World War, the club finished in the bottom five places.

In an effort to change its fortunes, Halifax began to sport claret and light blue shirts. After all, it worked for Aston Villa and Burnley! In the 1952/53 season, it seemed to do the trick. The club reached the fifth round of the FA Cup before going out to Tottenham Hotspur in front of a record gate of 36,995.

However, tradition soon returned, blue shirts and a life at the bottom of the League. In fact, other than one spell of minor success, after 1959 it was all pretty much gloom and doom until 1971.

George Kirby had begun the first of his managerial spells with The Shaymen. The excitement and interest was intense as the club almost achieved the impossible again. Eventually Halifax just missed out, finishing third in division three, just ahead of the great Aston Villa, and their blue shirts with white sleeves had featured on television more than once.

Life since then has not been kind, and the modern striped shirts have created little success on the field.

In 1993 the club's luck finally ran out altogether. They were relegated to the GM Vauxhall Conference and for a while looked close to going out of business. However, in 1998 under the management of George Mulhall, they boldly struck out to the top of the Conference and at the end of the season were promoted back to the Football League!

Hope is still strong. Halifax are one of football's great survivors.

Halifax (founded 1911) records and strips

1911

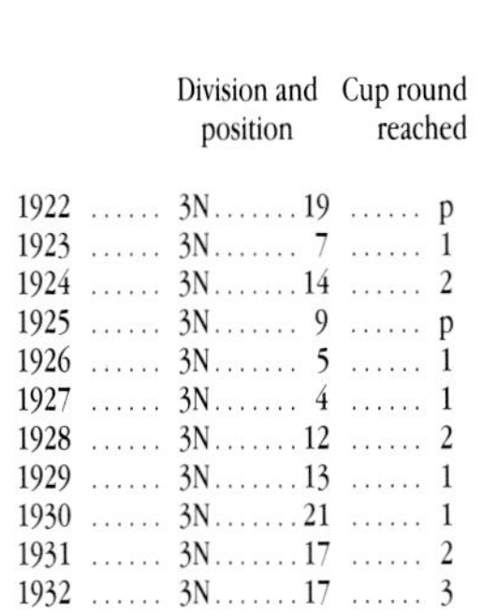

Year	Division	Position	Cup round reached
1922	3N	19	p
1923	3N	7	1
1924	3N	14	2
1925	3N	9	p
1926	3N	5	1
1927	3N	4	1
1928	3N	12	2
1929	3N	13	1
1930	3N	21	1
1931	3N	17	2
1932	3N	17	3

1926-27

1952

Year	Division	Position	Cup round reached
1933	3N	15	5
1934	3N	9	3
1935	3N	2	1
1936	3N	17	2
1937	3N	7	1

1960

Year	Division	Position	Cup round reached
1938	3N	18	1
1939	3N	12	3
1946			1
1947	3N	22	2
1948	3N	21	1
1949	3N	19	1
1950	3N	21	1
1951	3N	22	1
1952	3N	20	1
1953	3N	14	5
1954	3N	23	1
1955	3N	14	1
1956	3N	19	2
1957	3N	11	1
1958	3N	7	1
1959	3	9	2
1960	3	15	1
1961	3	9	2
1962	3	18	1

Year	Division	Position	Cup round reached
1963	3	24R	2
1964	4	10	1
1965	4	23	1
1966	4	15	1
1967	4	12	3
1968	4	11	3

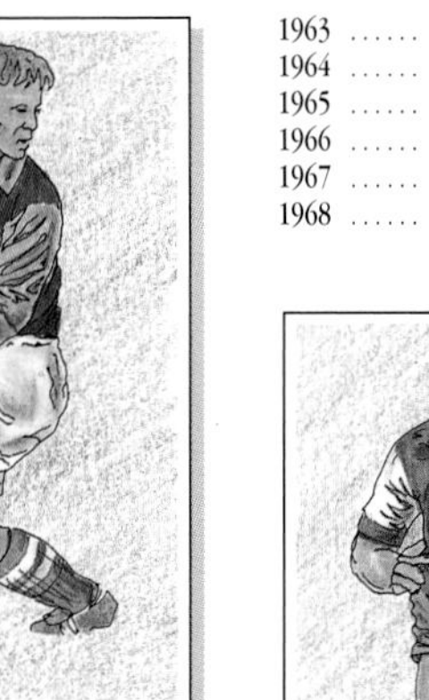

1971

Year	Division	Position	Cup round reached
1969	4	2P	4
1970	3	18	1
1971	3	3	1
1972	3	16	1
1973	3	20	2
1974	3	9	2

1973

Year	Division	Position	Cup round reached
1975	3	17	2
1976	3	24R	3
1977	4	21	1
1978	4	20	1
1979	4	23	1
1980	4	18	4
1981	4	23	1
1982	4	19	1
1983	4	11	1

1988

Year	Division	Position	Cup round reached
1984	4	21	1
1985	4	21	2
1986	4	20	1
1987	4	15	1
1988	4	18	3

1998

Year	Division	Position	Cup round reached
1989	4	21	3
1990	4	23	2
1991	4	22	2
1992	4	20	1
1993	4	24R	1
1994	GMVC	13	2
1995	GMVC	8	q4
1996	GMVC	15	q2
1997	GMVC	19	q2
1998	GMVC	1P	q4

Halifax even tried a Real Madrid, all white strip, trimmed with orange and blue.

HARTLEPOOL UNITED

This humble club belongs to that small exclusive band, mainly in the north of England, for whom escape from the re-election zone represents a major success. Over the years, these successes have been isolated blips on the graph of achievement and, as in Darlington's case, the challenge of the north-east's 'big three' has always been overwhelming.

From those early days back in the 1890s when the original club, West Hartlepool, used to play other top amateurs such as Bishop Auckland, and Stockton, the team sported blue and white, usually as stripes. Hartlepools United, as it was then called, was formed in 1908, and by 1921 had progressed to third division (north) status, and although most seasons were spent in the lower half of the table, survival was always ensured. At this stage the shirts became blue with a large white 'V', whilst later in the 1930s, when re-election was still a major problem, a plain light blue shirt was a regular feature.

The fight against the odds continued after the Second World War for many years until the mid-1950s, when manager Fred Westgarth finally put a strong team together. Clad in blue shirts with a broad white stripe and sleeves, players like Ken Johnson put fear into other teams in the northern division. In 1957 a really strong push for promotion was thwarted only by a fine Derby side.

After this, even though the players wore a progressive blue shirt with white pinstripes, the on-pitch performances diminished greatly. For a while even the fourth division could offer nothing other than constant re-election worries. Things were looking particularly bad in 1965, with the club virtually bankrupt without any resources. It needed a larger-than-life character to change it all, and in walked Brian Clough. The man who painted the ground, trained the players and gave the club some hope eventually moved on in 1967, but he left a team which won promotion the following season. The success was short-lived as relegation followed the next term but it proved the 'impossible' was achievable.

There was no magic formula for the next two decades, just the usual re-election tensions. Then enter a second 'messiah' in the shape of Cyril Knowles. In 1991 the first 'mission impossible' was another promotion, but even more exciting was the top-half finish the following season in the third division. The players wore a strip to match with a fabulous light blue, white and dark blue checkered shirt. All the old traditional colours had come together in a moment of glory.

Since then came relegation and a battle to survive. It was hoped widely that Hartlepool United would win through. Such a plucky club deserved their good fortune.

This wonderful strip was worn during Hartlepool's best season for years, as the club finished in the top half of the third division in 1992.

Hartlepool (founded 1908) records and strips

1908-1920

Year	Division and position		Cup round reached
1922	3N	4	p
1923	3N	15	p
1924	3N	21	p
1925	3N	20	1
1926	3N	6	p
1927	3N	17	1
1928	3N	15	1
1929	3N	21	1
1930	3N	8	1
1931	3N	20	1
1932	3N	13	1
1933	3N	14	2
1934	3N	11	2

1925-1928

1936-1939

Year	Division	Position	Cup round
1935	3N	12	2
1936	3N	8	3
1937	3N	6	2
1938	3N	20	2
1939	3N	21	2
1946			1

1956-1960

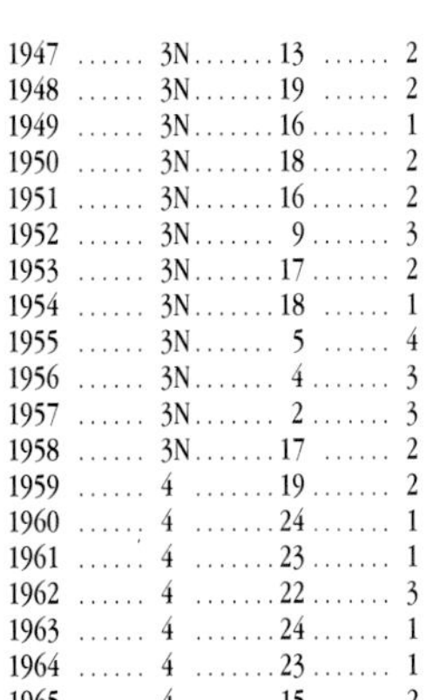

Year	Division	Position	Cup round
1947	3N	13	2
1948	3N	19	2
1949	3N	16	1
1950	3N	18	2
1951	3N	16	2
1952	3N	9	3
1953	3N	17	2
1954	3N	18	1
1955	3N	5	4
1956	3N	4	3
1957	3N	2	3
1958	3N	17	2
1959	4	19	2
1960	4	24	1
1961	4	23	1
1962	4	22	3
1963	4	24	1
1964	4	23	1
1965	4	15	2

One of the very early pinstriped shirts worn at the end of the successful late 1950s period.

1965-1969

Year	Division	Position	Cup round
1966	4	18	3
1967	4	8	1
1968	4	3P	1
1969	3	22R	1
1970	4	23	2
1971	4	23	1
1972	4	18	2

1988-1989

Year	Division	Position	Cup round
1973	4	20	1
1974	4	11	1
1975	4	13	2
1976	4	14	3
1977	4	22	1
1978	4	21	4
1979	4	13	3
1980	4	19	1
1981	4	9	1
1982	4	14	2
1983	4	22	2

1991-1992

Year	Division	Position	Cup round
1984	4	23	1
1985	4	19	2
1986	4	7	2
1987	4	18	1
1988	4	21	3
1989	4	23	4

1998

Year	Division	Position	Cup round
1990	4	22	1
1991	4	3P	2
1992	3	11	3
1993	N2	16	4
1994	N2	23R	1
1995	N3	18	1
1996	N3	20	1
1997	N3	20	1
1998	N3	17	1

HEREFORD UNITED

Geographical isolation and limited local interest in the game ensured a late start to senior football in this beautiful border town. Although there were several amateur clubs in the area, it was not until 1924 that there was sufficient confidence in Hereford to assemble a semi-professional squad.

In the years before the Second World War, clad in white shirts and black shorts, United progressed through local leagues before eventually joining the Southern League. Competing at this higher level did much to increase the club's status but it wasn't until after the War that the world began to take notice.

The extension of the Football League in 1951 was an opportunity which came too early for Hereford and for the next two decades it was a case of persistence and perseverance. United continued to exercise both; in 21 successive seasons the club won through the qualifying rounds to the FA Cup first round proper, constantly reminding the League of their potential.

There were several highlights in the competition, the 11-0 win over Thynnes and the 18,000 -plus crowd which saw Sheffield Wednesday in 1958, but it was a wonderful television performance which finally and undeniably proved the club's worth. The cameras had turned up following Hereford's shock draw at Newcastle in 1972 and the replay offered a newsworthy result either way. It all seemed predictable early on as the Tynesiders scored first, but in a constantly replayed sequence first Ronnie Radford lashed in a 30-yard opener and then Rickie George squeezed in the winner. The border town went mad, both on the pitch and in the streets, and the result provided enough impetus to break into the League. Their excellent manager Colin Addison continued to inspire success, and in the very first season United were promoted to division three. Of course, Addison was quickly whisked away, but his successor John Sillett continued the momentum and took the club into the second division. By this time, red had been added to the black trim on the shirts (perhaps reflecting the colour of the beef cattle used as the club's emblem), but all the sartorial innovations did nothing to hide the fact that too much had happened too quickly.

Hereford were not capable of taking on the likes of Wolves, Chelsea and Southampton, and in a traumatic dive were back in the fourth division within two years. Life has not been kind since, season after season being a constant battle hampered by insufficient resources and a limited catchment area. There have been odd moments of relief, however. In 1985 promotion was missed by one position and in 1990 Edgar Street entertained the mighty Manchester United, a single-goal defeat being no disgrace.

The 1990s offered the extra pressures of instant relegation to the GM Vauxhall Conference, but although United battled away gamely, in 1997 after an unprecedented slide down the table, they were dumped out of the League in a dramatic and traumatic final day showdown with Brighton.

Life in the Conference has not been easy and the club faces a new fight to regain their hard won Football League status. Everyone wishes them well.

This famous kit is still shown on TV as glimpses of the FA Cup win over Newcastle in 1972 are repeated.

Hereford (founded 1924) records and strips

1924-1939

Year	Division and position		Cup round reached
1946	SL		q1
1947	SL		q4
1948	SL		q2
1949	SL		2
1950	SL		2
1951	SL		2

1946-1957

Year	Division and position		Cup round reached
1952	SL		1
1953	SL		2
1954	SL		2
1955	SL		q4
1956	SL		1
1957	SL		2
1958	SL		3
1959	SL		2
1960	SL		1
1961	SL		1
1962	SL		1

1964-1967

Year	Division and position		Cup round reached
1963	SL		1
1964	SL		1
1965	SL		1
1966	SL		3
1967	SL		1

1973-1974

Year	Division and position		Cup round reached
1968	SL		2
1969	SL		1
1970	SL		2
1971	SL		2
1972	SL		4
1973	4	2P	1
1974	3	18	4

1976-1978

Year	Division and position		Cup round reached
1975	3	12	2
1976	3	1P	3
1977	2	22R	4
1978	3	23R	1
1979	4	14	1
1980	4	21	2
1981	4	22	2
1982	4	10	4
1983	4	24	1

Year	Division and position		Cup round reached
1984	4	11	1
1985	4	5	3
1986	4	10	2
1987	4	16	1
1988	4	19	2
1989	4	15	1
1990	4	17	4

1984-1985

Year	Division and position		Cup round reached
1991	4	17	1
1992	4	17	4
1993	4	17	2
1994	N3	20	2
1995	N3	16	1
1996	N3	6	3
1997	N3	24R	1
1998	GMVC		3

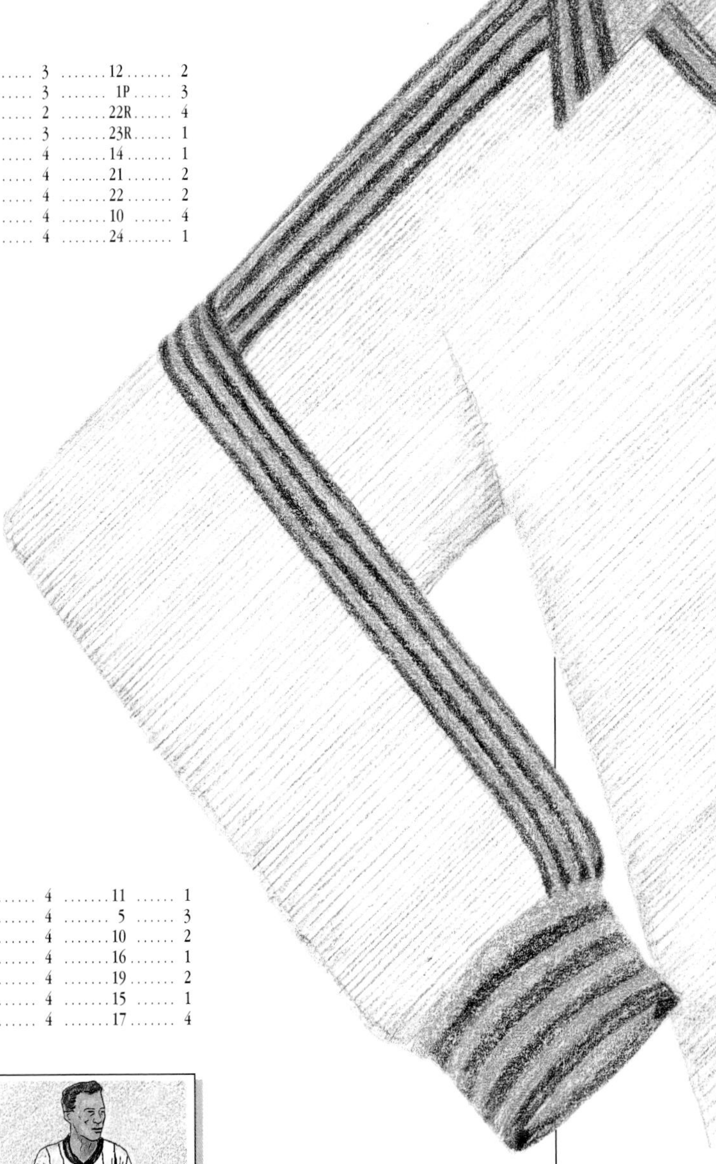

The multi-striped sleeve trim was very popular in the late 1970s.

1998

HUDDERSFIELD TOWN

Too much too soon' is the theory to explain the frustration of this famous club for the last 70 years. Although this period has produced a record many clubs would love to boast about, those glorious years of the early 1920s make everything since seem second best.

The club wasn't founded until 1908. There was an earlier amateur organisation but it never managed to attract sufficient support away from the rugby codes. One early uniform (another was salmon pink) was the same maroon with gold hoops that was worn by both the town's Rugby League and Rugby Union clubs. In fact, it was probably the desire to be a strong independent attraction which led to the first major change of strip, white shirts with a light blue yoke, a style which survived until 1913.

By this time the club had been elected to the second division of the Football League, performing steadily if not spectacularly. The only dramatic change was the style of the shirts, now adorned by blue and white stripes, soon to be feared around the land.

Just after the First Worls War Herbert Chapman was appointed manager and the club's fortunes took a quantum leap forward. In the first season Chapman's team won promotion and reached the FA Cup final. The next three years resulted in League consolidation and a dramatic Cup win over Preston, with Billy Smith scoring the only goal from a penalty in the final. Then followed three seasons of total domination and three consecutive League titles, a feat repeated only twice since. Chapman, arguably the most successful club manager in the League's history, had left by the end of this period and although the club continued to finish high in the League and appeared in three more Cup finals before the Second World War (losing them all including the 1938 show-down with Preston who gained revenge from the penalty spot), the dominant force had gone.

After the War it soon became obvious that Huddersfield had not the same talent or resources to challenge for titles or cups. The team were eventually relegated in 1952, and though they came straight back, went down again in 1956. Although Bill Shankly and his young star Denis Law promised great things, they both left before any concrete successes arrived. In fact, only Ian Greaves in 1970 managed to take Huddersfield back to the top flight. They remained among the elite for only two years, but it was a major success compared to the following 20 years.

The introduction of the all-blue shirts in 1975 even saw a period of five years in the fourth division. The stripes returned, as did a slow painful climb back to division two. Sadly there was a subsequent drop to division three, but the club continued to show the capacity for better things. After promotion to the the new division one in 1995 and moving to their new stadium there were suggestions that the addition of greater consistency, which ensured promotion, would guarantee a longer stay in the higher divisions.

The stripes of one of the most successful teams in Football League history, 1923-1926.

Huddersfield (founded 1908) records and strips

Year	Division	Position	Cup round reached
1937	1	15	3
1938	1	15	F
1939	1	19	sf
1946			3
1947	1	20	3
1948	1	19	3
1949	1	20	4
1950	1	15	3
1951	1	19	5
1952	1	21R	3

1908-1919

Year	Division and position		Cup round reached
1911	2	13	
1912	2	17	1
1913	2	5	2
1914	2	13	2
1915	2	8	1
1920	2	2P	F
1921	1	17	3
1922	1	14	W

Year	Division	Position	Cup round reached
1953	2	2P	4
1954	1	3	3
1955	1	12	qf
1956	1	21R	3
1957	2	12	5
1958	2	9	3
1959	2	14	3
1960	2	6	4
1961	2	20	4
1962	2	7	4

1919-1936

1951-1957

Year	Division	Position	Cup round reached
1923	1	3	3
1924	1	1C	3
1925	1	1C	1
1926	1	1C	4
1927	1	2	3
1928	1	2	F
1929	1	16	sf
1930	1	10	F
1931	1	5	3
1932	1	4	qf
1933	1	6	4
1934	1	2	4
1935	1	16	3
1936	1	3	4

Year	Division	Position	Cup round reached
1963	2	6	3
1964	2	12	5
1965	2	8	4
1966	2	4	5
1967	2	6	3
1968	2	14	3
1969	2	6	4
1970	2	1P	3
1971	1	15	4
1972	1	22R	qf
1973	2	21R	3
1974	3	10	2
1975	3	24R	1
1976	4	5	4

1966-1969

1994-1996

Year	Division	Position	Cup round reached
1977	4	9	1
1978	4	11	1
1979	4	9	1
1980	4	1P	1

Year	Division	Position	Cup round reached
1988	2	23R	3
1989	3	14	3
1990	3	8	4
1991	3	11	2

1977-1980

1998

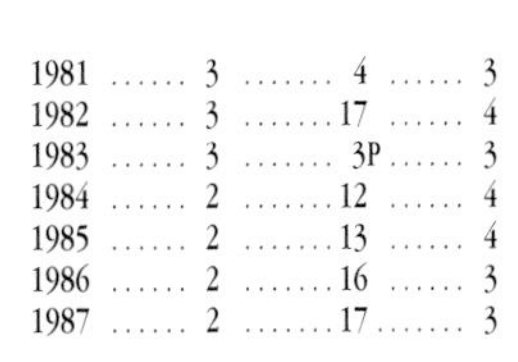

Year	Division	Position	Cup round reached
1981	3	4	3
1982	3	17	4
1983	3	3P	3
1984	2	12	4
1985	2	13	4
1986	2	16	3
1987	2	17	3

Year	Division	Position	Cup round reached
1992	3	3	3
1993	N2	15	4
1994	N2	11	2
1995	N2	5P(pl)	2
1996	N1	8	5
1997	N1	20	3
1998	N1	16	4

An unusual white panel shape enabled a clever use of stripes in this dramatic style.

HULL CITY

Despite having the huge potential of Humberside to tap, Hull City have never truly reached the heights. Indeed, they and neighbours Grimsby seem to operate a see-saw of relative successes and failures.

In 1904 Kingston-upon-Hull became a city and it was felt that a respectable football side should represent it, in addition to the rugby league clubs. The black and amber stripes prompted the local newspaper to christen them the Tigers and the two symbols have remained ever since.

After only a year Hull City were elected to the second division of the Football League and for a quarter of a century the club performed well without quite progressing to the top flight. The breakthrough almost came in 1910 but the Tigers missed out on goal average. Another high spot in the club's history came with an FA Cup semi-final in 1930, when they drew 2-2 with eventual winners Arsenal, before losing the replay 1-0. They had beaten Newcastle United in the sixth round. By the mid-1930s, although the shorts had become white, the amber and black stripes remained, but the successes had become less frequent. There had been one period when the club believed a change of strip would produce a change of luck. Sadly it did. In the first season Hull City donned sky blue shirts the team was relegated. The stripes returned but it was too late and remained in the third division until after the Second World War.

On resumption of peacetime football, an intended blue-trimmed orange shirt failed to materialise because of the Board of Trade restriction during the osterity period at the time. For a while, sky blue shirts were used but the traditional black and amber returned in 1947 just in time to see the exciting period when Raich Carter and his protege Don Revie promised so much. Unfortunately success did not come quickly enough, Carter retired and Revie moved on to greater things.

By the 1960s, after a few experiments with black bands and stripes, the club streamlined its kit to plain amber shirts and black shorts. Cliff Britton developed great young talent like Chris Chilton and Ken Wagstaff and a healthy second division spot was maintained for over a decade. There were two great Cup runs which almost emulated the sixth-round excitement of 1930. But towards the end of the 1970s, a long period of fluctuation came to Boothferry Park. The team dropped to the fourth division, fought their way back to the second and then dropped back to the third. New strips were introduced to revive old standards; broad stripes, narrow stripes, chestbands and shoulder stripes, but although looking exciting, they did not inspire the consistency of old.
One of the latest moves was to return to black and amber striped shirts (some literally quite tigerish!), and with this the locals hoped that Hull could join other old Yorkshire clubs which have enjoyed revivals in fortunes.

Sadly on the pitch events seem to have taken a different turn. Even the arrival of former England star Mark Hateley has so far failed to take the club away from football's basement!

Raich Carter and Don Revie wore this kit in 1950, when the club had great ambitions.

Hull (founded 1904) records and strips

Year	Division	Position	Cup round reached
1906	2	5	1
1907	2	9	1
1908	2	8	2
1909	2	4	1
1910	2	3	1
1911	2	5	3
1912	2	7	1
1913	2	12	2
1914	2	7	1
1915	2	7	qf
1920	2	11	1
1921	2	13	qf
1922	2	5	2
1923	2	12	1
1924	2	17	1
1925	2	10	3
1926	2	13	3
1927	2	7	5
1928	2	14	3
1929	2	12	3
1930	2	21R	sf
1931	3N	6	3
1932	3N	8	3
1933	3N	1P	3
1934	2	15	4
1935	2	13	3
1936	2	22R	3
1937	3N	5	1
1938	3N	3	3
1939	3N	7	2
1947	3N	11	3
1948	3N	5	3
1949	3N	1P	qf
1950	2	7	4
1951	2	10	5
1952	2	18	5
1953	2	18	4
1954	2	15	5
1955	2	19	3
1956	2	22R	3
1957	3N	8	3
1958	3N	5	4
1959	3	2P	1
1960	2	21R	3
1961	3	11	3
1962	3	10	2
1963	3	10	3
1964	3	8	3
1965	3	4	2
1966	3	1P	qf
1967	2	12	3
1968	2	17	3
1969	2	11	3
1970	2	13	3
1971	2	5	qf
1972	2	12	5
1973	2	13	5
1974	2	9	3
1975	2	8	3
1976	2	14	4
1977	2	14	3
1978	2	22R	3
1979	3	8	2
1980	3	20	1
1981	3	24R	4
1982	4	8	3
1983	4	2P	1
1984	3	4	2
1985	3	3P	3
1986	2	6	4
1987	2	14	5
1988	2	15	3
1989	2	21	5
1990	2	14	3
1991	2	24R	3
1992	3	14	3
1993	N2	20	2
1994	N2	9	2
1995	N2	8	1
1996	N2	24R	1
1997	N3	17	2
1998	N3	22	1

1904-1920

1920-1935

1935-36 & 1946-47

1947-1957

1964-1976

1975-1978

1986-1988

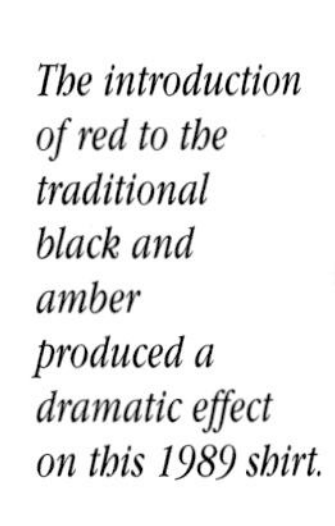
The introduction of red to the traditional black and amber produced a dramatic effect on this 1989 shirt.

1998

IPSWICH TOWN

The history of the Football League is littered with stories of big city clubs who have never lived up to their potential, and of ones with small town support which have little chance of a permanent placing at the top. However, Ipswich Town, despite a long spawning period in the minor leagues, have managed to challenge the best and fill a very impressive trophy room.

An Ipswich Town club was formed in 1878 and in the early days were clad in blue and white striped shirts, a style which has occasionally returned in modern styles. At that time, neither staff nor fans displayed great ambition, and it was not until 1936, when the Town were re-organised and took on the services of Scott Duncan as secretary/manager, that things began to happen. A supporters' association contributed £13,000, then a lot of money, and by 1938 Ipswich Town were considered good enough to join the third division (south).

By this time they were wearing blue, adding white sleeves only after the Second World War. The early post-War years were very inconsistent in terms of playing results, but following a series of low finishes promotion was achieved in 1954. Sadly the Town weren't quite ready, but the subsequent relegation prompted the club to make a decision which changed their history forever.

Former Englandfull-back Alf Ramsey became manager and, using new tactical ideas and maximising the talent available, he not only took Ipswich back into the second division, but by the beginning of the1960s astounded the football world with another promotion, immediately followed by the first division championship! A sound defence and midfield provided the platform for the goal-scoring skills of Crawford and Phillips to pick up the points. Sadly for the club, Ramsey left to apply the same successful formula to England teams, and within two seasons Ipswich were back in the second division.

However, this was not the end for the East Anglian club. In 1968 Bill McGarry had already led the team back to division one, when another ex-England player, Bobby Robson was asked to take charge. This was the beginning of another highly successful era. After a period of consolidation, and now wearing all-blue shirts again, the club regularly finished in the top three or four. And during one poor year in the League, the team crowned a glorious FA Cup run with a Wembley victory over the favourites, Arsenal.

The League successes meant regular European football, and in 1981, Ipswich brought home the UEFA Cup by beating AZ67 Alkmaar. Ironically it was the two Dutchmen, Arnold Muhren and Frans Thijssen, who were most influential at this time.

When this team of stars broke up, then so did the run of success. Relegation followed but in John Lyall the club seemed to have another manager capable of great things. Top flight football (and the white sleeves) were back; the fans awaited success but sadly Lyall was replaced and the team went down.

The signs of another full recovery are still not quite there.

Nobody expected players wearing this strip to lift the League championship trophy in 1962. But they did!

Ipswich (founded 1878) records and strips

1880-1914

	Division and position		Cup round reached
1939	3S	7	3
1946			2
1947	3S	6	2

1929-1939

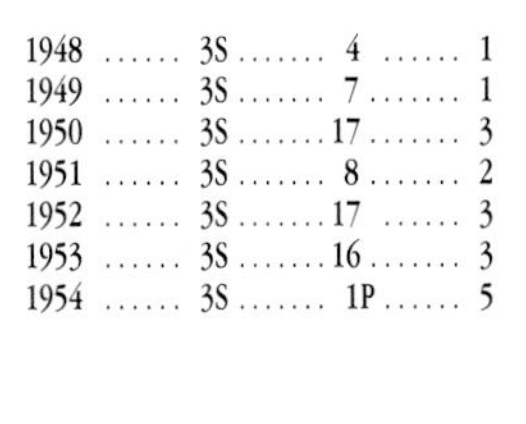

1948	3S	4	1
1949	3S	7	1
1950	3S	17	3
1951	3S	8	2
1952	3S	17	3
1953	3S	16	3
1954	3S	1P	5

1958-1962

1955	2	21R	3
1956	3S	3	1
1957	3S	1P	3
1958	2	8	4
1959	2	16	5
1960	2	11	3
1961	2	1P	3

1964-1970

1962	1	1C	4
1963	1	17	4
1964	1	22R	4
1965	2	5	4
1966	2	15	3

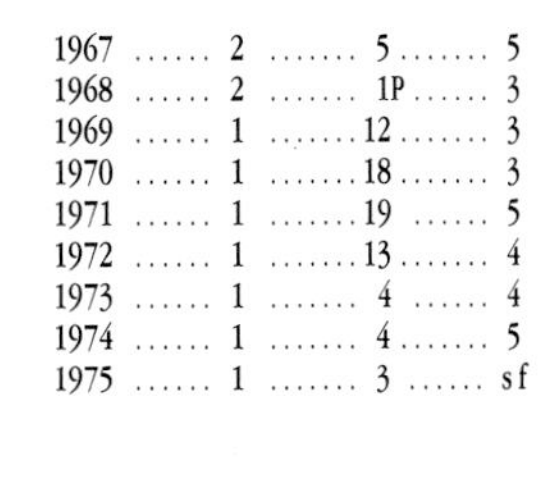

1967	2	5	5
1968	2	1P	3
1969	1	12	3
1970	1	18	3
1971	1	19	5
1972	1	13	4
1973	1	4	4
1974	1	4	5
1975	1	3	sf

1977-1978

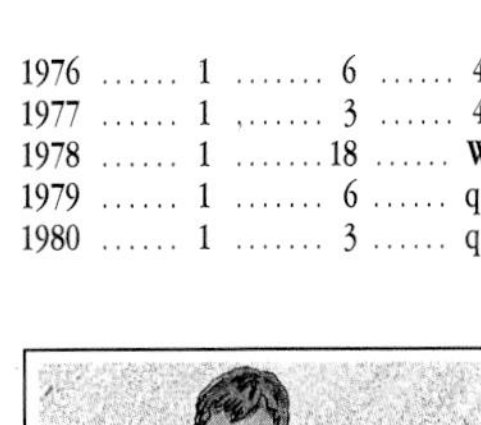

1976	1	6	4
1977	1	3	4
1978	1	18	W
1979	1	6	qf
1980	1	3	qf

1981-1985

The 1992 shirt incorporated this elaborate collar with a return to of the white sleeves of the league winning version.

1992-1993

1981	1	2	sf
1982	1	2	5
1983	1	9	5
1984	1	12	4
1985	1	17	6
1986	1	20R	4
1987	2	5	3
1988	2	8	3
1989	2	8	3

1998

1990	2	9	4
1991	2	14	3
1992	2	1P	5
1993	Pr	16	qf
1994	Pr	19	5
1995	Pr	22R	3
1996	N1	7	5
1997	N1	4	3
1998	N1	5	4

LEEDS UNITED

The history of football in this great Yorkshire city falls into three distinctive phases: first as Leeds City and then the pre- and post-Revie periods. Based roughly on the foundations laid by Hunslet FC, a club going back to 1880, Leeds City were formed in 1904 to represent the great Yorkshire city in the Football League. They were elected the following year, sporting the blue and white striped shirts.

A fairly unspectacular decade of League performances had not prepared the fans for shock of the first season after the First World War, when after eight games Leeds were expelled from the League for irregular payments to players. Although the city was stunned, a Leeds solicitor quickly called a meeting to form a new organisation and a year later Leeds United were elected to division two.

Now clad in the blue and gold associated with the borough, but having exchanged the previous stripes for a striking halved shirt, the players of the new club at first displayed no improvement in form, but in 1924 promotion to the first division was achieved. From then to the outbreak of Second World War, with the exception of two instances of relegation and immediate promotion, an unspectacular mid-table position was the norm.

In fact, even after the War it was only the excitement of mighty John Charles' attacking and defending skills which lit up Elland Road until the beginning of the 1960s. By then Charles had gone to Italy and United were on the verge of descending to the third division. Luckily the club had the foresight to appoint Don Revie as player/manager. Revie had already indicated he held radical ideas for tactical and administrative improvements when a player at Hull and Manchester City; and after his arrival in Leeds, Elland Road was never the same again.

The 'English Real Madrid' as envisaged by Don Revie in the 1960s.

A change of strip became, unusually, a very positive move. The all-white outfit was to encourage players and fans alike to believe that the club could, and should, be as successful as Real Madrid. The team based on Jack Charlton, a bunch of talented youngsters plus some great strategic buys like Bobby Collins and Johnny Giles, began to challenge for every title.

Leeds United did win most competitions, but perhaps the intensity of the search for extreme success sometimes backfired and there were also many sad, jittery near misses.

Eventually Revie left for international management and for a while Leeds became an ordinary club again. Even the strip would echo small touches of the blue and gold, reflecting some of the pre-Revie days. However, in recent years the arrival of another talented, thinking manager, Howard Wilkinson, brought glory back to Elland Road with a third League championship, the last before the formation of the Premiership.

Some kind of continuity had to be found before the club was really great again, but whether in white or blue and gold, the future looked pretty healthy in the 1990s and in 1998, under the managership of George Graham, the club won a place back in European competition.

Leeds United (founded 1920) records and strips

1904-1920

	Division and position		Cup round reached
1906	*2*	*6*	
1907	*2*	*10*	*1*
1908	*2*	*12*	*1*
1909	*2*	*12*	*2*
1910	*2*	*17*	*1*
1911	*2*	*11*	*1*
1912	*2*	*19*	*2*
1913	*2*	*6*	*1*
1914	*2*	*4*	*2*
1915	*2*	*15*	*2*
1920	*2*		
1921	2	14	1q
1922	2	8	1
1923	2	7	2

1921-1939

1924	2	1P	3
1925	1	18	1
1926	1	19	3
1927	1	21R	4
1928	2	2P	3
1929	1	13	4
1930	1	5	4
1931	1	21R	5
1932	2	2P	3
1933	1	8	5
1934	1	9	3

1947-1956

1935	1	18	4
1936	1	11	5
1937	1	19	3
1938	1	9	4
1939	1	13	4
1946			3
1947	1	22R	3
1948	2	18	3
1949	2	15	3
1950	2	5	qf
1951	2	5	4

1959-1963

1952	2	6	5
1953	2	10	3
1954	2	10	3
1955	2	4	3
1956	2	2P	3
1957	1	8	3
1958	1	17	3
1959	1	15	3
1960	1	21R	3
1961	2	14	3
1962	2	19	3
1963	2	5	5
1964	2	1P	4
1965	1	2	F
1966	1	2	4
1967	1	4	sf
1968	1	4	sf
1969	1	1C	3
1970	1	2	F
1971	1	2	5

1972	1	2	W
1973	1	3	F
1974	1	1C	5
1975	1	9	qf
1976	1	5	4
1977	1	10	sf
1978	1	9	3
1979	1	5	3
1980	1	11	3
1981	1	9	3
1982	1	20R	4
1983	2	8	4

1963-1973

1984	2	13	3
1985	2	7	3
1986	2	14	3
1987	2	4	sf
1988	2	7	3
1989	2	10	4

1980-1984

A truly unique feature was the stocking-tie numbered tag of 1973. Certainly a great publicity exercise, as the players threw them to the fans after the game.

1990-1992

1990	2	1P	3
1991	1	4	4
1992	1	1C	3
1993	Pr	17	4
1994	Pr	5	4
1995	Pr	5	5

1998

1996	Pr	13	6
1997	Pr.	11	5
1998	Pr.	5	6

The record of Leeds City 1906-1920 is in italics.

LEICESTER CITY

It seems strange to describe a club as 'nearly great', but in the case of Leicester City it is apt. On many occasions they have been on the verge of success in the League and even more so in the FA Cup, but until 1997 never did a major trophy come to Filbert Street.

The club was founded in 1884 as Leicester Fosse, named after the old Roman dyke nearby. At first it was amateur and self-supporting, and this might explain the great variety of playing strips. Leicester teams have always worn blue somewhere on part of their uniforms, but at first there was no regular pattern. A blue sash on black shirts was followed by chocolate and blue halves, then white shirts and blue shorts, and by the turn of the century various combinations of light and dark blue. Even after the famous royal blue version arrived, there had to be one last dabble, i.e. striped shirts at the time of Huddersfield's dominance.

By this time, the Filberts were regular members of the second division, just one period in the top flight breaking the sequence. However, the 1920s saw a change of attitude at the club; the name 'Fosse' was dropped for the larger appeal of 'City', the plain blue shirts returned and an aggressive push for promotion was realised in 1925. The following few years saw high positions in division one and long Cup runs, but no trophies; and by the 1930s the momentum was lost. Even the treasured first division status went just before the Second World War.

In the following peacetime, Leicester experienced their first Wembley Cup final, and later the fans were thrilled by big Arthur Rowley's goalscoring, but it was not until 1957 that the first division place was regained. Manager Matt Gillies assembled a strong team including internationals such as Gordon Banks and Frank McLintock, but again the 'nearly' situation remained. Poor McLintock had to join Arsenal to get a Cup-winner's medal, after taking two runners-up versions with Leicester. Somehow, City always seemed to come against another club who were at the height of their success, first Spurs, then Manchester United and later still Manchester City.

In the 1960s Leicester kept meeting great sides in Cup finals. This strip failed to frighten off Spurs in 1961.

Since that time the names which have worn the blue of Filbert Street have included Gary Lineker, Alan Smith, Frank Worthington, Keith Weller and Peter Shilton; the list of stars seems endless, but sadly they were never welded into a cohesive unit.

Leicester remained able to attract good management, so with more support to create consistency, the Filberts had hopes of breaking the 'nearly' image and winning one of the major trophies in the 1990s.

With the arrival of Martin O'Neill some of these dreams were turned into reality as the Filberts won the League Cup and had a taste of European competition.

Leicester (founded 1884) records and strips

Year	Division	Position	Cup round
1923	2	3	2
1924	2	12	1
1925	2	1P	qf
1926	1	17	3
1927	1	7	1
1928	1	3	5
1929	1	2	5
1930	1	8	3
1931	1	16	3

1884-1915

	Division and position		Cup round reached
1894			2
1895	2	4	1
1896	2	8	4q
1897	2	9	4q
1898	2	7	1
1899	2	3	4q
1900	2	5	1
1901	2	11	1
1902	2	14	p
1903	2	15	2q
1904	2	18	4q
1905	2	14	1
1906	2	7	1
1907	2	3	1

1915-1922

Year	Division	Position	Cup round
1908	2	2P	2
1909	1	20R	2
1910	2	5	qf
1911	2	15	2
1912	2	10	2
1913	2	15	1
1914	2	18	1
1915	2	19	6q
1920	2	14	3
1921	2	12	1
1922	2	9	3

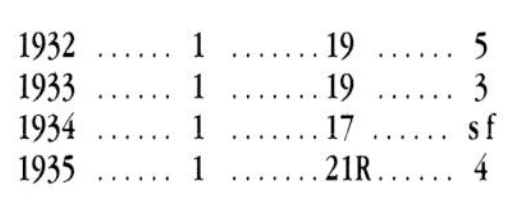

Year	Division	Position	Cup round
1932	1	19	5
1933	1	19	3
1934	1	17	sf
1935	1	21R	4

1932-1958

Year	Division	Position	Cup round
1936	2	6	5
1937	2	1P	4
1938	1	16	4
1939	1	22R	4
1946			3
1947	2	9	5
1948	2	9	5
1949	2	19	F
1950	2	15	3
1951	2	14	3
1952	2	5	3
1953	2	5	3
1954	2	1P	qf
1955	1	21R	3
1956	2	5	4
1957	2	1P	3
1958	1	18	3
1959	1	19	4
1960	1	12	qf
1961	1	6	F

1962-1967

Year	Division	Position	Cup round
1962	1	14	3
1963	1	4	F
1964	1	11	3
1965	1	18	qf
1966	1	7	5

1983-1985

Year	Division	Position	Cup round
1967	1	8	3
1968	1	13	qf
1969	1	21R	F
1970	2	3	5
1971	2	1P	qf
1972	1	12	4
1973	1	16	3
1974	1	9	sf
1975	1	18	5
1976	1	7	5
1977	1	11	3
1978	1	22R	4
1979	2	17	4
1980	2	1P	3
1981	1	21R	4
1982	2	8	sf
1983	2	3P	3

A smart early multi-coloured stocking of 1910, never since repeated.

1993-1994

Year	Division	Position	Cup round
1984	1	15	3
1985	1	15	5
1986	1	19	3
1987	1	20R	3
1988	2	13	3
1989	2	15	3
1990	2	13	3
1991	2	22	3
1992	2	4	4
1993	N1	6	3
1994	N1	4P(pl)	3

1998

Year	Division	Position	Cup round
1995	Pr	21R	5
1996	N1	5P(pl)	3
1997	Pr.	9	5
1998	Pr.	10	4

LEYTON ORIENT

Trying to describe the history of Leyton Orient is like talking about several different clubs. There have been so many different names, grounds and colours, it is difficult to trace a common thread.

The current club dates from the Glyn Cricket and and Football Club, founded in 1881. As Clapton Orient it had been playing in the East End long before it was reorganised and became professional in 1903. In 1905, when players sported red and white hooped jerseys, the club was elected to the second division of the Football League. There they started badly, improved just before the First World War and then slowly drifted to a regular spot near the bottom of the table by the late 1920s. At this stage, even the highly fashionable white shirts with a large red 'V', could not prevent relegation and a terrible cash crisis. The club would probably have gone out of existence but for Arsenal using it as a nursery and so taking on much of the expense.

After the Second World War, in a brave new world, the club changed the name to Leyton Orient, the colours to blue shirts, and finally settled on a regular ground Brisbane Road. Of course, Cinderella still did not go to the ball; Arsenal and Spurs took all the local talent and support, but slowly mangager Alec Stock pulled the club into shape, finally getting promotion to division two in 1956. Stock consolidated further, and later new manager Johnny Carey did something thought previously impossible by gaining promotion to the top flight in 1962.

Not ready for such a huge leap in playing demands, the O's finished ten points adrift at the bottom and such was the trauma that four years later they were in division three again.

However, undaunted, they began another phase, renamed just Orient and now wearing a smart all-red strip. Another cash crisis was overcome thanks to fans' contributions, and in 1970 they were back in the second division for a hard-fought 12-year period. These were colourful times at last, and the all-white outfit with red stripes running through shirts and shorts were sported by Peter Taylor and the Nigerian internationals John Chiedozie and Tunji Banjo.

The early 1980s saw a drop into the fourth division, but the consistency provided by ex-European Cup winner Frank Clark as manager and managing director ensured a stability which appeared to turn the tide. In 1988 the club became Leyton Orient again, promotion was achieved and the team battled hard to retain that momentum before going down in 1995.

Experience probably tells all at the club that the first division (or Premier League) is not the healthiest spot for the O's to be, but it doesn't stop them dreaming of the days when Norman Deeley and company faced the super clubs.

The blue period of the 1960s, when Orient reached the first division

Leyton Orient (founded 1881) records and strips

1885-1899

1950

1973

1992

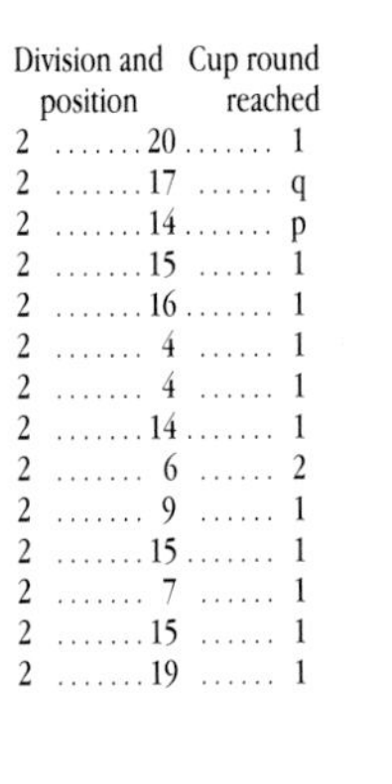

1963

1981

1928

1998

	Division and position		Cup round reached
1906	2	20	1
1907	2	17	q
1908	2	14	p
1909	2	15	1
1910	2	16	1
1911	2	4	1
1912	2	4	1
1913	2	14	1
1914	2	6	2
1915	2	9	1
1920	2	15	1
1921	2	7	1
1922	2	15	1
1923	2	19	1
1924	2	10	1
1925	2	11	1
1926	2	20	qf
1927	2	20	3
1928	2	20	3
1929	2	22R	4
1930	3S	12	4
1931	3S	19	1
1932	3S	16	2
1933	3S	20	1
1934	3S	11	3
1935	3S	14	2
1936	3S	14	4
1937	3S	12	2
1938	3S	19	2
1939	3S	20	2
1946			1
1947	3S	19	1
1948	3S	17	1
1949	3S	19	2
1950	3S	18	1
1951	3S	17	1
1952	3S	16	5
1953	3S	14	1
1954	3S	11	qf
1955	3S	2	2
1956	3S	1P	4
1957	2	15	3
1958	2	12	4
1959	2	17	3
1960	2	10	3
1961	2	19	5
1962	2	2P	4
1963	1	22R	5
1964	2	16	4
1965	2	19	3
1966	2	22R	3
1967	3	14	2
1968	3	18	4
1969	3	18	1
1970	3	1P	1
1971	2	17	4
1972	2	17	qf
1973	2	15	3
1974	2	4	4
1975	2	12	3
1976	2	13	3
1977	2	19	4
1978	2	14	sf
1979	2	11	4
1980	2	14	4
1981	2	17	3
1982	2	22R	5
1983	3	20	2
1984	3	11	1
1985	3	22R	4
1986	4	5	2
1987	4	7	3
1988	4	8	4
1989	4	6P(pl)	1
1990	3	14	1
1991	3	13	3
1992	3	10	4
1993	N2	7	2
1994	N2	18	2
1995	N2	24R	2
1996	N3	21	1
1997	N3	16	2
1998	N3	11	1

In the red period, the club tried its own version of the Coventry style, shirt and shorts striped special.

LINCOLN CITY

Located in an area not noted for football success or tradition, Lincoln have done well to have enjoyed so many years at a reasonable level and, indeed, survived at all.

Yet the first club in the city was formed as far back as 1861, when the uniform was described as 'red caps, belts and socks, with white jerseys, bearing on the left breast the Lincoln arms'. By the time the club was re-founded in 1883 the players wore striped jerseys, but the red and white have remained as club colours evers since.

In 1892 Lincoln City were founder members of the second division of the Football League and there they stayed with varying degrees of success until after the First World War. Three times they had failed to gain re-election but each time they bounced back after a gap of one year.

Following the last of these occasions, the club had to endure a decade of third division football. A short promotion excitement did no more to prove that, although Lincoln were above third division status, they were not properly equipped to survive at the next level.

It was the same after the Second World War, until in 1952 manager Bill Anderson inspired Andy Graver to fire with all guns blazing. Some 121 goals were scored in obtaining promotion including 11 in one match against Crewe. For a while, the Imps looked a respectable second division outfit, but the collapse, when it came, was rapid. From being a second division side in 1961, by 1967 the club had applied for re-election four times.

As usual at times like this, the club played around with the strip. All-red shirts were followed by white-sleeved ones and red shorts, but it was not until the arrival of a young manager, Graham Taylor, that the gloom began to lift. In 1976 Taylor's team, now happily back in red and white stripes, revived memories of the early 1950s – 111 goals were scored in the acquisition of a record 74 points.

Of course, a talent such as Taylor's was snapped up quickly, and there was nobody of his calibre to continue. Although a fine team played at Sincil Bank at the beginning of the 1980s, just missing promotion to division two, soon the Imps were back in the basement.

In 1987, following a double demotion, Lincoln City found themselves in non-League football. Luckily for them, the GM Vauxhall Conference doorway operates both ways and fourth division status was immediately regained. However, this traumatic experience made the club a sounder, more practical outfit, and in 1998 they won promotion to the second division.

In this strip, the Imps scored 111 goals and amassed 74 points in 1976.

Lincoln (founded 1883) records and strips

1861-1923

	Division and	position	Cup round reached
1885			3
1886			1
1887			1
1888			p
1889			p
1890			2
1891			1
1892			p
1893	2	9	p
1894	2	8	p
1895	2	13	q
1896	2	13	p
1897	2	16	p

1937-1957

1898	2	14	p
1899	2	12	p
1900	2	9	p
1901	2	8	p
1902	2	5	2
1903	2	10	1
1904	2	12	q
1905	2	9	1
1906	2	13	2
1907	2	19	2
1908	2	20L	1
1909			1

1958-1962

1910	2	15	p
1911	2	21L	p
1912			2
1913	2	8	p
1914	2	19	1
1915	2	16	1
1920	2	21L	1
1921			2
1922	3N	14	p
1923	3N	13	q
1924	3N	19	p

1972-1973

1925	3N	8	p
1926	3N	15	1
1927	3N	11	3
1928	3N	2	3
1929	3N	6	3
1930	3N	5	2
1931	3N	2	2
1932	3N	1P	2
1933	2	18	3
1934	2	22R	3
1935	3N	4	2
1936	3N	4	1
1937	3N	2	2
1938	3N	7	2
1939	3N	17	3
1946			2
1947	3N	12	3
1948	3N	1P	1
1949	2	22R	3
1950	3N	4	1
1951	3N	5	1
1952	3N	1P	3
1953	2	15	3
1954	2	16	4

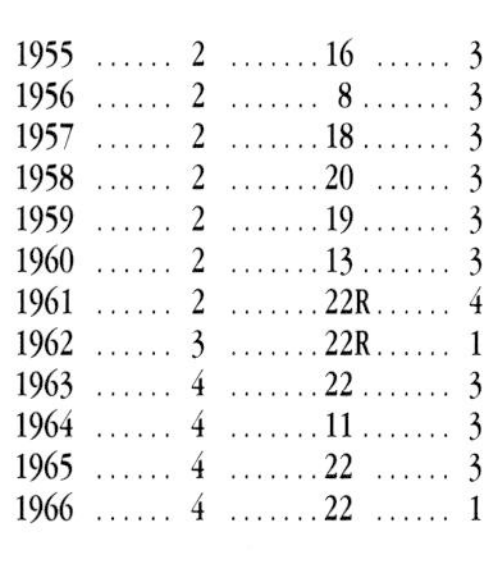

1955	2	16	3
1956	2	8	3
1957	2	18	3
1958	2	20	3
1959	2	19	3
1960	2	13	3
1961	2	22R	4
1962	3	22R	1
1963	4	22	3
1964	4	11	3
1965	4	22	3
1966	4	22	1

1976

1967	4	24	1
1968	4	13	1
1969	4	8	3
1970	4	8	2
1971	4	21	3
1972	4	5	1
1973	4	10	1
1974	4	12	1
1975	4	5	3
1976	4	1P	4
1977	3	9	3
1978	3	16	1
1979	3	24R	1
1980	4	7	1
1981	4	2P	2
1982	3	4	1
1983	3	6	1
1984	3	14	2
1985	3	19	1
1986	3	21R	1
1987	4	24R	1
1988	GMVC		2
1989	4	10	1

1981

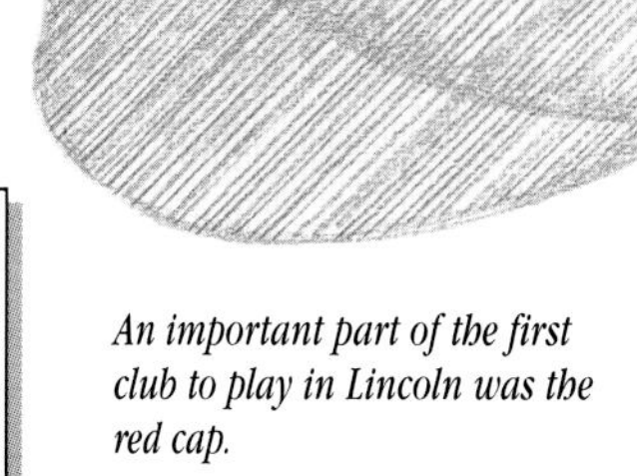

An important part of the first club to play in Lincoln was the red cap.

1988

1990	4	10	2
1991	4	14	1
1992	4	10	1
1993	N3	8	1
1994	N3	18	2
1995	N3	12	3
1996	N3	18	1
1997	N3	9	2
1998	N3	3P	2

1998

CLUBS NO LONGER IN THE LEAGUE
(Those which left before the First World War)

Usually the definition of a Football League club is one currently holding that status, but over the last 100 years or so there have been many others, successful in their day, who are sadly no longer competing at this top level.

Some lasted only a few years, enjoying perhaps one do-or-die period, in which they defied the odds of geography and limited financial resources, but there were others who had comparatively long League careers.

Unfortunately some of these once famous clubs are no longer with us, but there are others still competing healthily in different leagues, and in fact, the more ambitious are hoping to make a glorious come-back.

In this first section, illustrating clubs which have left the Football League before the First World War, only about half still survive, but these clubs were amongst the pioneers of Football League development, helping to make it what it is today, and therefore well worthy of a mention.

ACCRINGTON
One of the original founder members of the Football League in 1888, Accrington were not the same club as the later and more famous Stanley. In 1890, playing in red shirts, the team finished sixth in the first division.

BOOTLE
Bootle survived only one season in division two in 1892/93, but that year they beat Sheffield United, Grimsby Town and Walsall (by 7-1). The blue and white stripes were worn throughout. Today they play in the North West Counties League in an all-blue strip.

BURTON SWIFTS
The first of the Burton teams in the League, Swifts experienced two successful seasons, finishing sixth on each occasion. In the following few seasons, the teams also turned out in maroon and orange quarters and red and white quarters.

BURTON WANDERERS
Wanderers followed the Swifts into the second division and in 1895/96 ended up in fourth position, but the next year they were out. On both occasions the team wore blue and white halves.

DARWEN
1891-1899

GLOSSOP (NORTH END)
1898-1915

BURTON SWIFTS
1892-1900

NORTHWICH VICTORIA
1892-1894

BURTON UNITED
1901-1907

NEW BRIGHTON TOWE
1898-1901

OUGHBOROUGH
1895-1900

BOOTLE
1892-1893

ACCRINGTON
1888-1893

BURTON WANDERERS
1894-1897

GAINSBOROUGH TRINITY
1896-1912

MIDDLESBROUGH IRONOPOLIS
1893-1894

BURTON UNITED
Strangely the amalgamation of the earlier clubs produced no better results, Burton United's best being in 1901/02, their first season. In subsequent seasons, the players wore maroon, then geen shirts with red collars and finally, brown and blue quarters.

DARWEN
Darwen had two seasons in the first division during their eight-year stay. Later they wore black and white stripes, and also plain white shirts. Currently in the North-West Counties League with Bootle, they play in red and white shirts.

GAINSBOROUGH TRINITY
Trinity played in the second division for 16 years, once finishing sixth in 1904/05, always wearing blue shirts, white shorts. After a long and fairly successful non-League history, their blue shirts now appear in the HFS Loans League.

GLOSSOP (NORTH END)
Glossop spent one splendid year in the first division and another 16 in the second. They also wore white shirts with either violet or blue trim. They are yet another club currently in the North-West Counties League, and now sporting a blue kit.

LOUGHBOROUGH
Twelfth in 1895/96, their first season, Loughborough struggled in the other four, before failing to gain re-election and becoming defunct. The team wore black and white stripes throughout.

MIDDLESBROUGH IRONOPOLIS
Ironopolis just played one season in division two in 1893/94. Although they wore red and white shirts, they are not to be confused with Middlesbrough FC, then an entirely separate club.

NEW BRIGHTON TOWER
The Tower had three successful seasons (the third finishing in fourth spot) in the second division, before financial collapse closed the club. They also wore white shirts with blue shorts.

NORTHWICH VICTORIA
The Vics lasted only two seasons in the League, both in division two, but have always been a strong non-League side. The current side wear green and white and have finished in the top half of the GM Vauxhall League.

CLUBS NO LONGER IN THE LEAGUE
(Those whose best days were between the wars)

Most of the clubs which left in the period between the two world wars were ones which had joined in the mad scramble which accompanied the founding of the third divisions when the League was extended in 1921 and 1922.

Many of these were not ready to face the stiff opposition of clubs who had had tougher paths to League status, and returned to local football, mostly in the extreme north-east, the border area between Lancashire and Cheshire, and South Wales.

Happily, many of these clubs continue to survive. Included in this category are Bradford Park Avenue, re-formed in 1988 and now playing in the Northern Premier League. Although the original club did not leave the League until 1970, their most successful period was between the wars.

Perhaps they will follow the example of Stalybridge Celtic and rise to within striking distance of the League again.

ABERDARE ATHLETIC
Aberdaer had a successful first season in 1921/22, when they finished eighth in division three (south). Always wearing blue and yellow, they eventually failed to gain re-election in 1927. They finally folded in 1948 after many efforts to re-form.

ASHINGTON
Ashington played in the third division (north) for eight seasons, the best finish being eighth in 1923/24. The club still wore black and white stripes in the Northern League until the late 1980's.

BRADFORD PARK AVENUE
Bradford PA were really a major League club, spending three seasons in the first division and 22 in the second, out of a total of 51. They had two distinctly different colour schemes: green and white; and red, amber, black and white. They used to alternate at regular intervals. The revived club is on its way back in the Unibond Northern Premier League.

STALYBRIDGE CELTIC
1921-1923

SOUTH SHIELDS
1919-1930

DURHAM CITY
1921-1927

ASHINGTON
1921-1929

NELSON
1921-1931

DURHAM CITY
Durham are yet another club whose first season was probably the best (11th in 1922), the other six being a constant struggle. The team also wore blue and gold stripes, as well as plain red shirts. They are still playing in the Northern League.

MERTHYR TOWN
Merthyr, too, had a successful opening season, followed by a decline. They also played in red and green stripes before leaving the League after ten years. Modern Merthyr Tydfil play in black and white.

NELSON
More successful than most, Nelson were promoted to division two once and just missed out two years later. They wore only the blue shirts throughout, as they still do today in the North-West Counties League.

NEW BRIGHTON
New Brighton were a different club to the Tower of 20 years earlier. They played 21 seasons, incuding five just after the Second World War. Their best year was in 1925 when they finished third in white shirts. They also appeared in red and white, and maroon and white jerseys. Sadly they went out of existence in 1983.

SOUTH SHIELDS
South Shields spent 11 years in division three (north), once finishing sixth in 1923. They had other good seasons, but were eventually replaced by Gateshead. The club also played in blue shirts and white shorts.

STALYBRIDGE CELTIC
Celtic played only two seasons in the League, but like Cheshire neighbours Northwich, they have retained a good level of football, and have recently been flourishing in the GM Vauxhall Conference.

THAMES ASSOCIATION
Thames Association survived only two seasons in the third division (south). The red and blue quarters failed to impress the fans and the club soon folded.

CLUBS NO LONGER IN THE LEAGUE
(Those which left since the Second World War)

With the sad exception of Maidstone United, most of the clubs to have left the Football League since the Second World War had been members for about half a century. Usually they have battled against the odds of geographical isolation, the competition of a nearby big city club, or most often, an insufficient catchment area to swell small gates.

These clubs had held their own until the abolition of the maximum wage. Then, their previous excellent scouting systems were useless when the big cheques were waved about.The resulting lack of playing success had a disastrous effect on the clubs' resources.

Yet all of them, at some time or other, had been on the verge of promotion to the second division and better things. Accrington Stanley, for example, finished consecutively second, third, third and second in the third division only three seasons before resigning their League place.

With the doorway to the GM Vauxhall Conference now in place, there are likely to be more clubs to add to this list soon, but at least they will have the opportunity to fight their way back with results on the pitch.

ACCRINGTON STANLEY
Stanley were not the same club as the earlier Accrington, although they both wore exactly the same strip of all-red shirts and white shorts. The club declined rapidly in the late 1950s. A revived version of Stanley now plays in the Unibond Northern Premier League.

ALDERSHOT
Although usually struggling, the Shots did reach eighth in the third division in 1973/74. Eventually, though, they couldn't pay their way. A reformed club is now in the Diadora League. Other red-shirted strips included blue sleeves as well as a striped version.

BARROW
Barrow finished a creditable eighth in the third division in 1967/68, after years of combating the problems of geographical isolation. Sadly, within four years they were out, but have fought their way back to the higher levels of non-League football. Other strips include white as well as striped shirts.

BARROW
1921-1972

ACCRINGTON STANLEY
1921-1962

SOUTHPORT
1921-1978

GATESHEAD
After the Second World War, Gateshead had eight great seasons in succession, in 1949/50 being just two points off the second division. Within five seasons of that run, they too were out, but a reformed club has recently fought its way back to the GM Vauxhall Conference. They first played in claret shirts with light blue sleeves.

MAIDSTONE UNITED
After a long wait, promotion to the League in 1989 came at the wrong time for the Stones. They had no home and dwindling support. The gold shirts and black shorts were long-standing and traditional colours.

NEWPORT COUNTY
In the early 1980s County nearly repeated their 1946/47 one-year stay in the second division. Five years later they had slipped into non-League oblivion. The illustrated strip shows the 1960 three-black-banded version of the traditional amber shirts.

SOUTHPORT
A battling eighth position in the third division in 1969 was the highlight in a League record which ended for Southport nine years later. Other strips worn by Southport include all-red, black and white stripes, green and white hoops, and yellow. The Sandgrounders look to be on their way back following promotion to the GM Vauxhall Conference.

WORKINGTON TOWN
In 1966 the Cumbrian club, finishing fifth, Workington Town went very close to promotion to division two, but from that time on fell prey to the same problems as neighbours Barrow. Just relegated from the Unibond Northern Premier League, they still play in red shirts.

LIVERPOOL

To the modern fan, describing Liverpool is easy. They wear red shirts and shorts, and they win most trophies - but of course the club is over 100 years old and life, even before Bill Shankly, was extremely rich in history, with one or two strange facts cropping up.

Liverpool came into existence only because of a split between Everton and the owner of Anfield (then the home of the Toffeemen). Furthermore Liverpool, the club formed by the players left at Anfield, decided at first to wear a blue and white halved jersey to distinguish them from Everton, who were at the time sporting various strips with red in them. Eventually, the two clubs switched to their current shirts and the rivalry between the two has ensured no further tinkering with colours.

The early Liverpool were immediately successful and by 1906 they had been League champions twice and Cup semi-finalists three times. The great Sam Hardy starred in those early teams and it was another fine goalkeeper, Elisha Scott, and the long-serving full back Ephraim Longworth who were largely responsible for another grand period in the early 1920s. Liverpool triumphed in two other consecutive championship seasons and it was only the rise of the Herbert Chapman-inspired Huddersfield which prevented further successes.

In 1914, there had been a Cup final defeat by Burnley and, strangely enough for such a successful side in the League, Cup glory had always eluded Liverpool. Indeed, after the 1923 League win, Anfield did not have anything much to celebrate until after the Second World War. Everton had picked up trophies in the 1930s and the Reds were eager for success.

After the War, Liverpool started well, winning the first League title, then lost yet another Cup final, this time to an Arsenal side captained by old Evertonian favourite Joe Mercer. But somehow standards dropped, as did the club – into the second division. There followed a frustrating period as promotion was just missed year after year, and it took the arrival of Bill Shankly to shake the club out of a state of self-doubt; the modern era had begun.

Shankly changed everything. Liverpool were the first club regularly to wear an all-red strip and the 'Pool became fashion setters. As we all know, there followed a never-ending list of League successes, but it still seems strange that it was not until 1965 that the Reds first won the Cup against Leeds United, surprisingly in their first final.

The heroes of the last three decades are now household names and all the glory days, including those in Europe, can be recited by their legions of fans. All because of Everton's row with a landlord!

Probably of all the successful Liverpool strips, the simple 'V' collar version is best remembered.

Liverpool (founded 1892) records and strips

	Division and position		Cup round reached
1894	2	1P	qf
1895	1	16R	2
1896	2	1P	2
1897	1	5	sf
1898	1	9	qf
1899	1	2	sf
1900	1	19	2
1901	1	1C	1
1902	1	11	2
1903	1	5	1
1904	1	17R	1
1905	2	1P	1
1906	1	1C	sf
1907	1	15	qf
1908	1	8	3
1909	1	16	2
1910	1	2	1
1911	1	13	2
1912	1	17	2
1913	1	12	3
1914	1	16	F
1915	1	14	2
1920	1	4	qf
1921	1	4	2
1922	1	1C	2
1923	1	1C	3
1924	1	12	qf
1925	1	4	qf
1926	1	7	4
1927	1	9	5
1928	1	16	4
1929	1	5	4
1930	1	12	3
1931	1	9	3
1932	1	10	qf
1933	1	14	3
1934	1	18	5
1935	1	7	4
1936	1	19	4
1937	1	18	3
1938	1	11	5
1939	1	11	5
1946			4
1947	1	1C	sf
1948	1	11	4
1949	1	12	5
1950	1	8	F
1951	1	9	3
1952	1	11	5
1953	1	17	3
1954	1	22R	3
1955	2	11	5
1956	2	3	5
1957	2	3	3
1958	2	4	qf
1959	2	4	3
1960	2	3	4
1961	2	3	4
1962	2	1P	5
1963	1	8	sf
1964	1	1C	qf
1965	1	7	W
1966	1	1C	3
1967	1	5	5
1968	1	3	qf
1969	1	2	5
1970	1	5	qf
1971	1	5	F
1972	1	3	4
1973	1	1C	qf
1974	1	2	W
1975	1	2	4
1976	1	1C	4
1977	1	1C	F
1978	1	2	3
1979	1	1C	sf
1980	1	1C	sf
1981	1	5	4
1982	1	1C	sf
1983	1	1C	5
1984	1	1C	4
1985	1	2	sf
1986	1	1C	W
1987	1	2	3
1988	1	1C	F
1989	1	2	W
1990	1	1C	sf
1991	1	2	5
1992	1	6	W
1993	Pr	6	3
1994	Pr	8	3
1995	Pr	4	qf
1996	Pr	3	F
1997	Pr.	4	4
1998	Pr.	3	3

1892-1915

1920-1937

1938-1956

1957-1962

1977-1983

1985-1987

1998

Although a manufacturer's style, the three-panelled kit is a striking example of modern design.

LUTON TOWN

Luton Town are yet another club whose current supporters would never have recognised the early outfits worn by the 19th century players. Back in 1885, the first Luton team turned out in an immaculate strip of navy blue and pink halved shirts and caps. Four years later this had been replaced by a splendid cochineal red ensemble, before, at the turn of the century, a more sober, sky blue shirt was preferred.

At this stage the game in Luton was thriving, and feeling that Southern League football was not sufficiently demanding, the club applied for, and were granted, election to the Football League's second division. Sadly, Luton had more ambition than talent at this stage and three years later they lost their League status. Back in the Southern League, the Hatters now sported a large black 'V' and belt on their shirts, but this unique sartorial combination failed to produce any improvement within the club.

In fact by the time Luton returned to the League with the introduction of the third division in 1920, they had changed to their now traditional white shirts and the black shorts which they wore for over half a century.

The Town, despite performing well, stayed in the third division until 1937. This dramatic season was packed with goals, 55 alone from Joe Payne, the centre-forward who the previous season had scored ten in his first match up front!

The club held its elevated position this time and after the Second World War, manager Dally Duncan built an even better side, led by intelligent skipper Syd Owen, which made Luton the first Bedfordshire club to reach the top flight. Four years later in 1959, the Hatters reached their only FA Cup final, going down 2-1 to an inspired Nottingham Forest.

The rapid drop to the fourth division which followed in the 1960s was extremely traumatic as well as unexpected. However, slowly, good fortunes returned and the club even managed one brief season back in division one.

At this time yet another colour scheme was advanced. The orange of a startling design in 1975 eventually diminished in emphasis, but blue had replaced black as the support to the white shirts, and it was in this strip during a recent return to the top flight that Luton Town won their first trophy. In 1988, in an exciting League Cup final, Brian Stein grabbed a last-minute winner against Arsenal. The fans still remembered the celebrations of that day as the team struggled for inspiration in the 1990s.

The club's first major trophy was won in this smart outfit in the 1988 League Cup final.

Luton (founded 1885) records and strips

Year	Division and position		Cup round reached
1931	3S	7	2
1932	3S	6	3
1933	3S	14	qf
1934	3S	6	3
1935	3S	4	4
1936	3S	2	4
1937	3S	1P	4
1938	2	12	5

1957-1962

Luton's flirtation with orange provided many remarkable combinations like this one in 1975.

1885-1914

1988

Year	Division and position		Cup round reached
1960	1	22R	5
1961	2	13	5
1962	2	13	3
1963	2	22R	3
1964	3	18	3
1965	3	21R	3
1966	4	6	2
1967	4	17	2
1968	4	1P	2

Year	Division and position		Cup round reached
1898	2	8	1
1899	2	15	p
1900	2	17L	p
1921	3S	9	3
1922	3S	4	2
1923	3S	5	1

Year	Division and position		Cup round reached
1939	2	7	3
1946			3
1947	2	13	5
1948	2	13	5
1949	2	10	5
1950	2	17	3
1951	2	19	4
1952	2	8	qf

1975-1976

Year	Division and position		Cup round reached
1988	1	9	sf
1989	1	16	3
1990	1	17	3
1991	1	18	3
1992	1	20R	3
1993	N1	20	4
1994	N1	20	sf
1995	N1	16	4
1996	N1	24R	3
1997	N2	3	3
1997	N2	17	1

1928-1935

1935-1956

1998

Year	Division and position		Cup round reached
1924	3S	7	1
1925	3S	16	1
1926	3S	7	2
1927	3S	8	3
1928	3S	13	3
1929	3S	7	3
1930	3S	13	1

Year	Division and position		Cup round reached
1953	2	3	5
1954	2	6	3
1955	2	2P	5
1956	1	10	3
1957	1	16	3
1958	1	8	3
1959	1	17	F

Year	Division and position		Cup round reached
1969	3	3	3
1970	3	2P	2
1971	2	6	3
1972	2	13	3
1973	2	12	qf
1974	2	2P	5
1975	1	20R	3
1976	2	7	4
1977	2	6	4
1978	2	13	4
1979	2	18	3
1980	2	6	3
1981	2	5	4
1982	2	1P	4
1983	1	18	4
1984	1	16	3
1985	1	13	sf
1986	1	9	6
1987	1	7	4

MACCLESFIELD TOWN

In 1997, after three decades of being one of the superstars of non-League football, Macclesfield finally took their deserved place in the Football League.

The Silkmen had seen many of their peers progress to national status whilst they had been the victims of unfortunate mistiming. Every season where there had been an opportunity to break through, the club had witnessed a temporary dip in form. Even the automatic promotion spot in 1995 was denied because of inadequate ground standards – this after Chester City had used the Moss Rose Ground themselves for a season!

However, back in 1874 when the club was formed, appearing in the Football League lists was a remote possibility. The early years were spent in the Manchester League. They were twice champions, but the proximity of the silk manufacturing town to the northern metropolis was a double-edged sword. Manchester provided a lot of high quality competition but also took away a lot of much needed support.

Eventually Macclesfield looked southwards and joined the powerful Cheshire League. Playing against former and future Football League sides increased the Town's reputation and a particularly successful spell in the 1930s made them a team to fear. Players like Albert Valentine, who scored 84 goals in 1934, were greatly respected in the north-west.

All through this period, the club remained faithful to its blue and white uniform, and after the Second World War, the blue shirted Silkmen were still finding success in the Cheshire League and Senior Cup. However, at that time progress from senior non-League status was difficult and it was only the streamlining of non-League football which allowed the club to illustrate its full potential. Macclesfield won the first two Northern Premier League titles as well as the 1970 FA Trophy, the replacement for the Amateur Cup.

When the non-League pyramid was completed by the formation of the GM Vauxhall Conference, the Silkmen, still sporting their blue shirts, were the obvious contenders for the offered prize of a place in the Football League. However, although the club had the potential, the next step was to prove frustrating.

The mixed blessing of the proximity of Manchester eventually turned full circle when ex-Busby Babe, Sammy McIlroy was appointed manager. The club survived the trauma of the first GMVC title and subsequent Football League rejection, by continuing to challenge for non-League supremacy, and one FA Trophy and GMVC title later, the momentum was undeniable and the Silkmen became one of the 'big boys'.

The 'Old Trafford' professionalism offered by McIlroy showed in the inaugural season and the Silkmen looked forward to an exciting new future in the Football League as they immediately gained promotion to the second division.

This kit proudly worn by the Silkmen in their first season in the Football League.

Macclesfield (founded 1874) records and strips

1911

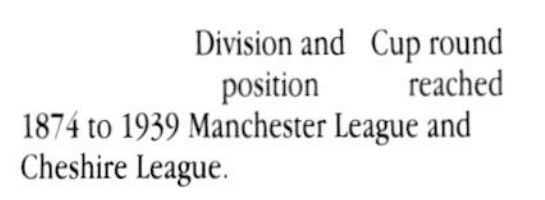

	Division and position		Cup round reached
1874 to 1939 Manchester League and Cheshire League.			
1946	CL		
1947	CL		
1948	CL		p

1934

1949	CL		p
1950	CL		q1
1951	CL		q1
1952	CL		q1
1953	CL		q2
1954	CL		q1
1955	CL		q2
1956	CL		q1
1957	CL		q3
1958	CL		q1
1959	CL		p
1960	CL		q1
1961	CL		1

1955

1962	CL		q2
1963	CL		q1
1964	CL		q4
1965	CL		1

1960

1966	CL		q3
1967	CL		q4
1968	CL		3
1969	NP	1	1
1970	NP	1	1
1971	NP	5	1
1972	NP	6	q4
1973	NP	10	q4

1967

The half-sleeve style was similar to the one worn by Cheshire neighbours, Crewe Alexandra in the Football League.

1974	NP	8	q4
1975	NP	17	q2
1976	NP	15	1
1977	NP	19	q1

1974

1978	NP	22	q1
1979	NP	23	p
1980	NP	8	q2

1980

1981	NP	13	q1
1982	NP	10	p
1983	NP	5	1
1984	NP	6	1
1985	NP	2	1
1986	NP	9	1
1987	NP	1	q4
1988	GMVC	11	2
1989	GMVC	7	1
1990	GMVC	4	4
1991	GMVC	7	1
1992	GMVC	13	4
1993	GMVC	18	2

1990

1994	GMVC	7	2
1995	GMVC	1	1
1996	GMVC	4	3
1997	GMVC	1	q2
1998	N3	2P	2

1998

MANCHESTER CITY

The beginnings of Manchester City were both inauspicious and humble. Under the various names of West Gorton, Gorton and Ardwick, and playing at an even greater variety of venues, the club achieved little of significance outside local league circles.

Even the eventual election to the second division of the Football League provided only extra pressures and it was only in 1894, when the name was changed to Manchester City, that the club finally began to satisfy the ambitions of fans and board alike. Ardwick's old colours of red and black stripes were dropped, although they did reappear as a second strip in the great successes eighty years later.

The now famous sky blue shirts figured in the promotion struggle regularly until 1899, when the achievement of first division status was followed five years later by an FA Cup final win over Bolton, the only goal coming from Welsh international star Billy Meredith.

However, this success also brought allegations of illegal payments and although the punishments and humiliations which followed did not affect the club's first division status immediately, it did allow something more significant to happen. Their chief rivals Newton Heath, by now renamed Manchester United, took advantage of City's traumas to emerge as Manchester's premier club for the first time.

After the First World War City began to illustrate the contrast of circumstances the Maine Road fans would experience over the years. A long run of relative League success was followed by relegation in the same year as a near miss in the FA Cup final versus Bolton. Promotion back to the first division in 1928 seemed to signal the beginning of good times to come in the 1930s. Another Wembley defeat in 1933 was followed by a second success a year later, 2-1 over Portsmouth in the final. With a team considered by many as the club's best, City even became champions for the first time in 1937, yet unbelievably were relegated the following season.

After the Second World War, early promotion was followed by two other yo-yo years. Then in the mid-1950s, with astute management by Les McDowall and the early illustration of Don Revie's tactical skills, there was another pair of consecutive FA Cup finals, with again the second being successful, in 1956 against Birmingham City.

Sadly for the Sky Blues, their Manchester rivals United were beginning their own period of domination, so to some degree City's potential never really materialised.

It was only in the late 1960s, after the Old Trafford outfit had become satiated with success, that the leadership of Joe Mercer and Malcolm Allison produced a wonderful team capable of great results. They went on to win the League, the Cup, and on a famous night in Vienna beat the crack Poles, Gornik Zabrze, to lift the European Cup Winners' Cup.

Since those heady days, life has been up and down again, and managers have come and gone. In 1998 the Sky Blues sank for the first time into the third flight – a sad day.

City added maroon to their kit when winning the League, FA Cup and European Cup Winners' Cup in successive years.

City (founded 1887) records and strips

1887-1924

1924-1936

1936-1953

1955-1960

1969-1971

1991-1993

1981-1983

1998

	Division and position		Cup round reached
1893	2	5	
1894	2	13	
1895	2	9	
1896	2	2	
1897	2	6	1
1898	2	3	2
1899	2	1P	2
1900	1	7	1
1901	1	11	1
1902	1	18R	2
1903	2	1P	1
1904	1	2	W
1905	1	3	2
1906	1	5	1
1907	1	17	1
1908	1	3	3
1909	1	19R	1
1910	2	1P	qf
1911	1	17	2
1912	1	15	2
1913	1	6	2
1914	1	13	qf
1915	1	5	3
1920	1	7	2
1921	1	2	1
1922	1	10	3
1923	1	8	1
1924	1	11	sf
1925	1	10	1
1926	1	21R	F
1927	2	3	3
1928	2	1P	5
1929	1	8	3
1930	1	3	5
1931	1	8	3
1932	1	14	sf
1933	1	16	F
1934	1	5	W
1935	1	4	3
1936	1	9	5
1937	1	1C	qf
1938	1	21R	qf
1939	2	5	4
1946			4
1947	2	1P	5
1948	1	10	5
1949	1	7	3
1950	1	21R	3
1951	2	2P	3
1952	1	15	3
1953	1	20	4
1954	1	17	4
1955	1	7	F
1956	1	4	W
1957	1	18	3
1958	1	5	3
1959	1	20	3
1960	1	16	3
1961	1	13	4
1962	1	12	4
1963	1	21R	5
1964	2	6	3
1965	2	11	3
1966	2	1P	qf
1967	1	15	qf
1968	1	1C	4
1969	1	13	W
1970	1	9	4
1971	1	11	5
1972	1	4	3
1973	1	11	5
1974	1	14	4
1975	1	8	3
1976	1	8	4
1977	1	2	5
1978	1	4	4
1979	1	15	4
1980	1	17	3
1981	1	12	F
1982	1	10	4
1983	1	20R	4
1984	2	4	3
1985	2	3P	3
1986	1	15	4
1987	1	21R	3
1988	2	9	qf
1989	2	2P	4
1990	1	14	3
1991	1	5	5
1992	1	5	3
1993	Pr	9	qf
1994	Pr	16	4
1995	Pr	17	5
1996	Pr	18R	5
1997	N1	14	5
1998	N1	22R	4

The maroon and white topped stockings of the late 1960s.

MANCHESTER UNITED

Despite the modern publicity given to their early strip, it's still difficult to imagine the Red devils from Old Trafford wearing anything else but red. In fact, it's now difficult to comprehend those same humble beginnings in 19th century Manchester as experienced by their City rivals. As Newton Heath and clad in yellow and green halves, the club had just managed to enter the enlarged Football League first division. However, the team was just not good enough and was soon relegated. So by the turn of the century, following Ardwick's example, the name was changed to indicate a new status and Manchester United became a big city club.

A white shirt was tried before the now-famous red version was finally adopted and indeed it was not until 1906 that the first division status was regained. However, this was the beginning of a glorious if short-lived period. The 1909 FA Cup final win over Bristol City was sandwiched between two championship successes, all inspired by the transfer of Manchester City favourite Billy Meredith.

Current fans, however, find it difficult to believe that in the period between the Wars this great club never finished better than ninth in the League or the semi-final in the Cup. City dominated Manchester and only Everton brought other success to the north-west.

After the Second World War the future looked bleak. Old Trafford had been destroyed by bombs and the playing staff seemed fairly old, but nobody had allowed for the vision and vitality of Matt Busby. After four runners-up spots in five years, plus a wonderful FA Cup final win over Blackpool, his first United team won the League in 1952 – and as the Old Trafford ground was rebuilt, so the manager did the same with the team. The Busby Babes were born out of a revolutionary youth policy and the new team soon dominated the League championship.

Sadly, the Munich air tragedy of 1958 prematurely crushed this team's potential but Busby, who survived, and assistant Jimmy Murphy built another around the young Bobby Charlton. When Denis Law and George Best were added, the trophy-winning became almost an annual event. A Cup win and two further championships preceded the club's finest hour, when they became the first English team to win the European Cup. That 4-1 win over Benfica at Wembley was just reward for Busby's ambition over a decade earlier.

Sir Matt, as he became, moved upstairs to the board room, and there followed a quarter of a century of frustration. Great Cup wins, but no further League titles. However, in the 1990s there was yet another Cup win, followed by a second European trophy, thanks to victory over Barcelona, which gave the club a renewed self-belief. The near miss in the 1992 League campaign proved only a final frustration before United became the inaugural Premier League champions a year later. Other League titles and Cup wins promised the beginning of another all-conquering era. Alex Ferguson's United were now big enough to take on the world's best.

It seems a simple strip now, but it was much discussed when introduced by Matt Busby's third great team.

United (founded 1878) records and strips

	Division and position		Cup round reached
1890			1
1891			
1892			
1893	1	16	1
1894	1	16R	2
1895	2	3	1
1896	2	6	2
1897	2	2	qf
1898	2	4	2
1899	2	4	1
1900	2	4	
1901	2	10	1
1902	2	15	
1903	2	5	2
1904	2	3	2
1905	2	3	
1906	2	2P	qf
1907	1	8	1
1908	1	1C	qf
1909	1	13	W
1910	1	5	1
1911	1	1C	3
1912	1	13	qf
1913	1	4	3
1914	1	14	1
1915	1	18	1
1920	1	12	2
1921	1	13	1
1922	1	22R	1
1923	2	4	2
1924	2	14	2
1925	2	2P	1
1926	1	9	sf
1927	1	15	3
1928	1	19	qf
1929	1	12	4
1930	1	17	3
1931	1	22R	4
1932	2	12	3
1933	2	6	3
1934	2	20	3
1935	2	5	4
1936	2	1P	4
1937	1	21R	4
1938	2	2P	5
1939	1	14	3
1946			4
1947	1	2	4
1948	1	2	W
1949	1	2	sf
1950	1	4	qf
1951	1	2	qf
1952	1	1C	3
1953	1	8	5
1954	1	4	3
1955	1	5	4
1956	1	1C	3
1957	1	1C	F
1958	1	9	F
1959	1	2	3
1960	1	7	5
1961	1	7	4
1962	1	15	sf
1963	1	19	W
1964	1	2	sf
1965	1	1C	sf
1966	1	4	sf
1967	1	1C	4
1968	1	2	3
1969	1	11	qf
1970	1	8	sf
1971	1	8	3
1972	1	8	4
1973	1	18	3
1974	1	21R	4
1975	2	1P	3
1976	1	3	F
1977	1	6	W
1978	1	10	4
1979	1	9	F
1980	1	2	3
1981	1	8	4
1982	1	3	3
1983	1	3	W
1984	1	4	3
1985	1	4	W
1986	1	4	5
1987	1	11	4
1988	1	2	5
1989	1	11	qf
1990	1	13	W
1991	1	6	5
1992	1	2	4
1993	Pr	1C	5
1994	Pr	1C	W
1995	Pr	2	F
1996	Pr	1C	W
1997	Pr.	1C	4
1998	Pr.	2	5

1878-1925

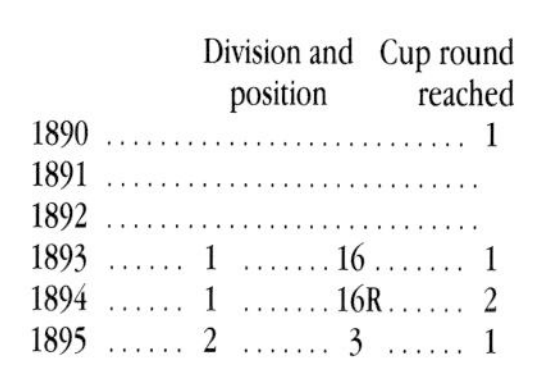

1926-1928

1935-1955

1963-1971

1988-1989

1993-1994

1998

Another United innovation was their continental 'V' collar in the 1950s.

MANSFIELD TOWN

Football in Mansfield has a long and colourful history, but it was a long time before the club acquired Football League status, and apart from some early highlights, success has come in limited quantities.

As long ago as 1870 a team called Mansfield were competing in local leagues, clad in scarlet and black and having their base at Parr's Cricket field. By 1891 Mansfield Wesleyans had become the foundation of the modern club, and wore blue shirts and white shorts, but it was not until 1910 that Mansfield Town were re-founded in their present form.

Years in the Notts and District League followed by a spell in the Central Alliance saw the club's performance improve at a gradual pace. Two of the now traditional colour schemes were first worn at this stage; amber and blue halves were eventually superseded by white shirts and black shorts. The two versions were often changed, but by the time League status was eventually achieved in 1931, white was more commonly used.

Successes before the First World War were very limited and the club often struggled. After the War the same continued until during a wonderful 1950/51 season, when only a very strong Rotherham side denied the Stags promotion to division two. That season Mansfield wore blue shirts with amber sleeves, but it was in white shirts again that mediocrity returned for a further decade. It took many years of struggle before the Town scrambled promotion from the fourth division, on goal average over Gillingham. However, two years later in 1965, this amber-shirted team missed a second division place only by another goal average decision. In fact, one more win would have seen them divisional champions.

In 1970, during another promotion push, the two colour schemes were mixed in a smart white shirt trimmed with blue and amber. Sadly this strip eventually saw the club drop into the lower regions of the fourth division, and since then most kits have been predominantly amber trimmed with blue. Thus clad, Mansfield have enjoyed some good times. In 1977 after two promotions in three years, this little club, after constantly being dominated by the Nottingham clubs, finally made it to the second division. The glory lasted only one season and fourth division football has been played at the Field Mill Ground often since. However, life has never been dull and Mansfield are always involved in a contest to either go up or stay up.

In 1987 the Stags experienced an occasion denied many top professionals, i.e. a Wembley success, this time in the Freight Rover Trophy. Days like these, plus a search for new stars to replace heroes such as Mike Stringfellow, Ken Wagstaff and Ted Haston, kept the Mansfield faithful forever in hope.

The Stags proudly wore this amber and blue kit in the second division in 1978.

Mansfield (founded 1891) records and strips

Year	Division	Position	Cup round reached
1956	3N	18	2
1957	3N	16	1
1958	3N	6	3
1959	3	20	1
1960	3	22R	3
1961	4	20	2
1962	4	14	2
1963	4	4P	3
1964	3	7	1

1891-1939

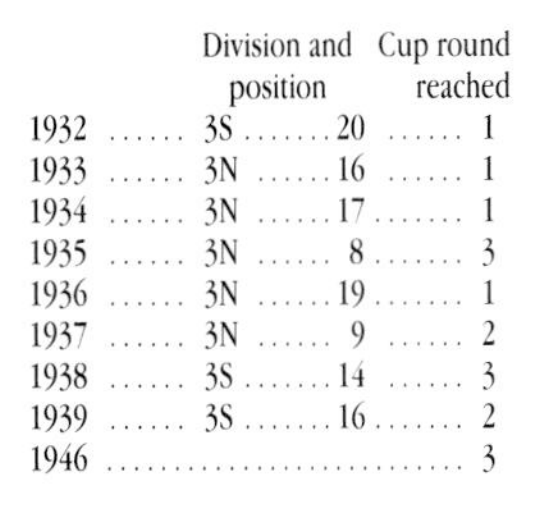

Year	Division and position		Cup round reached
1932	3S	20	1
1933	3N	16	1
1934	3N	17	1
1935	3N	8	3
1936	3N	19	1
1937	3N	9	2
1938	3S	14	3
1939	3S	16	2
1946			3

1947-1954

Year	Division	Position	Cup round reached
1947	3S	22	1
1948	3N	8	3
1949	3N	10	3
1950	3N	8	2
1951	3N	2	5
1952	3N	6	1
1953	3N	18	3
1954	3N	7	1
1955	3N	13	1

1964-1969

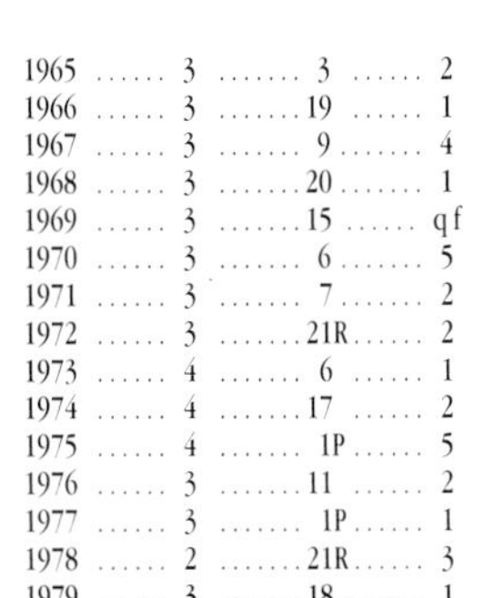

Year	Division	Position	Cup round reached
1965	3	3	2
1966	3	19	1
1967	3	9	4
1968	3	20	1
1969	3	15	qf
1970	3	6	5
1971	3	7	2
1972	3	21R	2
1973	4	6	1
1974	4	17	2
1975	4	1P	5
1976	3	11	2
1977	3	1P	1
1978	2	21R	3
1979	3	18	1

1970-1974

Year	Division	Position	Cup round reached
1980	3	23R	3
1981	4	7	3
1982	4	20	1
1983	4	10	2
1984	4	19	2
1985	4	14	2
1986	4	3P	1
1987	3	10	1
1988	3	19	4
1989	3	15	1
1990	3	15	1
1991	3	24R	3
1992	4	3P	1

1975-1978

The early 1970s saw this stylish stocking, which accompanied the white shirt of that era.

1986-1987

Year	Division	Position	Cup round reached
1993	N2	22R	1
1994	N3	12	1
1995	N3	6	3
1996	N3	19	2
1997	N3	11	2
1998	N3	12	1

1998

MIDDLESBROUGH

Despite being the dominant club on Teesside, with large potential support and a good ground, Middlesbrough have consistently failed to achieve any major success in the League or Cup.

Formed in 1876 and wearing red and black stripes, the club had a top-class amateur reputation when the professional League format swept into the north-east. By 1889, Middlesbrough had also been converted but within four years local pressure obliged a return to amateur status. In many ways it was a good move. In the 1890s, there were two Amateur Cup wins and many local league championships. The white-shirted Ironsides had become a major force. With the demise of local rivals Middlesbrough Ironopolis the club returned to professionalism, and by 1900 had been elected into the Football League second division. By this stage the colours had been changed to red shirts with a white yoke, a style which continued to reappear at many stages of the club's history.

Within three years, first division status had been achieved and was retained for over two decades. Strangely it was the subsequent relegation in the late 1920s which produced the first memorable events since the first £1,000 transfer of Alf Common in 1905. In the promotion success of 1927, Boro's deadly attack scored 122 goals, with George Camsell netting an incredible 59, still a second division record.

For the 25 years after 1930, Middlesbrough battled away in the top flight, occasionally even pushing for the championship itself, before eventually dropping back into the second division. Yet despite the lack of team glory, certain individuals were to become part of the game's folklore. The multi-talented Wilf Mannion entertained thousands of adoring fans when playing before huge gates.after the Second World War, and in the late 1950s when crowd figures and defences were becoming meaner, the goal machine called Brian Clough brought back memories of the Camsell days.

During the last thirty years, until recently, only the managerial efforts of Jack Charlton and Lenny Lawrence enabled Middlesbrough to fight back to the first division. Once there, the club still found it difficult to look the part, often displaying a lack of confidence.

The playing strip, although often changing, usually retained some reference to the early white shoulder/yoke format, but the repeat of the old-type jersey usually failed to inspire a return to pre-War playing standards. However, in the mid-1990s Brian Robson's team, playing in Manchester United style shirts, fought its way back to to top flight. Perhaps an Old Trafford style of confidence would come with it.

Despite all the relegation and Cup final disappointments of 1997, Robson remained and the top flight was regained at the first attempt.

After the War, Wilf Mannion's red-shirted men challenged for League honours.

Boro (founded 1876) records and strips

	Division and position		Cup round reached
1914	1	4	1
1915	1	12	2
1920	1	13	2
1921	1	8	1
1922	1	8	1
1923	1	18	2
1924	1	22R	1

	Division and position		Cup round reached
1958	2	7	4
1959	2	13	3
1960	2	5	3
1961	2	5	3
1962	2	12	5
1963	2	4	4
1964	2	10	3
1965	2	17	5
1966	2	21R	3
1967	3	2P	3
1968	2	6	4

The white centre hoop, like the yoke, is a repeating theme in Middlesbrough's history.

1876-1936

1973-1978

1995-1996

	Division and position		Cup round reached
1888			qf
1889			q
1890			q
1891			q
1892			2
1893			2
1894			1
1895			2
1896			2q
1897			1q
1898			5q
1899			2q
1900	2	14	p

	Division and position		Cup round reached
1925	2	13	1
1926	2	10	4

1957-1963

	Division and position		Cup round reached
1969	2	4	3
1970	2	4	qf
1971	2	7	4
1972	2	9	5
1973	2	4	3
1974	2	1P	4
1975	1	7	qf
1976	1	13	3
1977	1	12	qf
1978	1	14	qf

1947-1956

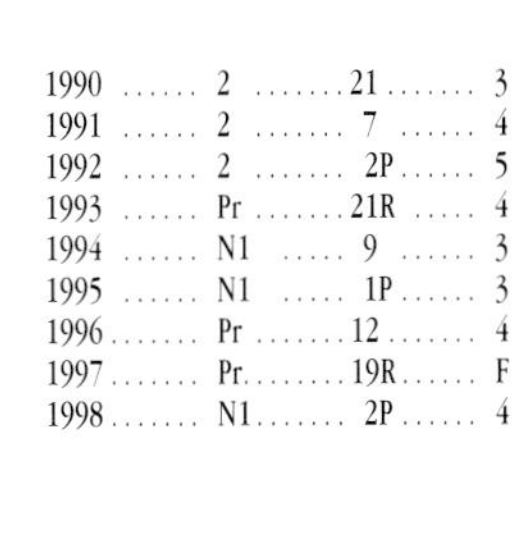

	Division and position		Cup round reached
1990	2	21	3
1991	2	7	4
1992	2	2P	5
1993	Pr	21R	4
1994	N1	9	3
1995	N1	1P	3
1996	Pr	12	4
1997	Pr.	19R	F
1998	N1	2P	4

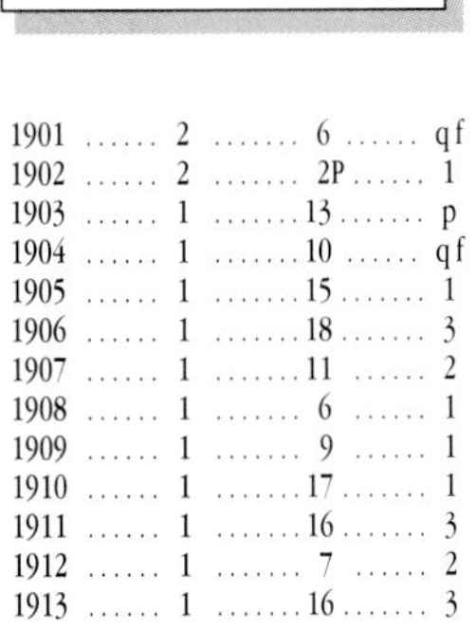

	Division and position		Cup round reached
1901	2	6	qf
1902	2	2P	1
1903	1	13	p
1904	1	10	qf
1905	1	15	1
1906	1	18	3
1907	1	11	2
1908	1	6	1
1909	1	9	1
1910	1	17	1
1911	1	16	3
1912	1	7	2
1913	1	16	3

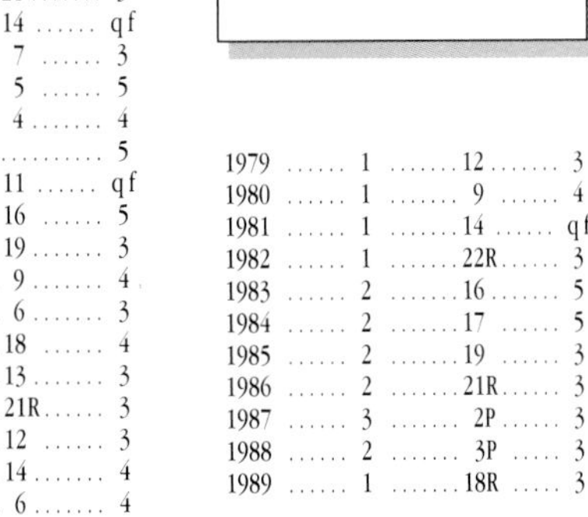

	Division and position		Cup round reached
1927	2	1P	5
1928	1	22R	5
1929	2	1P	4
1930	1	16	5
1931	1	7	3
1932	1	18	3
1933	1	17	5
1934	1	16	3
1935	1	20	3
1936	1	14	qf
1937	1	7	3
1938	1	5	5
1939	1	4	4
1946			5
1947	1	11	qf
1948	1	16	5
1949	1	19	3
1950	1	9	4
1951	1	6	3
1952	1	18	4
1953	1	13	3
1954	1	21R	3
1955	2	12	3
1956	2	14	4
1957	2	6	4

	Division and position		Cup round reached
1979	1	12	3
1980	1	9	4
1981	1	14	qf
1982	1	22R	3
1983	2	16	5
1984	2	17	5
1985	2	19	3
1986	2	21R	3
1987	3	2P	3
1988	2	3P	3
1989	1	18R	3

1998

MILLWALL

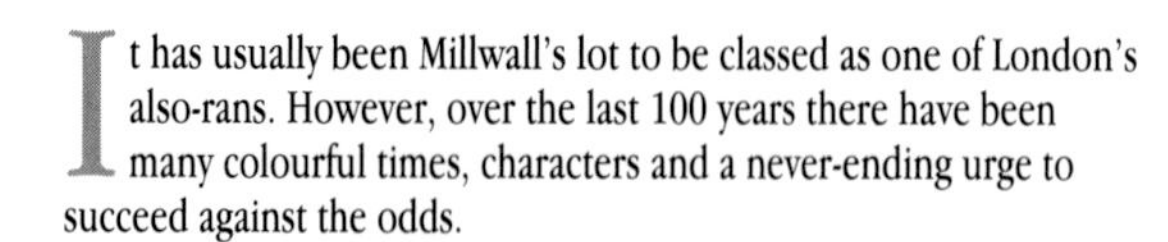

It has usually been Millwall's lot to be classed as one of London's also-rans. However, over the last 100 years there have been many colourful times, characters and a never-ending urge to succeed against the odds.

This was the kit worn at the Den when the team finally reached the first division in 1988.

Founded in 1885 by employees of Messrs Morton, a jam manufacturer, Millwall Rovers' first strip was dark blue shirts and white shorts – obviously reflecting the interests of the many exiled Scots involved in those early days. Often in the first decade, there were colour changes. Financial limitations usually meant wearing whatever was available. Red and white stripes were followed by a black and white version, then an all-blue kit, before in 1895 the navy blue shirts and white shorts were back, this time to last until 1936.

On the pitch, Millwall Athletic, as they had become in 1893, had turned professional, and were influential members of the Southern League. There were two runs to the semi-finals of the FA Cup and many other local successes before they gained admittance to the Football League in 1920.

The club adjusted well to the third division and after many high positions were eventually promoted to the second in 1928. There they stayed until the late 1930s and upon relegation, manager Charles Hewitt decided to change the shirt colours to royal blue, probably in an attempt to change the club's luck. To a certain extent, it did. A third semi-final appearance, the first by a third division club, was followed by promotion in 1938.

After the Second World War, the Lions returned to the third division and sadly, by 1960, the fourth. Once again strip changes were used to help improve fortunes on the pitch. Various versions were introduced, including white shirts with blue and white striped shorts! Again the changes seemed to have a positive effect. Whilst wearing blue and white striped shirts, followed by a return to dark blue and finally all-white, Millwall fought their way back to a respectable place in the top half of the second division. Great characters at the Den at this time included Harry 'Boy' Cripps, Keith Weller and Derek Possee.

Strangely enough, when Gordon Jago reintroduced royal blue shirts, in the mistaken belief that these were the club's traditional colours, it had a negative effect and a six-year period in division three followed.

Eventually two managers, George Graham before he went to Arsenal, and then John Doherty, took the Lions to new and great heights by reaching division one for the first time. With the successful strike force of Tony Cascarino and Teddy Sheringham, the club even topped the League for a short while. Sadly, two years later the pressure was too much and Millwall were relegated. Although, for a while, Mick McCarthy produced more exciting times in the new Lion's Den, when he went, the club's second flight status surprisingly went with him.

The famous striped shorts of the early 1960s which prompted much wolf-whistling.

Millwall (founded 1885) records and strips

1885-1936

1965-1967

1988-1989

1960-1965

1936-1956

1968-1975

1998

Year	Division and	position	Cup round reached
1895			1
1896			1
1897			1
1898			q
1899			q
1900			sf
1901			1
1902			p
1903			sf
1904			1
1905			1
1906			2
1907			2
1908			1
1909			3
1910			1
1911			1
1912			1
1913			1
1914			3
1915			2
1920			1
1921	3	7	1
1922	3S	12	qf
1923	3S	6	2
1924	3S	3	1
1925	3S	5	1
1926	3S	3	5
1927	3S	3	qf
1928	3S	1P	3
1929	2	14	4
1930	2	14	5
1931	2	14	3
1932	2	9	3
1933	2	7	4
1934	2	21R	4
1935	3S	12	4
1936	3S	12	3
1937	3S	8	sf
1938	3S	1P	3
1939	2	13	4
1946			4
1947	2	18	3
1948	2	22R	3
1949	3S	8	2
1950	3S	22	1
1951	3S	5	4
1952	3S	4	2
1953	3S	2	3
1954	3S	12	2
1955	3S	5	3
1956	3S	22	1
1957	3S	17	5
1958	3S	23	2
1959	4	9	2
1960	4	5	1
1961	4	6	1
1962	4	1P	1
1963	3	16	2
1964	3	21R	1
1965	4	2P	4
1966	3	2P	2
1967	2	8	3
1968	2	7	3
1969	2	10	4
1970	2	10	3
1971	2	8	3
1972	2	3	4
1973	2	11	5
1974	2	12	3
1975	2	20R	3
1976	3	3P	2
1977	2	10	3
1978	2	16	qf
1979	2	21R	3
1980	3	14	4
1981	3	16	2
1982	3	9	3
1983	3	17	1
1984	3	9	2
1985	3	2P	6
1986	2	9	5
1987	2	16	3
1988	2	1P	4
1989	1	10	4
1990	1	20R	4
1991	2	5	4
1992	2	14	4
1993	N1	7	3
1994	N1	3	3
1995	N1	12	5
1996	N1	22R	3
1997	N2	14	1
1998	N2	18	1

NEWCASTLE UNITED

The trophy room at St James' Park is full of evidence of a wonderful past, but such is the potential in terms of talent and support in the north-east that one is left with the feeling that it could have been so much more.

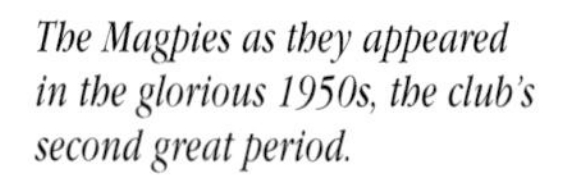

The Magpies as they appeared in the glorious 1950s, the club's second great period.

Back in 1885, after a great local rivalry between Newcastle East End and Newcastle West End, the clubs amalgamated to form Newcastle United. As the East End club had been dominant, their colours of red and white were chosen. It seems hard to believe now, particularly down the road in Sunderland.

It wasn't until about 1904 that the famous black and white version was introduced. Those were the county colours, but strangely the chief reason for the change was purely because of regularly clashing with the colours of other clubs.

The new colours certainly coincided with a glorious time in the club's history. After a decade in the first and second divisions with only average success, the next seven years produced three League championships and five FA Cup finals, including a win in 1910 over Barnsley.

Although the break for the First World War slowed down the success, there was still another championship and two more Cup wins in ten years, and the club remained a major force until the early 1930s. Sadly, in 1934 the Magpies were relegated to division two, where they remained until 1948.

Then in a second great period which coincided with the emergence of stars such as 'Wor' Jackie Milburn, Bobby Mitchell, the Robledos and Joe Harvey, promotion was followed by three FA Cup wins in five seasons. Indeed until a sad defeat versus Liverpool in 1974, Wembley offered no fears for the Geordies.

At the beginning of the 1960s playing standards dropped, just as the club experimented with the strip. White trimmings at the base of the shorts and vertical stripes on the stocking tops were major fashion changes, the like of which the League has rarely witnessed.

Later in the decade, Joe Harvey returned as manager and with Bobby Moncur, Pop Robson, Wyn Davies and company playing in a more traditional garb, Newcastle shocked the football world by winning the UEFA Cup. In a thrilling two-legged final, United overcame the crack Hungarian team, Ujpesti Dozsa.

Since then there have been many ups and downs, with most of the ups associated with the presence of Kevin Keegan. After promototion in 1993 there were genuine hopes that if the ex-England international could keep his team together, then Geordie fans would no longer talk of the lost potential of the likes of Waddle, Beardsley and Gascoigne. Although the signs were that the Keegan/Sir John Hall combination could emulate all those former glories, the major trophies frustratingly eluded them in those first few years. Even after Kenny Dalglish had replaced a fraught Keegan, the Geordies had still failed to climb the final rung of the ladder.

Newcastle (founded 1881) records and strips

1893-1903

	Division and position		Cup round reached
1893			1
1894	2	4	2
1895	2	10	2
1896	2	5	2
1897	2	5	1
1898	2	2P	2
1899	1	13	2
1900	1	5	2
1901	1	6	1
1902	1	3	qf
1903	1	14	1

1904-1930

1904	1	4	1
1905	1	1C	F
1906	1	4	F
1907	1	1C	1
1908	1	4	F
1909	1	1C	sf
1910	1	4	W
1911	1	8	F

The white trim on the shorts in 1960 was a radical change for the traditionally minded club.

1912	1	3	1
1913	1	14	qf
1914	1	11	1
1915	1	15	qf
1920	1	8	2
1921	1	5	3
1922	1	7	2
1923	1	4	1
1924	1	9	W
1925	1	6	2
1926	1	10	5
1927	1	1C	5
1928	1	9	3
1929	1	10	3
1930	1	19	qf
1931	1	17	4

1931-1955

1932	1	11	W
1933	1	5	3
1934	1	21R	3
1935	2	6	4
1936	2	8	5
1937	2	4	3
1938	2	19	3

1957-1961

1971-1974

1939	2	9	5
1946			3
1947	2	5	sf
1948	2	2P	3
1949	1	4	3
1950	1	5	4
1951	1	4	W
1952	1	8	W
1953	1	16	4
1954	1	15	5
1955	1	8	W
1956	1	11	qf

1983-1986

1957	1	17	4
1958	1	19	4
1959	1	11	3
1960	1	8	3
1961	1	21R	qf
1962	2	11	3
1963	2	7	4
1964	2	8	3
1965	2	1P	3
1966	1	15	4
1967	1	20	4
1968	1	10	3
1969	1	9	4

1970	1	7	3
1971	1	12	3
1972	1	11	3
1973	1	9	4
1974	1	15	F
1975	1	15	4
1976	1	15	qf
1977	1	5	4
1978	1	21R	4
1979	2	8	4
1980	2	9	3
1981	2	11	5
1982	2	9	4
1983	2	5	3
1984	2	3P	3
1985	1	14	3
1986	1	11	3
1987	1	17	5
1988	1	8	5
1989	1	20R	3
1990	2	3	5
1991	2	11	4
1992	2	20	3

1995-1996

1993	N1	1P	5
1994	Pr	3	4
1995	Pr	6	qf
1996	Pr	2	3
1997	Pr.	2	4
1998	Pr.	13	F

1998

NORTHAMPTON TOWN

Apart from one unbelievable period in the mid-1960s, the history of Northampton Town has had few major highlights, but for the imaginative use of colour and pattern, the club has had few rivals.

When the Cobblers first put out a team in 1897, the players sported an attractive blue and chocolate halved jersey. However, although it was a much admired kit, once the club had entered local league football two years later it was decided to adopt the county colours of claret and white. It was hoped that the Town would attract support from all over the county, and over the years this has been the case. In fact, one former Cobblers fan became chairman of Chelmsford City and insisted that they, too, adopt this colour combination.

For the first two decades of the century, Northampton played in the Southern League wearing in turn claret and white stripes, white shirts and claret shorts, then the reverse.

After the First World War, the Cobblers were elected into division three (south) along with several other Southern League sides. Although no major successes were gained, they certainly held their own, regularly turning out in a smart strip of claret with white shorts. This kit remained until after the Second World War when three white chest-bands were added, but the playing consistency of the early period had been replaced by a see-saw sequence of League finishes, culminating in a drop into the fourth division in 1958.

Three years later saw a whole series of kit changes which coincided with a wide range of League successes and failures. A plain claret shirt saw the Cobblers out of division four, a white shirt with a claret hoop was worn when promotion to division two followed in 1963, and two years later a further change, this time to claret shirts with white sleeves became the most famous strip yet worn by the club.

The stay in division one lasted just one season, but it had been a brave effort by the Cobblers and with a bit more luck survival might have been achieved. Sadly, once the slide began, the momentum was uncontrollable and within four years, they were back in the basement.

There were three following promotion seasons since, but Northampton Town have never really recovered. The only notable events at the County Ground have been the odd decent Cup runs and yet another range of claret and white sartorial specials. Most of the recent versions have been white with fine claret stripes including a unique zig-zag version in 1989.

Come the 1990s, club and supporters alike were yearning for a successful team to pull in large crowds to their brand-new stadium, all sporting some extravagant claret and white ensemble.

In 1998 the Cobblers had just completed their most successful season for ten years. Perhaps they were on their way back?

To most fans, 1966 will go down as the year England won the World Cup, but for the people of Northampton it was a season in the first division.

Northampton (founded 1897) records and strips

1897-1910

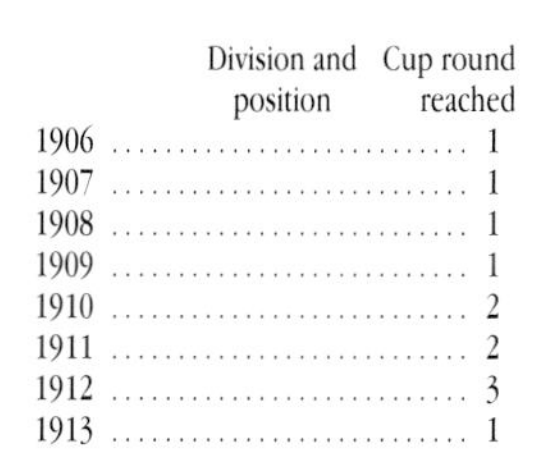

	Division and position		Cup round reached
1906			1
1907			1
1908			1
1909			1
1910			2
1911			2
1912			3
1913			1

1910-1939

1914			p
1915			2
1920			p
1921	3	14	1
1922	3S	17	2
1923	3S	8	p
1924	3S	8	1
1925	3S	9	1
1926	3S	12	3
1927	3S	18	2
1928	3S	2	3
1929	3S	3	3
1930	3S	4	3

1931	3S	6	1
1932	3S	14	4
1933	3S	8	2
1934	3S	13	5
1935	3S	7	3
1936	3S	15	1
1937	3S	7	1
1938	3S	9	1

1939	3S	17	1
1946			3
1947	3S	13	3
1948	3S	14	2
1949	3S	20	2
1950	3S	2	5

1946-1952

1951	3S	21	4
1952	3S	8	1
1953	3S	3	2
1954	3S	5	2
1955	3S	13	1
1956	3S	11	3
1957	3S	14	1
1958	3S	13	4
1959	4	8	2
1960	4	6	1
1961	4	3P	3
1962	3	8	3
1963	3	1P	1
1964	2	11	3
1965	2	2P	3
1966	1	21R	3
1967	2	21R	3
1968	3	17	1

1963-1964

1969	3	21R	3
1970	4	14	5
1971	4	7	1
1972	4	21	2

1964-1967

1973	4	23	1
1974	4	5	2
1975	4	16	2
1976	4	2P	1
1977	3	22R	1
1978	4	10	2
1979	4	19	1
1980	4	13	1

1983-1988

1981	4	10	1
1982	4	22	2
1983	4	15	3
1984	4	18	2
1985	4	23	2
1986	4	8	1
1987	4	1P	3
1988	3	6	3
1989	3	20	1
1990	3	22R	4
1991	4	10	2

1998

1992	4	16	1
1993	N3	20	3
1994	N3	24	1
1995	N3	17	1
1996	N3	11	2
1997	N3	4P(pl)	1
1998	N2	4	3

The three-striped chest-band of the post-War years, unique in its day.

NORWICH CITY

Imagine the picture; the players attacking, clad in blue and white halved shirts, the crowd shouting 'Play up, the Citizens'. Probably none of us would imagine this scene depicted the newly formed Norwich City. However, by 1907, five years after its foundation, the club had been christened with the now-familiar nickname of the Canaries. The tag was due to the city being famous as the centre for the breeding and exporting of the pet birds. Eventually, at the end of the season, Norwich decided to live up to their label and changed their strip to canary yellow and green shirts. A rare example of this sequence of events.

Norwich were regularly competing in the Southern League, where they stayed until joining the third division (south) in 1920. There were no early successes and, probably looking for a change of fortune, white shirts were introduced by the club in 1923. The canary badge remained but as the new version effected no great improvement, the yellow and green returned, this time in dramatic halved shirts.

Now there was a marked improvement and in 1934 the club were promoted, staying in the second division until just before the Second Word War.

In the post-War years, an all-yellow shirt trimmed with green saw many see-saw years. Early successes in the League were followed by a dip in quality before, in 1959, the Canaries became only the fourth club from division three to reach the semi-finals of the FA Cup. Manchester United, Spurs and Sheffield United had been overcome before Luton just squeezed past them in a replay. In the next season, more was to come with long-serving captain Ron Ashman leading them to the second division.

Norwich City's rise in stature was growing steadily; their Cup successes received more and more publicity, and in the League, by 1973, the Canaries finally flew to the top of the tree. They have been relegated from the first division four times, but until recently, each time have been immediately promoted again and their small-time beginnings belie a new-found confidence on the highest stage.

Modern versions of the yellow and green outfits have appeared three times at Wembley in League Cup finals, the most recent one in 1985 against Sunderland, adding to the early win in the competition versus Rochdale. Once again these Cup successes were the precursor of improved results in the League.

During the 1990s, this well-run East Anglian club was capable of challenging for a League championship but Canaries fans were never sure the club had sufficient resources to maintain that challenge. The 1995 relegation would test those doubts to the full.

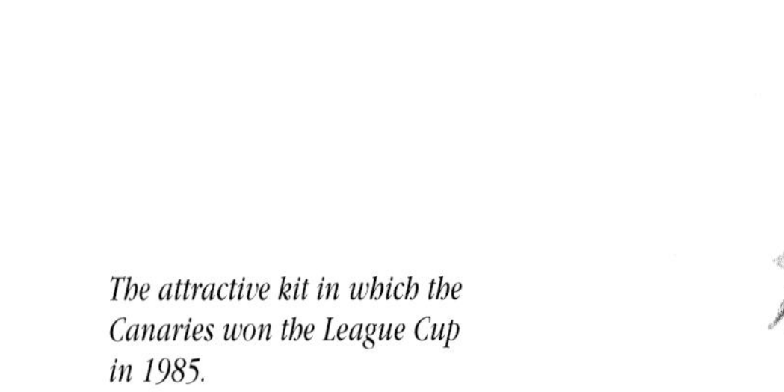

The attractive kit in which the Canaries won the League Cup in 1985.

Norwich (founded 1902) records and strips

	Division and	Cup round
	position	reached
1906		2
1907		2
1908		2
1909		3
1910		1
1911		2
1912		1
1913		2
1914		1
1915		3
1920		qf
1921	3 16	1
1922	3S 15	1
1923	3S 18	1
1924	3S 11	1
1925	3S 12	2
1926	3S 16	1
1927	3S 16	3
1928	3S 17	2
1929	3S 17	3
1930	3S 8	1
1931	3S 21	2
1932	3S 10	2
1933	3S 3	1
1934	3S 1P	1
1935	2 14	5
1936	2 11	3
1937	2 17	4
1938	2 14	3
1939	2 .... 21R	3
1946		3
1947	3S 21	2
1948	3S 21	2
1949	3S 9	2
1950	3S 11	3
1951	3S 2	5
1952	3S 3	3
1953	3S 4	2
1954	3S 7	5
1955	3S 11	2
1956	3S 7	3
1957	3S 24	1
1958	3S 8	3
1959	3 4	sf
1960	3 .... 2P	1
1961	2 4	5
1962	2 17	5
1963	2 11	qf
1964	2 17	3
1965	2 6	3
1966	2 13	5
1967	2 11	5
1968	2 9	4
1969	2 13	3
1970	2 11	3
1971	2 10	3
1972	2 .... 1P	3
1973	1 20	3
1974	1 .... 22R	3
1975	2 .... 3P	3
1976	1 10	5
1977	1 16	3
1978	1 13	3
1979	1 16	3
1980	1 12	3
1981	1 .... 20R	4
1982	2 .... 3P	5
1983	1 14	6
1984	1 14	5
1985	1 .... 20R	4
1986	2 .... 1P	3
1987	1 5	4
1988	1 14	3
1989	1 4	sf
1990	1 10	4
1991	1 15	qf
1992	1 18	sf
1993	Pr 3	4
1994	Pr 12	4
1995	Pr 20R	5
1996	N1 16	3
1997	N1 13	4
1998	N1 15	3

1902-1927

1971-1974

1989-1992

1984-1986

1947-1957

1998

1927-1947

The striking diagonal stripes of the 1990 shirts.

NOTTINGHAM FOREST

Sport had been played in and around the forest in Nottingham for centuries, and during the Victorian era a group of young men regularly took part in a game called shinney. In 1865 these same young men decided to form themselves into a football club taking the name of Forest. Nottingham Forest - never Notts - became a very organised and soon ordered the first uniform, a dozen red caps. These colours have remained unchanged until today.

Although in the early days there was not a great deal of competition other than from city rivals County, the club prospered and early adventures in the FA Cup ended only at the semi-final stage in both 1879 and the following year. Election into the Football League came in 1892 and the team fared well without winning any trophies. In the Cup, however, Forest were still a major force and in the next few years there were many more semi-final visits, plus a final victory when goals from Capes and McPherson overcame Derby County in 1898.

The all-red shirts were now nationally famous, but slowly the power of the club faded as the game's popularity grew, and from 1911 to the beginning of the Second World War, Forest were no more than a humble member of division two.

After the War, for a while, things became even worse. There were two seasons in the third division (north), but Forest have always stood by their managers and Billy Walker stayed to take the club not only back to the second, but into the top flight again. Two years later Forest overcame Luton 2-1 in the FA Cup final, despite playing much of the match with only ten men. Later, Johnny Carey built a fine team, including gifted players such as Ian Storey-Moore and Terry Hennessey, which went close to achieving the League and Cup double in 1967.

Sadly this side was allowed to break up and relegation again followed. It took the larger-than-life figure of Brian Clough to turn things around at the City Ground. With Peter Taylor, Clough confounded the English football world by immediately following promotion with Forest's first title in 1978. However, during the next two seasons, the whole of Europe had to stand and watch as the red-shirted men from Nottingham twice won the European Cup.

Clough's story is, of course, legend, and although life at Forest was to become less spectacular, there have been several League Cup wins, plus yet another FA Cup final, unhappily lost to Spurs. Sales of top stars put Forest's accepted place in the top division in jeopardy, and it was hoped the 1993 relegation and the end of the Clough era would prove to be only a temporary hiccup in the club's history.

Indeed, the revival under new manager Frank Clark at first seemed to offer as much hope, and even European glory, as ever before, but subsequent events left much in doubt until a new board appointed promotion specialist Dave Bassett as the manager to take them back to the top flight in 1998.

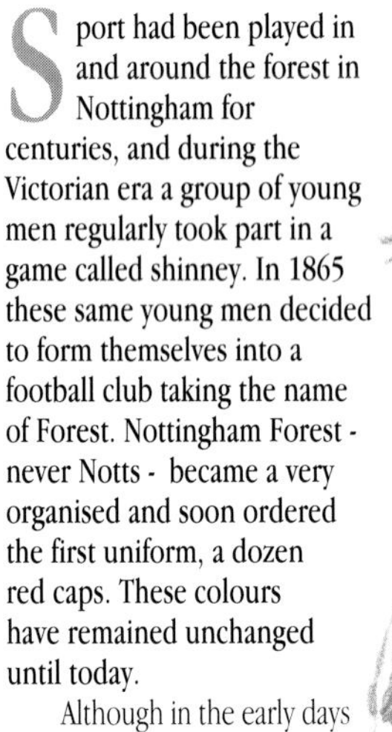

This simple strip was worn by a club promoted from the second division to become League champions and double European champions in successive years.

Forest (founded 1865) records and strips

1865-1906

1907-1928

1936-1955

1958-1962

1966-1972

1978-1982

1989-1992

1998

Year	Division	Position	Cup round reached
1879			sf
1880			sf
1881			2
1882			1
1883			3
1884			2
1885			sf
1886			3
1887			3
1888			5
1889			2
1890			1
1891			qf
1892			sf
1893	1	10	2
1894	1	7	qf
1895	1	7	qf
1896	1	13	1
1897	1	11	qf
1898	1	8	W
1899	1	11	qf
1900	1	8	sf
1901	1	4	2
1902	1	5	sf
1903	1	10	2
1904	1	9	2
1905	1	16	2
1906	1	19R	3
1907	2	1P	1
1908	1	9	1
1909	1	14	qf
1910	1	14	3
1911	1	20R	1
1912	2	15	1
1913	2	17	2
1914	2	20	1
1915	2	18	1
1920	2	18	1
1921	2	18	1
1922	2	1P	3
1923	1	20	1
1924	1	20	1
1925	1	22R	2
1926	2	17	qf
1927	2	5	4
1931	2	17	3
1932	2	11	3
1933	2	5	3
1934	2	17	4
1935	2	9	5
1936	2	19	4
1937	2	19	3
1938	2	20	4
1939	2	20	3
1946			3
1947	2	11	5
1948	2	19	3
1949	2	21R	3
1950	3S	4	2
1951	3S	1P	2
1952	2	4	3
1953	2	7	4
1954	2	4	3
1955	2	15	5
1956	2	7	3
1957	2	2P	qf
1958	1	10	4
1959	1	13	W
1960	1	20	4
1961	1	14	3
1962	1	19	4
1963	1	9	qf
1964	1	13	3
1965	1	5	5
1966	1	18	4
1967	1	2	sf
1968	1	11	4
1969	1	18	3
1970	1	15	3
1971	1	16	5
1972	1	21R	3
1973	2	14	3
1974	2	7	qf
1975	2	16	4
1976	2	8	3
1977	2	3P	4
1978	1	1C	qf
1979	1	2	5
1980	1	5	4
1981	1	7	qf
1982	1	12	3
1983	1	3	3
1984	1	3	2
1985	1	9	4
1986	1	8	3
1987	1	8	3
1988	1	3	sf
1989	1	3	sf
1990	1	9	3
1991	1	8	F
1992	1	8	qf
1993	Pr	22R	5
1994	N1	2P	3
1995	Pr	3	4
1996	Pr	9	6
1997	Pr.	20R	5
1998	N1	1P	3

Although it has sad associations, the 1993 shirt was a rare diversion from the normally plain format.

NOTTS COUNTY

For over a century Notts County have proudly worn their black and white striped shirts, and for most clubs that would have covered their entire history. However, this is not just a club with a long history. County are the oldest surviving senior club in Britain and in those first three decades the team sported very different colours.

The first County sides wore amber and black striped shirts with black shorts, and this amber tradition has reappeared on several occasions since to adorn the dominant black and white theme. During this early period the club enjoyed a great reputation playing against sides such as the Wanderers, Queen's Park and the Sheffield clubs, and in E H Greenhalgh County had their first international player.

By the 1880s the club had changed strip to chocolate and blue halves with white shorts and were known as the team of brothers, with at least eight pairs appearing together at various times. There were great Cup runs, to the semi- and quarter-finals, before in 1888 County became founder members of the Football League.

Three years later a third-place spot in the League was accompanied by an FA Cup final visit which ended in defeat by the then mighty Blackburn Rovers. A further three years on, despite having been relegated, County surprised everyone outside of Nottingham by winning the Cup, the only second division to do so before 1910. By this stage the black and white stripes had been introduced and had become famous.

The club returned to division one and stayed there until the First World War, before drifting into a long period of relative mediocrity until after the Second World War. Then for a while, exciting times returned. There was a smart white shirt, trimmed with black and an amber top to the stockings as a reminder of the very early days. Stars such as Tommy Lawton, Jackie Sewell, Leon Leuty and Frank Broome played in front of huge gates such as the 49,000 crowd who saw the 1950 derby with the Forest.

Sadly after this there followed another period of decline and long spells were spent in the lower divisions. Then manager Jimmy Sirrel took the club by the scruff of the neck and, with Don Masson to control events on the field, gradually took the County through the divisions to the top flight.

When Sirrel and Masson left, there was another five-year spell in the second division. Neil Warnock reintroduced amber trim to the club colours and another promotion was achieved, but County had yet to prove they had the resources and self-belief to survive at the top and in 1992 they returned to the second flight. Three years later followed another drop and as Forest's star began to rise again County faced an even greater challenge.

The runaway championship of the third division in 1998 was a great response.

The Cup-winning strip of 1894 is not very different from that of 104 years later.

County (founded 1862) records and strips

Year	Division	Position	Cup round reached
1905	1	18	1
1906	1	16	1
1907	1	18	qf
1908	1	18	2
1909	1	15	1
1910	1	19	1
1911	1	11	1
1912	1	16	2

Year	Division	Position	Cup round reached
1952	2	15	4
1953	2	19	4
1954	2	14	3
1955	2	7	qf
1956	2	20	3
1957	2	20	3
1958	2	21R	4
1959	3	23R	1
1960	4	2P	2
1961	3	5	1
1962	3	13	2
1963	3	7	1
1964	3	24R	2
1965	4	13	2
1966	4	8	1
1967	4	20	1
1968	4	17	1
1969	4	19	1
1970	4	7	1
1971	4	1P	3

1862-1925

1973-1976

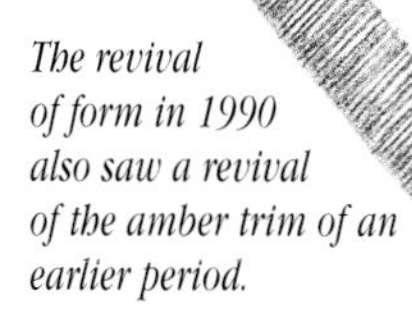

The revival of form in 1990 also saw a revival of the amber trim of an earlier period.

1990-1992

Year	Division and position		Cup round reached
1878			1
1879			1
1880			1
1881			3
1882			3
1883			sf
1884			sf
1885			qf
1886			5
1887			qf
1888			q
1889	1	11	2
1890	1	10	3
1891	1	3	F

Year	Division	Position	Cup round reached
1913	1	19R	1
1914	2	1P	1
1915	1	16	
1920	1	21R	3
1921	2	6	2
1922	2	13	sf
1923	2	1P	1
1924	1	10	2
1925	1	9	3
1926	1	22R	5
1927	2	16	3
1928	2	15	3
1929	2	5	3

Year	Division	Position	Cup round reached
1972	3	4	4
1973	3	2P	3
1974	2	10	3
1975	2	14	4
1976	2	5	3
1977	2	8	3
1978	2	15	5
1979	2	6	4

Year	Division	Position	Cup round reached
1990	3	3P	1
1991	2	4P	qf
1992	1	21R	5
1993	N1	17	3
1994	N1	7	4
1995	N1	24R	3
1996	N2	4	3
1997	N2	24R	3
1998	N3	1P	2

1926-1929

1948-1952

1978-1983

1998

Year	Division	Position	Cup round reached
1892	1	8	q
1893	1	14R	2
1894	2	3	W
1895	2	2	1
1896	2	10	1
1897	2	1P	2
1898	1	13	1
1899	1	5	2
1900	1	15	2
1901	1	3	2
1902	1	13	1
1903	1	15	3
1904	1	13	1

Year	Division	Position	Cup round reached
1930	2	22R	3
1931	3S	1P	4
1932	2	16	3
1933	2	15	3
1934	2	18	3
1935	2	22R	3
1936	3S	9	3
1937	3S	2	1
1938	3S	11	4
1939	3S	11	4
1946			2
1947	3S	12	3
1948	3S	6	4
1949	3S	11	4
1950	3S	1P	3
1951	2	17	3

Year	Division	Position	Cup round reached
1980	2	17	3
1981	2	2P	4
1982	1	15	3
1983	1	15	4
1984	1	21R	6
1985	2	20R	3
1986	3	8	4
1987	3	7	2
1988	3	4	2
1989	3	9	2

OLDHAM ATHLETIC

After five years of building a club of some stature under the name of Pine Villa, the players and officials decided to opt for the 'town' title of Oldham Athletic and seek national league status. The early Latics wore regular red and white stripes or hoops but had changed to blue and white by the time they played in the Manchester League and Lancashire Combination, before finally gaining admittance to the second division of the Football League in 1908.

The period up to the beginning of the First WorldWar was one of the club's brightest and most successful. Oldham coped confidently with second division football and in the third season were promoted to the first. More was to come; in the next five years, an FA Cup semi-final was followed by a third-placed league finish in 1914, whilst in the next season the Latics missed the championship by a mere two points!

The outbreak of the War impeded Oldham's momentum as it had many other clubs, and in the 1920s and 1930s results fell away badly. For the first time, the club tried a new style of white shirts with a broad blue stripe, but although fashion-wise it was quite revolutionary, the playing standards did not improve.

Relegation in 1935 saw a stay in the third division until after the Second World War. A season in hoops inspired no progress in 1947, and a return to the previous style provided only temporary improvement under the leadership of George Hardwick, but not enough to avoid joining division four when the third divisions were split in 1958. At this time new chairman Ken Bates decided the club needed a whole new start, and amongst other changes was the introduction of tangerine shirts.

There was no immediate change of fortune, but gradually things improved and in 1974 manager Jimmy Frizzell took the Latics back to the second division.

Probably as recognition of a return to former glories, the blue and white theme returned, although in a simpler, plain version, and it was thus when Joe Royle took over as manager in 1982. Slowly playing standards improved further and a greater professional attitude ran through the whole club. In 1987 promotion was just missed, and three years later two great runs in the League Cup (finalists) and the FA Cup (semi-finalists) were arguably responsible for yet another relative League 'failure'.

The next season Oldham made no mistake and finally won back their place in division one. Royle and his team looked comfortable competing against local rivals Manchester United and City, yet it was the proximity of the Lancashire giants and the restriction of the club's own revenue which seemed likely to cause the Latics' greatest problems in the search for permanent success. So it turned out as, despite being a few seconds away from an FA Cup final, the strain proved eventually too much. The club was relegated and even Joe Royle left for his old club Everton.

Today the struggle continues.

After a gap of 68 years, the blue of Oldham returned to the first division in 1991.

Oldham (founded 1895) records and strips

1895-1945

1965-1974

1987-1992

1976-1985

1946-1948

1948-1964

1998

Year	Division	Position	Cup round reached
1907			2
1908	2	3	2
1909	2	6	1
1910	2	2P	1
1911	1	7	2
1912	1	18	3
1913	1	9	sf
1914	1	3	1
1915	1	2	qf
1920	1	17	1
1921	1	19	1
1922	1	19	2
1923	1	22R	1
1924	2	7	2
1925	2	18	1
1926	2	7	3
1927	2	10	3
1928	2	7	4
1929	2	18	3
1930	2	3	4
1931	2	12	3
1932	2	18	3
1933	2	16	3
1934	2	9	4
1935	2	21R	3
1936	3N	7	2
1937	3N	4	3
1938	3N	4	1
1939	3N	5	1
1946			2
1947	3N	19	2
1948	3N	11	2
1949	3N	6	3
1950	3N	11	3
1951	3N	15	3
1952	3N	4	2
1953	3N	1P	3
1954	2	22R	3
1955	3N	10	2
1956	3N	20	1
1957	3N	19	2
1958	3N	15	2
1959	4	21	3
1960	4	23	2
1961	4	12	2
1962	4	11	4
1963	4	2P	1
1964	3	9	3
1965	3	20	3
1966	3	20	3
1967	3	10	3
1968	3	16	1
1969	3	24R	1
1970	4	19	2
1971	4	3P	1
1972	3	11	1
1973	3	4	1
1974	3	1P	4
1975	2	18	3
1976	2	17	3
1977	2	13	5
1978	2	8	3
1979	2	14	5
1980	2	11	3
1981	2	15	3
1982	2	11	3
1983	2	7	3
1984	2	19	3
1985	2	14	4
1986	2	8	3
1987	2	3	3
1988	2	10	3
1989	2	16	3
1990	2	8	sf
1991	2	1P	4
1992	1	17	3
1993	Pr	19	3
1994	Pr	21R	sf
1995	N1	14	4
1996	N1	18	4
1997	N1	23R	3
1998	N2	13	3

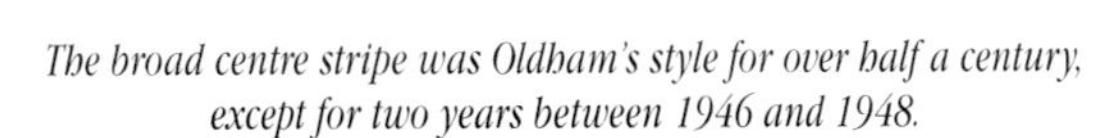

The broad centre stripe was Oldham's style for over half a century, except for two years between 1946 and 1948.

OXFORD UNITED

As in the case of the other famous university town, it was not the club which held the name of the city itself which eventually succeeded in reaching the top. Oxford City had been in existence for 11 years by the time Headington United were formed in 1893. The new club's colours were gold and Oxford blue, and in strikingly striped shirts they slowly worked their way through the local league system.

By the 1930s, Headington were performing well in the Southern League. The strip had changed to gold shirts with blue sleeves, but although well known in the upper levels of non-League football, there were no opportunities to break through into the Football League.

The club just missed out on the third division reshuffle in 1951 and at this time, the dark blue was replaced by black, so it was a Wolves look-alike which began the big push in the 1950s.

In 1959, the arrival of Arthur Turner as manager provided the catalyst for a total transformation of the club's fortunes. As ambitious as the club, he insisted the name should change to Oxford United.

After winning two Southern League championships, United were the obvious choice to replace the outgoing Accrington Stanley in the football league. The team was already a strong one, including Ron Atkinson, his brother Graham, and stalwarts such as John Shuker and Maurice Kyle. Two seasons of consolidation preceded promotion to division three, followed by an exact repeat at the higher level. Thus in 1968 United entered the dizzy heights of second division football.

The club coped confidently if not spectacularly, and it was surprising when Turner was sacked in 1972. The subsequent managerial changes probably proved unsettling and four years later Oxford were back in the third division, this time for a period of eight years. Yet it was the introduction of two more managers which heralded United's finest period. Jim Smith started the revival by reorganising club attitudes and playing methods, and eventually taking the side through to the first division in successive seasons. Strangely enough, having achieved this he decided to move on to Queen's Park Rangers, but his replacement Maurice Evans continued the good work, developing the likes of John Aldridge and Ray Houghton into major talents.

Ironically, when Oxford's greatest day arrived it was against Jim Smith's QPR in the 1986 League Cup final. As the team climbed the steps at Wembley after their 3-0 victory, those Southern League days before Arthur Turner arrived must have seemed a million miles away, particularly as by now the black trim had been replaced by the dark blue again.

Unfortunately it was the old enemy, that of limited resources, which proved the club's undoing. The team's stars, including the up-and-coming Dean Saunders, had to be sold. A proposed merger with Reading by owner Robert Maxwell was scrapped and eventually Oxford slipped back into the new second division. Life continued to be difficult and less glamorous, but at least United had managed to survive the dramatic collapse of other small clubs who have dared to take on the traditional giants and by 1996 had been promoted again.

Oxford shirts were spot on when the club struck gold in the 1986 League Cup final.

Oxford (founded 1893) records and strips

	Division and position		Cup round reached
1896-1939 Southern League			
1946	SL		e
1947	SL		q2

1896-1927

1948	SL		q1
1949	SL		p
1950	SL		p
1951	SL		p
1952	SL		q2
1953	SL		q4
1954	SL		4

1935-1955

1962-1965

1955	SL		1
1956	SL		q4
1957	SL		q4
1958	SL		q4
1959	SL		2
1960	SL		1
1961	SL		3
1962	SL		1

1973-1974

1963	4	18	3
1964	4	18	qf
1965	4	4P	1
1966	3	14	1
1967	3	15	1
1968	3	1P	1
1969	2	20	3
1970	2	15	3
1971	2	14	5

1974-1977

1972	2	15	3
1973	2	8	4
1974	2	18	3
1975	2	11	3
1976	2	20R	3
1977	3	17	1
1978	3	18	1
1979	3	11	1
1980	3	17	1

1986-1987

1981	3	14	2
1982	3	5	5
1983	3	5	3
1984	3	1P	5
1985	2	1P	4
1986	1	18	3
1987	1	18	3
1988	1	21R	4

1987-1989

1989	2	17	4
1990	2	17	4
1991	2	10	4
1992	2	21	4

1998

1993	N1	14	3
1994	N1	23R	5
1995	N2	7	1
1996	N2	2P	4
1997	N1	17	3
1998	N1	12	3

The multi-coloured striped shirts of the late 1980s, a rare sight in kit design.

PETERBOROUGH UNITED

Despite fine achievements at all levels for many years, Peterborough United are a relatively new club. It was not until 1934, when clubs such as fellow east midlanders Notts County were already 70 years old, that there was sufficient interest in the town to support a senior club. Peterborough and Fletton FC had been suspended by the FA, but locals were determined to carry on and the current club was formed.

The first shirts were green with a large white chevron, but by the outbreak of the Second World War, the green had been replaced by blue; and it was in blue that the club began to impress the football world.

With the resumption of peacetime football, the Posh had only five years of playing experience, but immediately the team's ability to perform well in the FA Cup attracted attention. In their all-blue shirts, Peterborough would brush aside fellow non-Leaguers, as they did Rushden 9-1 in 1945, and still managed to take on League sides. In the next 15 years, United beat eight clubs from the Football League and on at least four occasions were the last non-League team to be eliminated. They were also regular winners of the powerful Midland League, yet although the club applied for League membership every year, each time it was refused.

Finally, in 1960, poorly supported Gateshead were the victims of the Posh's momentum and United took on the challenge of the fourth division. What happened was a giant 'I told you so', with centre-forward Terry Bly getting 52 goals out of a massive total of 134.

The white-sleeved jersey worn by the players was exactly the same as the one worn by Ipswich, but whereas the Suffolk club went on to achieve great things, the Posh surprisingly did not. Probably the chief reason was that although the goals still flooded in, the defence was leaky. However, nothing had prepared the club for the traumas of 1968, when relegation was the punishment for irregular payments.

A six-year gloomy spell in the basement was difficult to bear, but in 1974 manager Noel Cantwell took them back to the third division. Again, times at London Road looked promising. In 1978 Peterborough were only two points off a rise to the second division, yet astonishingly the next season they were relegated again. The playing strip was all-blue at this time and so was the atmosphere.

There followed a period of frustration as the club, despite good support, never quite seemed to get going. Eventually it took the vision of a man who had seen better times to inject positive thinking. Ex-Liverpool star Mark Lawrenson introduced more professional attitudes and a crop of good young players, and unbelievably within two years the Posh were in the second flight (the new first division).

It seemed strange that the goal-scoring machine of 30 years ago never made it, whilst this relatively inexperienced one had. However, after their promising first season at the higher level, the team failed to last the pace and were eventually relegated. With the arrival of ebullient manager Barry Fry, Peterborough, received lots of attention. Despite immediate relegation, the fans hoped for accompanying success on the field in 1998.

The 1992 strip, worn by the Posh as they ascended to the second flight.

Peterborough (founded 1934) records and strips

1934-1937

	Division and position		Cup round reached
1934 to 1939 Midland League			
1946	ML		q3
1947	ML		2
1948	ML		q4
1949	ML		1
1950	ML		q3
1951	ML		q2

1938-1953

1959-1962

1952	ML		q4
1953	ML		2
1954	ML		3
1955	ML		q4
1956	ML		2
1957	ML		4

1970-1973

1958	ML		1
1959	ML		3
1960	ML		4
1961	4	1P	4
1962	3	5	4
1963	3	6	3
1964	3	10	1
1965	3	8	qf
1966	3	13	2
1967	3	15	4
1968	3	24R	3

1969	4	18	1
1970	4	9	4
1971	4	16	2
1972	4	8	3
1973	4	19	3
1974	4	1P	4
1975	3	7	5
1976	3	10	4

1975-1977

1977	3	16	2
1978	3	4	3
1979	3	21R	1
1980	4	8	1
1981	4	5	5
1982	4	5	3
1983	4	9	3
1984	4	7	1
1985	4	11	2

1986

1993

1986	4	17	5
1987	4	10	1
1988	4	7	2
1989	4	7	2
1990	4	9	3
1991	4	4P	3
1992	3	6P(pl)	2
1993	N1	10	2
1994	N1	24R	3

1998

1995	N2	15	2
1996	N2	19	4
1997	N2	21R	4
1998	N3	10	3

One of the first Peterborough shirts, with its large white 'V'.

PLYMOUTH ARGYLE

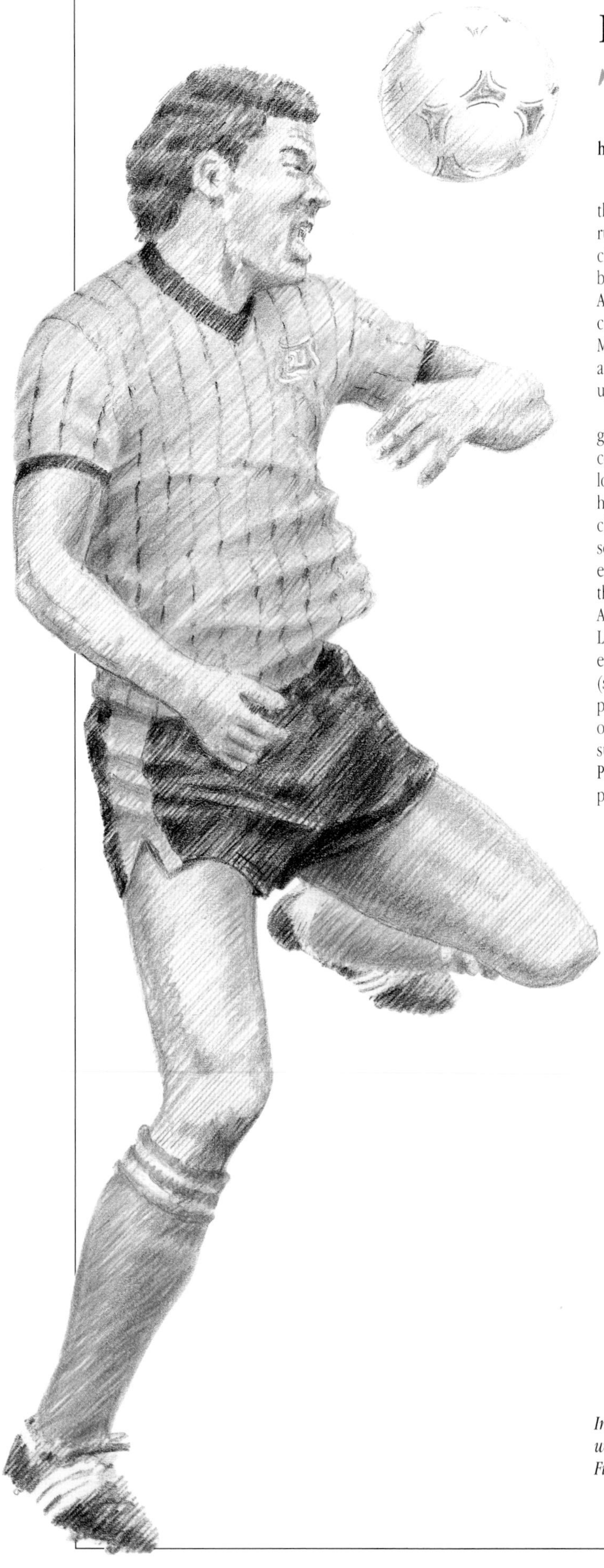

The very fact that Plymouth Argyle still exists is a major success story in itself. The whole of the south-west peninsular is a rugby stronghold and any soccer competition demands hundreds of miles of travel, causing a heavy drain on resources.

In fact, there was football in the city before the 1890s, but rugger was always the first choice. Home Park was originally built and laid out for Davenport Albion, but when the rugby club could not agree terms, Argyle's Mr Spooner quickly stepped in and the ground has indeed lived up to its name ever since.

The early teams sported a green, black and white combination, one influenced by local rugby tradition and which has remained throughout the club's history. After playing several highly publicised exhibition matches arranged by the enterprising Mr Spooner, Argyle joined the Southern League, where they stayed until election into the third division (south) in 1920. This first decade produced an extraordinary series of near misses. After six successive runners-up spots, the Pilgrims were eventually promoted to division two. The players had for many seasons worn green shirts with black collars and cuffs, and certainly looked the part, as the club never appeared in danger of losing its place.

After the Second World War, however, the kit lost its black trimmings, and the team, clad in green shirts with white sleeves, began to lose form and were relegated to the third division in 1950. Luckily the club didn't succumb to the anti-green paranoia, and wearing the same strip were promoted two years later. The following season a fourth place in division two plus a run to the fifth round of the FA Cup suggested great things to come, but sadly by 1958 Argyle were back in division three. The green and black returned as did a place in division two. But in the 1960s, a decade of semi-success, Plymouth wore one of the great individual and stylish strips.It was all-white with a green and black centre-band, way ahead of its time. It was hoped that it might inspire success for the future, but in fact financial limitations proved a stronger influence.

Since then limited resources have meant more years in division three than in the second. There have been odd highlights in the past 20 years, but these have usually been in the knockout competitions. In addition to two semi-final runs in the League Cup, in 1984 the Pilgrims got within a whisker of an FA Cup final appearance at Wembley. Only a single goal prevented a famous day and a confrontation with Everton.

The team that day, and those who subsequently battled away to attempt to maintain at least a second division place, continued to sport the unique green, black and white outfit. Unfortunately, 1998 brought relegation to the bottom of the league.

In 1984, the Pilgrims got within a whisker of an FA Cup Final appearance.

Plymouth (founded 1886) records and strips

	Division and position	Cup round reached
1904		1
1905		1
1906		2
1907		1
1908		2

1886-1914

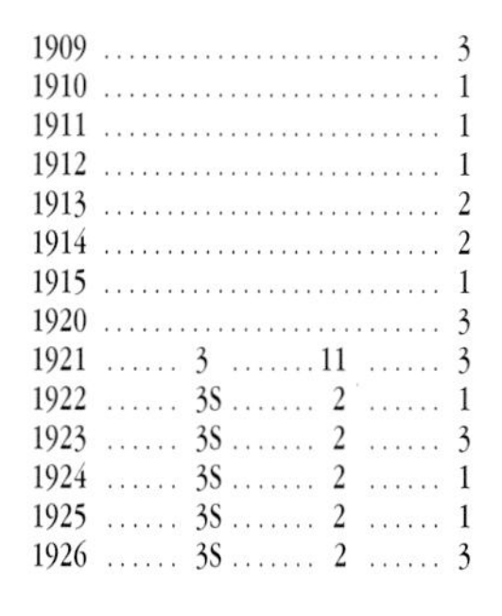

	Division	Position	Cup round reached
1909			3
1910			1
1911			1
1912			1
1913			2
1914			2
1915			1
1920			3
1921	3	11	3
1922	3S	2	1
1923	3S	2	3
1924	3S	2	1
1925	3S	2	1
1926	3S	2	3

1921-1939

	Division	Position	Cup round reached
1927	3S	2	3
1928	3S	3	1
1929	3S	4	4
1930	3S	1P	3
1931	2	18	3
1932	2	4	4
1933	2	14	3

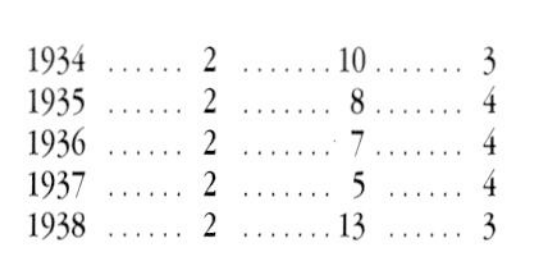

	Division	Position	Cup round reached
1934	2	10	3
1935	2	8	4
1936	2	7	4
1937	2	5	4
1938	2	13	3

	Division	Position	Cup round reached
1939	2	15	3
1946			3
1947	2	19	3
1948	2	17	3
1949	2	20	3
1950	2	21R	3
1951	3S	4	3
1952	3S	1P	1
1953	2	4	5
1954	2	19	4
1955	2	20	3

1946-1955

1956-1962

	Division	Position	Cup round reached
1956	2	21R	3
1957	3S	18	2
1958	3S	3	3
1959	3	1P	3
1960	2	19	3
1961	2	11	3
1962	2	5	4
1963	2	12	3
1964	2	20	3

1962-1967

One of the great individual and stylish shirts of the 1960s.

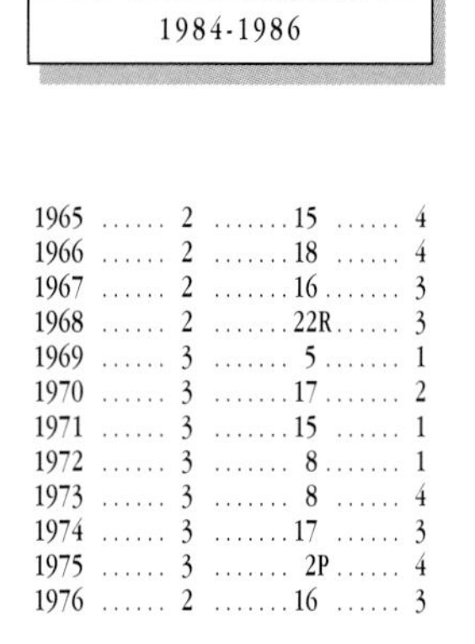

	Division	Position	Cup round reached
1965	2	15	4
1966	2	18	4
1967	2	16	3
1968	2	22R	3
1969	3	5	1
1970	3	17	2
1971	3	15	1
1972	3	8	1
1973	3	8	4
1974	3	17	3
1975	3	2P	4
1976	2	16	3

1975-1978

	Division	Position	Cup round reached
1977	2	21R	3
1978	3	19	3
1979	3	15	1
1980	3	15	1
1981	3	7	3
1982	3	10	1
1983	3	8	3
1984	3	19	sf
1985	3	15	2
1986	3	2P	3
1987	2	7	4
1988	2	16	5
1989	2	18	4
1990	2	16	3
1991	2	18	3
1992	2	22R	3
1993	N2	14	3
1994	N2	3	4
1995	N2	21R	3
1996	N3	4P(pl)	3
1997	N2	19	3
1998	N2	22R	1

1984-1986

1995-1996

1998

PORTSMOUTH

The very early Portsmouth teams were dressed in a striking strip of salmon pink jerseys trimmed with claret collars and cuffs, yet it is the blue, white and red, reflecting the town's link with the armed forces, which is the colour theme always associated with the club.

The earlier version of the club, Royal Artillery, appeared to have a very promising amateur future in store, when an illegal expenses scandal caused them to be ejected from the FA Amateur Cup. However, the fans still wanted first-class football, and the support of the navy and several branches of the army was sufficient to enable the establishment of a professional club and the purchase of Fratton Park.

Progress came through the usual channels of the Southern League and then the third division (south) in 1920, and it was soon obvious that the blue-shirted Hampshire team were a force to be reckoned with. Four years later promotion to the second division was achieved, and by 1928 Pompey were in the first division.

Although those first two seasons saw Portsmouth hang on by the skin of their teeth, in the second one the club reached their first FA Cup final, going down only to the great Cup fighters of the day, Bolton Wanderers. League performances improved and in 1934 there was a second trip to Wembley, and although on this occasion Manchester City won 2-1, Pompey were getting a reputation as Cup specialists as well as first division regulars.

In the last season, before the Second World War, there was another final, against a very strong Wolves side which had just been pipped for the League title. This time, however, Portsmouth were not to be denied and stunned the football world by winning 4-1.

In most cases the War had a negative effect on successful teams, but in the years immediately after the conflict manager Bob Jackson assembled a great team built around Jimmy Dickinson, Jimmy Scoular and wingers Peter Harris and Jack Froggatt. Two consecutive championships and another Cup semi-final appearance ensured the famous 'Pompey Chimes' were rendered with full gusto during those heady days.

Unfortunately, once this side broke up the club's fortunes waned and although Pompey managed to survive in the second division until 1976, fans even had to endure two seasons in the fourth. Eventually the financial crisis which had caused the slump was resolved and Portsmouth fought their way back. The famous blue kit trimmed with red and white had proudly remained throughout, and this pride was obvious in 1988 when first division football returned after a gap of 30 years.

Although the club was quickly relegated, first Jim Smith, then Glen Roeder put together other enterprising sides which still sometimes promised a bright future again. However, ten years later, after Terry Venables' temporary controlling influence, Pompey had still failed to deliver.

The blue, white and red of Pompey, which they wore for Cup and League triumphs each side of the Second World War.

Portsmouth (founded 1898) records and strips

1898-1910

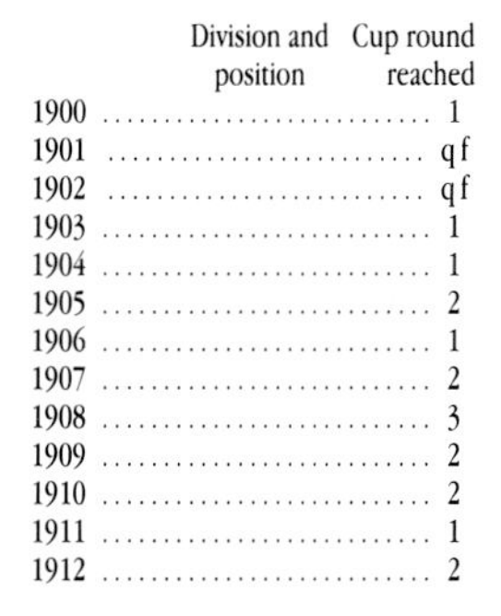

Year	Division and position		Cup round reached
1900			1
1901			qf
1902			qf
1903			1
1904			1
1905			2
1906			1
1907			2
1908			3
1909			2
1910			2
1911			1
1912			2

1921-1932

Year	Division	Position	Cup round
1913			1
1914			1
1915			1
1920			1
1921	3S	12	1
1922	3S	3	1
1923	3S	6	1
1924	3S	1P	1
1925	2	4	2
1926	2	11	3
1927	2	2P	4
1928	1	20	3

1937-1956

Year	Division	Position	Cup round
1929	1	20	F
1930	1	13	4
1931	1	4	5
1932	1	8	5
1933	1	9	3
1934	1	10	F
1935	1	14	4
1936	1	10	3
1937	1	9	3
1938	1	19	4

1958-1963

Year	Division	Position	Cup round
1939	1	17	**W**
1946			3
1947	1	12	4
1948	1	8	4
1949	1	1C	sf
1950	1	1C	5
1951	1	7	3
1952	1	4	qf
1953	1	15	3
1954	1	14	5
1955	1	3	3
1956	1	12	4
1957	1	19	4
1958	1	20	4
1959	1	22R	5
1960	2	20	3
1961	2	21R	3
1962	3	1P	1
1963	2	16	4
1964	2	9	3
1965	2	20	3
1966	2	12	3
1967	2	14	4

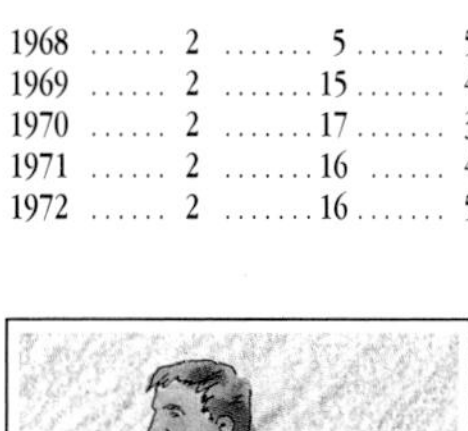

Year	Division	Position	Cup round
1968	2	5	5
1969	2	15	4
1970	2	17	3
1971	2	16	4
1972	2	16	5

1974-1975

Year	Division	Position	Cup round
1973	2	17	3
1974	2	15	5
1975	2	17	3

1985

Year	Division	Position	Cup round
1976	2	22R	1
1977	3	20	3
1978	3	24R	2
1979	4	7	2
1980	4	4P	3
1981	3	6	1
1982	3	13	1
1983	3	1P	2
1984	2	16	4

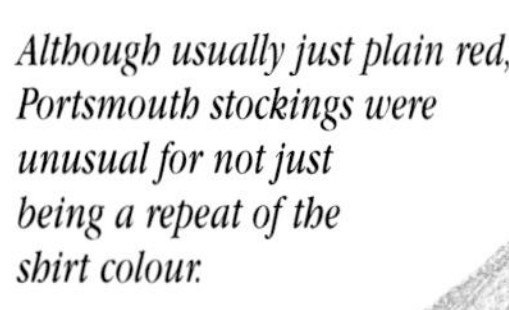

Although usually just plain red, Portsmouth stockings were unusual for not just being a repeat of the shirt colour.

1988-1990

Year	Division	Position	Cup round
1985	2	4	3
1986	2	4	3
1987	2	2P	4
1988	1	19R	qf
1989	2	20	3
1990	2	12	3
1991	2	17	5
1992	2	9	sf
1993	N1	3	3
1994	N1	17	3

1998

Year	Division	Position	Cup round
1995	N1	18	4
1996	N1	21	3
1997	N1	7	6
1998	N1	20	3

PORT VALE

In 1876 a group of young men met in a house in Longport called 'Vale', hence the name of the football club they were about to form. However, in those early days the team roamed around the Potteries searching for a permanent home, at one time being called Burslem Port Vale when located in that particular area. Even a regular uniform was not evident as amber and black, claret and blue and black and white were all recorded during this period.

By 1892 the Vale had been elected into the second division of the Football League, and life was always a struggle. At the end of the century, failure to be re-elected meant two years in the wilderness, and worse was to come when as Burslem Port Vale the club had to resign their newly re-acquired League status. However, despite the presence of city neighbours Stoke, the Vale continued to survive and eventually replaced Leeds City in the League 1919. Port Vale had become a reasonably successful club by the end of the 1920s and in the 1927 FA Cup campaign had been only one minute off an unbelievable win over the mighty Arsenal. Goal-scoring hero Wilf Kirkham starred on the day.

Just before the Second World War, relegation to the third division served only to emphasise their secondary status within the Potteries as Stoke City's star rose, and it was not until the mid-1950s that Vale's fortunes improved. They were sporting a black and white strip again, after an earlier spell in red shirts, and looked a formidable outfit in 1954 when they not only gained promotion, but reached the semi-final of the FA Cup against West Bromwich Albion. Only a penalty by England international Ronnie Allen, a Vale old boy, prevented the Potteries club from being the first ever third division finalists.

Perhaps the Cup glory was too much to live up to, but second division status was soon surrendered and by 1959 Port Vale found themselves in the fourth division. In an attempt to alter their luck, they changed the shirt style back to amber and black stripes. It worked instantly, Vale becoming divisional champions. However, the luck did not last, and even making Sir Stanley Matthews manager did not inspire any improvement, the club even being expelled from the League for making illegal payments. Fortunately the Vale were re-elected immediately, but not until the appointment of John Rudge as manager in 1983 did any concrete improvement begin to show itself. After eight years of consolidation, and clad in a striking ensemble of black and white shirts trimmed with the familiar old amber colours of the 1960s, Port Vale finally returned to the second division and city dominance.

The higher status has been difficult to maintain, but with Rudge still at the helm, strong League performances and exciting Cup runs should become the norm.

The 1954 team easily won promotion and became only the second side from division three to reach the semi-finals of the FA Cup.

Port Vale (founded 1876) records and strips

1886-1928

1975

1990-1993

1984

1947-1957

1960-1961

1998

	Division and	position	Cup round reached
1893	2	11	q
1894	2	7	q
1895	2	15	q
1896	2	14L	p
1897			p
1898			2
1899	2	9	1
1900	2	11	1
1901	2	9	1
1902	2	13	1
1903	2	9	p
1904	2	13	p
1905	2	16	2
1906	2	17	1
1907	2	16	2
1908			p
1909			p
1910			p
1911			p
1912			p
1913			p
1914			1
1915			q
1920	2	13	1
1921	2	17	p
1922	2	18	1
1923	2	17	p
1924	2	16	p
1925	2	8	1
1926	2	8	3
1927	2	8	4
1928	2	9	5
1929	2	21R	3
1930	3N	1P	2
1931	2	5	4
1932	2	20	4
1933	2	17	3
1934	2	8	3
1935	2	18	3
1936	2	21R	4
1937	3N	11	3
1938	3N	15	1
1939	3S	18	2
1946			3
1947	3S	10	4
1948	3S	8	1
1949	3S	13	1
1950	3S	13	4
1951	3S	12	3
1952	3S	13	3
1953	3N	2	2
1954	3N	1P	sf
1955	2	17	4
1956	2	12	4
1957	2	22R	3
1958	3S	15	2
1959	4	1P	1
1960	3	14	5
1961	3	7	3
1962	3	12	5
1963	3	3	4
1964	3	13	4
1965	3	22R	2
1966	4	19	3
1967	4	13	2
1968	4	18	1
1969	4	13	3
1970	4	4P	2
1971	3	17	1
1972	3	15	3
1973	3	6	3
1974	3	20	3
1975	3	6	1
1976	3	12	2
1977	3	19	5
1978	3	21R	2
1979	4	16	1
1980	4	20	1
1981	4	19	3
1982	4	7	3
1983	4	3P	1
1984	3	23R	1
1985	4	12	3
1986	4	4P	2
1987	3	12	2
1988	3	11	5
1989	3	3P	3
1990	2	11	4
1991	2	15	4
1992	2	24R	3
1993	N2	3	3
1994	N2	2P	4
1995	N1	16	2
1996	N1	12	5
1997	N1	8	3
1998	N1	19	3

The wonderful 'shadow' stripes of the 1990s Vale team.

PRESTON NORTH END

Sadly, most observers of modern Preston performances would find it difficult to comprehend the power, dominance and influence of the club over a century ago.

In the early 1880s, wearing either blue and white hooped or striped shirts, North End had to learn the finer points of football very quickly, such was the pressure and competition from nearby Blackburn Rovers.

However, by 1888 and now sporting the famous white shirts and navy blue shorts, Preston were strong enough to be founder members of the Football League. Strong they certainly were. In fact, they dominated the first season, winning the title without losing a match, as well as taking the FA Cup without conceding a goal. Perhaps their rivals should have been prepared for this tour de force, as the 'Old Invincibles' had only a year earlier beaten Hyde United 26-0! Preston also took the second championship, but as their rivals also took on the full professionalism that North End had introduced, the club's total dominance faded.

Three runners-up spots were followed by lower positions and, in 1901, relegation. By 1906 they were back in the top flight and had achieved a wonderful runners-up finish. However, the next 30 years produced no great League successes, many seasons being spent in the second division. The Cup did offer some relief and apart from several quarter-finals, there were three finals with contrasting outcomes. In 1922, only a controversial penalty by Huddersfield prevented Preston taking the trophy; 15 years on Sunderland were the victors, but a year later a return match with Huddersfield allowed North End to get revenge with a last-minute penalty!

After the Second World War following another relegation, the club bounced back with a strong team based around the great Tom Finney. During the 1950s, Preston became a major force in the land again, just missing the League title on three occasions and suffering an exciting defeat in the 1954 Cup final versus West Bromwich Albion.

Unfortunately Finney retired at the same time as the abolition of the maximum wage and from this moment on 'Proud Preston' had to sell to survive. Talent such as Peter Thompson and Howard Kendall departed to balance the books.

Third and fourth division football became the norm, and the grand revival of Blackburn added a further challenge. Come the 1990s Deepdale was yearning for a manager with the talent of Kenny Dalglish and the financial support of a Jack Walker.

In 1996, the Endsleigh League third division championship might be just the start. The Ribble Valley looks forward to more success.

The 'Old Invincibles' of 1889, undefeated in both Cup and League.

Preston (founded 1881) records and strips

A hundred years after the double, only the shirts offered style.

1882-1920

1921-1933

1934-1957

1963-1967

1974-1976

1988-89

1998

Year	Division	Position	Cup round reached
1884			4
1885			
1886			3
1887			sf
1888			F
1889	1	1C	W
1890	1	1C	qf
1891	1	2	1
1892	1	2	qf
1893	1	2	sf
1894	1	14	2
1895	1	4	2
1896	1	9	1
1897	1	4	qf
1898	1	12	1
1899	1	15	2
1900	1	16	qf
1901	1	17R	1
1902	2	3	1
1903	2	7	2
1904	2	1P	2
1905	1	8	qf
1906	1	2	1
1907	1	14	1
1908	1	12	1
1909	1	10	2
1910	1	12	1
1911	1	14	2
1912	1	19R	1
1913	2	1P	1
1914	1	19R	3
1915	2	2P	1
1920	1	19	3
1921	1	16	sf
1922	1	16	F
1923	1	16	2
1924	1	18	1
1925	1	21R	2
1926	2	12	3
1927	2	6	4
1928	2	4	3
1929	2	13	3
1930	2	16	3
1931	2	7	3
1932	2	13	5
1933	2	9	3
1934	2	2P	qf
1935	1	11	qf
1936	1	7	4
1937	1	14	F
1938	1	3	W
1939	1	9	qf
1946			5
1947	1	7	qf
1948	1	7	qf
1949	1	21R	4
1950	2	6	3
1951	2	1P	4
1952	1	7	3
1953	1	2	4
1954	1	11	F
1955	1	14	4
1956	1	19	3
1957	1	3	5
1958	1	2	3
1959	1	12	5
1960	1	9	qf
1961	1	22R	4
1962	2	10	qf
1963	2	17	3
1964	2	3	F
1965	2	12	4
1966	2	17	qf
1967	2	13	3
1968	2	20	4
1969	2	14	4
1970	2	22R	3
1971	3	1P	1
1972	2	18	4
1973	2	19	3
1974	2	21R	3
1975	3	9	3
1976	3	8	2
1977	3	6	2
1978	3	3P	2
1979	2	7	4
1980	2	10	3
1981	2	20R	3
1982	3	14	1
1983	3	16	3
1984	3	16	1
1985	3	23R	2
1986	4	23	1
1987	4	2P	4
1988	3	16	1
1989	3	6	1
1990	3	19	2
1991	3	17	1
1992	3	17	3
1993	N2	21R	1
1994	N3	5	4
1995	N3	5	2
1996	N3	1P	2
1997	N2	15	2
1998	N2	15	3

QUEEN'S PARK RANGERS

National trophies and European competitions were surely never within the ambitions of the two junior clubs from the Queen's Park Estate in west London when they merged in 1886. Christchurch Rangers and St Jude's Institution first took the name of the latter club, but four years later combined the area name with part of the Christchurch title and Queen's Park Rangers were born.

The hooped shirts of the 1960s as worn by Rodney Marsh and company.

In the early days the players wore Oxford and Cambridge blue halves, but by 1897 the club decided to change to green and white hoops to avoid clashing with local rivals Paddington. Soon QPR had left local football behind, gaining great prominence when playing against mighty Spurs and the famous Casuals. Southern League football was reasonably successful, but in the FA Cup QPR reached the quarter-finals on two occasions, again attracting attention from the football hierarchy, and it was no surprise when they were elected into the Football League.

The first two seasons in the third division were very successful, but the team's form waned and by 1926 drastic measures were required. Green was usually considered unlucky, and in an attempt to halt the decline the hoops became blue. The improvement came, but it was gradual, and after the Second World War QPR were still in the third division.

However, the early post-War years were sensational, promotion to the second division and another quarter-final appearance promising a bright future. But Rangers have often been pro-moted before they were ready and by 1953 they were back in the third. Again a change of strip was tried, but even an all-silk outfit of white shirts and blue shorts failed to lift the gloom.

By the 1960s Rangers' time had come, manager Alec Stock assembling an enterprising team around flamboyant star Rodney Marsh. The League Cup was won in glorious style against West Bromwich Albion in 1967 and that year saw also the first of two consecutive promotion successes. Again this came too quickly and the hoop-shirted Rangers were immediately relegated. But QPR had now become an established top club and later managers Gordon Jago and Dave Sexton built sides which not only returned to the top flight, but in 1976 missed the League championship by only one point. Back in the Second division, Rangers reached their first FA Cup final in 1982. The loss against London rivals Spurs was a disappointment as was a League Cup final reverse four years later, but in the 1980s and 1990s QPR looked a real top flight club with hopes of further glories in England and Europe.

The 1996 relegation therefore came as a shock and Rangers main task now is to regain Premiership status.

QPR (founded 1885) records and strips

1882-1896

Year	Division	Position	Cup round reached
1900			2
1901			q
1902			q
1903			q
1904			q
1905			q
1906			1
1907			1
1908			2

1897-1926

Year	Division	Position	Cup round reached
1909			1
1910			qf
1911			1
1912			1
1913			2
1914			qf
1915			3
1920			1
1921	3S	3	2
1922	3S	5	1

1926-1953

Year	Division	Position	Cup round reached
1923	3S	11	qf
1924	3S	22	1
1925	3S	19	1
1926	3S	22	2
1927	3S	14	
1928	3S	10	1
1929	3S	6	1
1930	3S	3	3
1931	3S	8	3
1932	3S	13	4
1933	3S	16	3
1934	3S	4	3
1935	3S	13	2

1953-1960

Year	Division	Position	Cup round reached
1936	3S	4	1
1937	3S	9	3
1938	3S	3	2
1939	3S	6	3
1946			5
1947	3S	2	3
1948	3S	1P	qf
1949	2	13	3
1950	2	20	3
1951	2	16	3
1952	2	22R	3
1953	3S	21	1

1960-1975

Year	Division	Position	Cup round reached
1954	3S	18	3
1955	3S	15	1
1956	3S	18	1
1957	3S	10	3
1958	3S	10	2
1959	3	13	2
1960	3	8	2
1961	3	3	2
1962	3	4	3
1963	3	13	3
1964	3	15	3
1965	3	14	2
1966	3	3	3

1983-1986

Year	Division	Position	Cup round reached
1967	3	1P	3
1968	2	2P	3
1969	1	22R	3
1970	2	9	qf
1971	2	10	3
1972	2	4	3
1973	2	2P	5
1974	1	8	qf
1975	1	11	5
1976	1	2	3
1977	1	14	4
1978	1	19	5

Year	Division	Position	Cup round reached
1979	1	20R	3
1980	2	5	3
1981	2	8	3
1982	2	5	F
1983	2	1P	3
1984	1	5	3
1985	1	19	3
1986	1	13	3
1987	1	16	5
1988	1	5	5
1989	1	9	3

1994-95

Year	Division	Position	Cup round reached
1990	1	11	qf
1991	1	12	3
1992	1	11	3
1993	Pr	5	4
1994	Pr	9	3
1995	Pr	8	qf
1996	Pr	19R	4
1997	N1	9	5
1998	N1	21	3

1998

In 1990, Rangers' shirts had a unique collar with a built-in blue panel.

READING

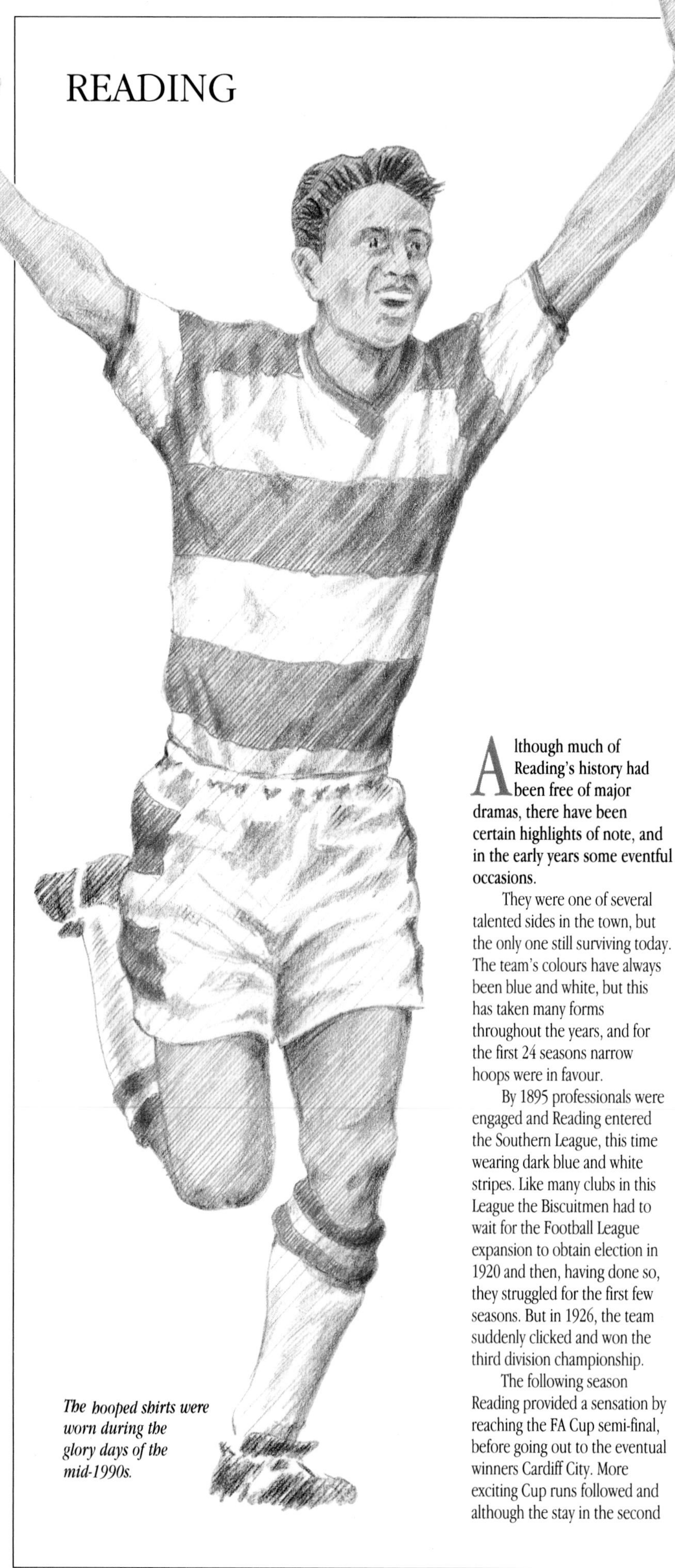

The hooped shirts were worn during the glory days of the mid-1990s.

Although much of Reading's history had been free of major dramas, there have been certain highlights of note, and in the early years some eventful occasions.

They were one of several talented sides in the town, but the only one still surviving today. The team's colours have always been blue and white, but this has taken many forms throughout the years, and for the first 24 seasons narrow hoops were in favour.

By 1895 professionals were engaged and Reading entered the Southern League, this time wearing dark blue and white stripes. Like many clubs in this League the Biscuitmen had to wait for the Football League expansion to obtain election in 1920 and then, having done so, they struggled for the first few seasons. But in 1926, the team suddenly clicked and won the third division championship.

The following season Reading provided a sensation by reaching the FA Cup semi-final, before going out to the eventual winners Cardiff City. More exciting Cup runs followed and although the stay in the second division lasted only five seasons, the 1930s provided lots of good football and many other pushes for promotion.

Just before the Second World War, the club's famous broad hoops appeared for the first time and were retained on the resumption of peacetime football, when Elm Park witnessed several other near misses in the League. Then in 1953, just like their fellow 'hoop men' Queen's Park Rangers, Reading experimented with white shirts and blue shorts. The change provided no improvement in form; in fact, playing standards dropped, so the hoops returned.

Why the club insisted in changing the strip so often is not clear, but yet another switch occurred in 1965. The new all-sky blue strip, inspired by Jimmy Hill's Coventry, did coincide with higher placings in the League for the next five years, surely a good reason to continue in that style, but in 1970 the hoops reappeared.

This time the effect was traumatic and the Biscuitmen slumped into the fourth division. There were several ups and downs, but by 1984 Reading were still at the lowest level. Then Ian Branfoot was appointed manager and immediately began assembling a side to support the goal-scoring feats of Trevor Senior.

Of course, there was a strip change to accompany the new era, but at least this time there was a happy association. Two promotions in three seasons, including one spell of 13 consecutive wins, saw the club return to the second division for the first time in over half a century. Although the second division proved too hot for the Biscuitmen on this visit, at least the club continued with the unusual light blue, white and navy blue strip for a while. By the mid-1990s, they were back in the second flight, and once more in the blue and white hoops until relegation again in 1998.

Reading (founded 1871) records and strips

1871-1938

	Division and position		Cup round reached
1900			1
1901			3
1902			2
1903			1
1904			1
1905			1
1906			1
1907			1
1908			1

1938-1953

	Division and position		Cup round reached
1909			1
1910			1
1911			q
1912			3
1913			3
1914			1
1915			1
1920			1
1921	3	20	1
1922	3S	13	1
1923	3S	19	1

1953-1955

	Division and position		Cup round reached
1924	3S	18	1
1925	3S	14	2
1926	3S	1P	3
1927	2	14	sf
1928	2	18	4
1929	2	15	5

1965-1970

	Division and position		Cup round reached
1930	2	19	3
1931	2	21R	3
1932	3S	2	1
1933	3S	4	3
1934	3S	3	3
1935	3S	2	5
1936	3S	3	3
1937	3S	5	3
1938	3S	6	1
1939	3S	5	1
1946			1
1947	3S	9	3
1948	3S	10	3
1949	3S	2	2
1950	3S	10	3
1951	3S	3	3
1952	3S	2	3
1953	3S	11	1
1954	3S	8	1

1970-1981

	Division and position		Cup round reached
1955	3S	18	3
1956	3S	17	2
1957	3S	13	3
1958	3S	5	3
1959	3	6	1
1960	3	11	3
1961	3	18	3
1962	3	7	1
1963	3	20	1
1964	3	6	2
1965	3	13	4
1966	3	8	3
1967	3	4	2
1968	3	5	3
1969	3	14	3
1970	3	8	1

1984-1991

1995

	Division and position		Cup round reached
1971	3	21R	3
1972	4	16	4
1973	4	7	4
1974	4	6	2
1975	4	7	1
1976	4	3P	1
1977	3	21R	3
1978	4	8	2
1979	4	1P	3
1980	3	7	4
1981	3	10	1

1998

	Division and position		Cup round reached
1982	3	12	1
1983	3	21R	1
1984	4	3P	2
1985	3	9	3
1986	3	1P	4
1987	2	13	3
1988	2	22R	3
1989	3	18	4
1990	3	10	4
1991	3	15	1
1992	3	12	3
1993	N2	8	3
1994	N2	1P	1
1995	N1	2	3
1996	N1	19	4
1997	N1	18	4
1998	N1	24R	5

A detail of the 1987 shirt and the multi-coloured collar.

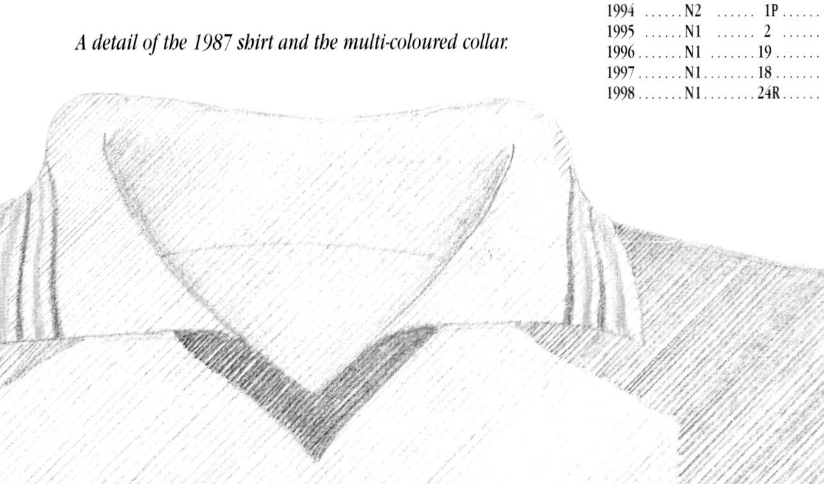

ROCHDALE

It was a struggle to establish a club at all in Rochdale. Indeed, one attempt had already failed by the time the Dale were founded in 1907. Tucked away in the rain-soaked foothills of the Pennines and surrounded by big city clubs which would claim much of the town's support, there would never be an easy ride.

At first the club played in the lower divisions of the Manchester League without impressing the people of Rochdale and only the ambition of the directors who promptly assembled a much better team enabled them to survive. However, the public eventually responded and the club progressed through the Lancashire Combination and Central League.

In fact, Rochdale improved to such a degree that by the time of the First World War, they were regularly playing against top teams and did so well that application to the second division followed. After the disappointment of rejection, Rochdale pushed for the extension of League football and became founder members of the third division (north).

The mid-1920s were wonderful times. Twice the club just missed promotion to the second division and all the early struggles were forgotten for a while, but eventually the competition improved and the remainder of the period before the Second World War was spent at the lower end of the division.

During the first 30 years, the club's colours varied between two different formats; either blue shirts or a black and white version. After the War, it was the blue-shirted team that put in another strong challenge for that elusive place in division two.

Once again a slump followed and in 1959 the Dale found themselves in the fourth division. But this very status provided a unique distinction when in 1962 Rochdale reached the final of the League Cup, losing to Norwich City. The competition was only in its infancy, but it was still a mighty achievement for a fourth division side.

The black and white strip came back for a short spell at this time, but by the end of the decade the blue shirts returned for another period of positive success. In 1969, the Spotland fans were treated to the realisation of a dream, promotion back to division three at last. It was a minor success compared to those of the Lancashire giants, but it was the first evidence of real promise for a long time.

Since that time, the blues have remained at Spotland, and with a mid-table position in the lower division being regarded as a success, though there were occasional lifts like the 1990 run to the fifth round of the FA Cup. Beyond that only the odd sartorial delight provided the club with any light relief.

1970 was a rare period of Dale success in the more usual blue shirt style.

Rochdale (founded 1907) records and strips

Year	Division and position		Cup round reached
1913			1
1914			p
1915			2
1920			1
1921			1
1922	3N	20	p
1923	3N	12	p
1924	3N	2	p
1925	3N	6	p
1926	3N	3	2
1927	3N	2	1
1928	3N	13	2
1929	3N	17	1
1930	3N	10	1
1931	3N	21	1
1932	3N	21	1
1933	3N	18	1
1934	3N	22	1
1935	3N	20	1
1936	3N	20	1
1937	3N	18	1
1938	3N	17	1
1939	3N	15	1
1946			3
1947	3N	6	3
1948	3N	12	2
1949	3N	7	1
1950	3N	3	2
1951	3N	11	3
1952	3N	21	3
1953	3N	22	1
1954	3N	19	1
1955	3N	12	3
1956	3N	12	1
1957	3N	13	1
1958	3N	10	1
1959	3	24R	1
1960	4	12	2
1961	4	17	1
1962	4	12	2
1963	4	7	1
1964	4	20	2
1965	4	6	1
1966	4	21	2
1967	4	21	1
1968	4	19	1
1969	4	3P	1
1970	3	9	1
1971	3	16	4
1972	3	18	1
1973	3	13	1
1974	3	24R	2
1975	4	19	2
1976	4	15	3
1977	4	18	1
1978	4	24	1
1979	4	20	1
1980	4	24	3
1981	4	15	1
1982	4	21	1
1983	4	20	1
1984	4	22	3
1985	4	18	1
1986	4	18	3
1987	4	21	2
1988	4	21	1
1989	4	18	1
1990	4	12	5
1991	4	12	1
1992	4	8	2
1993	N3	11	2
1994	N3	9	2
1995	N3	15	1
1996	N3	15	3
1997	N3	14	2
1998	N3	18	1

1907

1922

1950

1961

1970

1973

1992

1998

One of the rare sashed shirts in modern football, as worn during the 1973 season.

ROTHERHAM UNITED

The early history of Rotherham United is long and tortuous, taking many different twists before the present club came into being. In fact, there were two main sources which eventually amalgamated.

The first stirrings were in 1884 when a junior club called Thornhill United was formed. Having done well over the years, clad in black and white stripes, the ambitious club changed its name to Rotherham County and joined the Midland League. Eventually, wearing white shirts and black shorts (with red belt), County were elected into the second division of the Football League, but found the competition a bit too strong. A drop into the third division resulted in subsequent re-election.

Here we have to return to the 19th century, when Rotherham Town were gamely battling in the second division. The Town, first sporting chocolate and sky halves then blue shirts with white sleeves, also found Football League standards hard to cope with. After three difficult seasons they resigned, to face the wilderness of non-League football for 30 years.

In 1925 the resources of both clubs were amalgamated and at last Rotherham had a team to cope with the demands of the League and the big local clubs.

Before the Second World War little was achieved, but in the immediate post-War period under the management of Reg Freeman, a great side came runners-up during three consecutive seasons before finally being promoted to the second division in 1951. Thus, the Reds, for this was the adopted colour of the United club, had entered their finest period. In 1955, under the management of Andy Swailes, promotion to the first division was missed only on goal average. The club never quite came so close again, but were certainly at home at that level.

In 1961 Millmoor saw its team narrowly fail to win the first ever League Cup final and in retrospect one can only wonder what might have happened if Rotherham had converted any of these 'near miss' opportunities – particularly as so many of the following seasons were to be spent in the lower divisions, including three in the fourth.

There must always be a reason for optimism at the club though. Millmoor has managed to attract big-name managers such as Tommy Doherty and Emlyn Hughes, and has unearthed such talent as Dave Watson who went on to play for England.

Second division soccer returned for a short time in the 1980s, and in the 1990s it always looked a possibility that the all-red or Arsenal-style shirts would see the club reach better times again.

In 1955 the Reds missed promotion to the first division only on goal average and five years later were League Cup runners-up.

Rotherham (founded 1884) records and strips

	Division and position		Cup round reached
1894	2	14	q
1895	2	12	q

Town(l) & County(r) 1895

Town(l) & County(r) 1909

1896	2	15	1
1920	2	17	q
1921	2	19	q
1922	2	16	q
1923	2	21R	1
1924	3N	4	q
1925	3N	22	q
1926	3N	14	3
1927	3N	19	1
1928	3N	14	3
1929	3N	16	1
1930	3N	20	3
1931	3N	14	1
1932	3N	16	1
1933	3N	17	1
1934	3N	21	3
1935	3N	9	2

1925

1936	3N	11	2
1937	3N	17	1
1938	3N	6	2

1938

1939	3N	11	1
1946			4
1947	3N	2	3
1948	3N	2	3

1955

1949	3N	3	4
1950	3N	6	3
1951	3N	1P	4
1952	2	9	4

1961

1953	2	12	5
1954	2	5	4
1955	2	3	4
1956	2	19	3

1981

1957	2	17	3
1958	2	18	3
1959	2	20	3
1960	2	8	4
1961	2	15	4
1962	2	9	3
1963	2	14	3
1964	2	7	3
1965	2	14	4
1966	2	7	4
1967	2	18	4
1968	2	21R	5
1969	3	11	2
1970	3	14	3
1971	3	8	3
1972	3	5	4
1973	3	21R	2
1974	4	15	2
1975	4	3P	3
1976	3	16	2

1990

1977	3	4	3
1978	3	20	3
1979	3	17	3
1980	3	13	2
1981	3	1P	2
1982	2	7	3
1983	2	20R	3
1984	3	18	3
1985	3	12	1
1986	3	14	4

1998

1987	3	14	1
1988	3	21R	2
1989	4	1P	2
1990	3	9	2
1991	3	23R	4
1992	4	2P	2
1993	N2	11	4
1994	N2	15	1
1995	N2	17	2
1996	N2	16	1
1997	N2	23R	1
1998	N3	9	3

An early Rotherham side wore a wonderful bright red belt as part of their uniform.

SCARBOROUGH

Apart from the people closely associated with the club, most football fans regarded Scarborough as one of the less likely sides to enter Football League circles. Outside the non-League world, they had not received the same national recognition as some of their peers.

Yet the club's history goes back a long way. They were formed in 1879 and after a decade of playing friendlies went on to compete in both the Northern League and the Yorkshire Combination. These red-shirted enthusiasts added many wins in the East Riding and North Riding Cup competitions at this time.

In 1926 Scarborough took on professional status, although most of the players were part-time. For a while, the team wore claret and sky blue shirts (yet another seeking to become the second Aston Villa), and became members of the strong Midland League, eventually becoming champions in 1930. The following year the Boro reached the third round of the FA Cup, a feat repeated seven years later, and were obviously a team of standing in non-League football.

After the Second World War the club still competed in the Midland League, although by now the red shirts had returned. League performances were steady rather than spectacular, but by regularly winning the North Riding Senior Cup the club did enough to keep the fans happy.

During the 1960s, the North Eastern League championship was won and the club became more outwardly ambitious as non-League football streamlined its competitions. By 1968 the Northern Premier League had been formed, attracting the area's top clubs, and this proved the ideal platform for Scarborough. Although one of the stronger clubs, Boro never quite managed to take the title, but in the FA Trophy, a new competition for the country's best clubs outside the Football League, the Yorkshire coast side proved the tops.

The former Leicester City star Colin Appleton put together a highly efficient outfit and in the five years from 1973 Scarborough won the trophy three times, in addition to one runners-up spot. One of the teams beaten were Wigan Athletic, who eventually pipped Boro to a Football League place.

There were other important Cup wins before Scarborough joined the Alliance Premier, the unofficial fifth division. Once again the club, usually in all-red, did not take any of the early League honours, but in the season which really mattered, new manager Neil Warnock created a team which surprised the favourites. So in 1987 Scarborough became a Football League club.

The first season started sensationally as the team topped the division, but eventually Boro had to settle for a mid-table position. Limited finances and a scarcity of new talent were to delay further progress, but while the players continued to wear strikingly patterned red and white strips there was always a projection of optimism at the club.

After 110 years, the Yorkshire club made it to the Football League.

Scarborough (founded 1879) records and strips

1879 to 1939 Northern League, Yorkshire Combination, Northern League, Yorkshire League, Midland League

1953

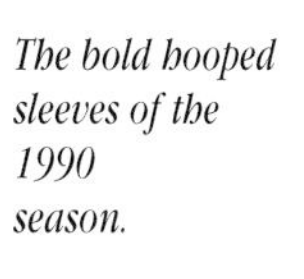

The bold hooped sleeves of the 1990 season.

1895

	Division and position		Cup round reached
1946	SD		q4
1947	ML		q4
1948	ML		q4
1949	ML		2
1950	ML		q4
1951	ML		1
1952	ML		q4
1953	ML		1
1954	ML		1
1955	ML		1
1956	ML		1
1957	ML		1
1958	ML		1
1959	ML		q4
1960	ML		1
1961	NC		1
1962	NC		q4
1963	NE		1
1964	ML		q3
1965	ML		2
1966	ML		1
1967	ML		q1
1968	NP		q1
1969	NP		q2
1970	NP		q4
1971	NP		1
1972	NP		1
1973	NP		2
1974	NP		2
1975	NP		q4
1976	NP		3
1977	NP		1
1978	NP		3
1979	NP		2
1980	APL		1
1981	APL		1
1982	APL		q4
1983	APL		1
1984	APL		q4
1985	GL		q4
1986	GL		1
1987	GMVC		q1
1988	4	12	1
1989	4	5	2
1990	4	18	1
1991	4	9	1
1992	4	12	1
1993	4	13	1
1994	N3	14	2
1995	N3	21	3
1996	N3	23	1
1997	N3	12	2
1998	N3	6	1

1960

1986

1998

1928

1977

1992

SCUNTHORPE UNITED

North Lincolnshire was always one of the remoter parts of England, and because of this and the associated transport problems, senior football was very slow to develop in the area.

It was the growth of the iron and steel industries which gave Scunthorpe its importance and it was the workers from these factories who provided the early support.

The club was formed in 1904, when they wore claret and sky halves, but it was not until a reorganisation 11 years later that the Iron moved beyond the levels of the local leagues. There were many years of building and consolidation before the 1930s, when as Scunthorpe and Lindsey United the club were amongst the leaders of the Midland League.

By now the team wore claret shirts with light blue sleeves and had ambitions to be as successful as Aston Villa or Burnley. However, the Lincolnshiremen had to be patient for some seasons to come, and it was not until soon after the Second World War that the Iron finally entered the Football League.

After three years of adjustment, full-back hero Jackie Brownsword and his men began to push for promotion, and in 1958 succeeded in reaching the dizzy heights of the second division. Nor were Scunthorpe overwhelmed by the experience; in 1962 they were only two places off promotion to the top flight itself.

Feeling their new status deserved a new look, United sported a very modern-looking white shirt with blue and amber trim, but there were no improvements in results and the claret and blue returned.

However, the resources of this small club were not sufficient to sustain second division football. Players such as chief goalscorer Barry Thomas had to be sold, and an inexperienced team dropped through the divisions. Once again a change of strip was introduced to help improve sagging fortunes, and the young Kevin Keegan wore an all-red outfit before he, too, had to move on. Ray Clemence was another famous Scunthorpe player of the era.

The all-red remained as did a regular position in the fourth division; crowds were poor and so were playing standards. Eventually, the claret and blue was reintroduced in the mid-1980s and many of the designs were both unique and eye-catching. In recent years there has been the occasional improvement on the pitch, including a short stay in the third division in 1983/84. The modern Scunthorpe was left to yearn for another Keegan or Brownsword to convert the string of near misses into tangible achievement.

The kit in which little Scunthorpe came within two places of the first division.

Scunthorpe (founded 1904) records and strips

1904 to 1939 Midland League

	Division and position	Cup round reached
1946	ML	q4

1904-1910

1947	ML	2
1948	ML	1
1949	ML	2
1950	ML	q4

1937-1956

1951	3N	12	q4
1952	3N	14	3
1953	3N	15	3
1954	3N	3	4
1955	3N	3	2
1956	3N	9	4
1957	3N	14	2
1958	3N	1P	5
1959	2	18	3
1960	2	15	4
1961	2	9	4
1962	2	4	3

1957-59 & 1961-64

1963	2	9	3
1964	2	22R	3
1965	3	18	1
1966	3	4	1
1967	3	18	2
1968	3	23R	2
1969	4	16	1
1970	4	12	5
1971	4	17	3

1960

1972	4	4P	1
1973	3	24R	3
1974	4	18	4
1975	4	24	1
1976	4	19	1
1977	4	20	1
1978	4	14	1
1979	4	12	1
1980	4	14	1
1981	4	16	2
1982	4	23	3
1983	4	4P	3
1984	3	21R	4
1985	4	9	2
1986	4	15	2

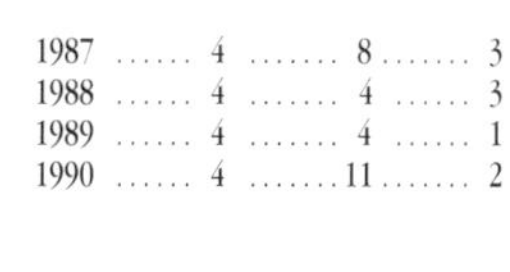

1987	4	8	3
1988	4	4	3
1989	4	4	1
1990	4	11	2

1973

1991	4	8	3
1992	4	5	1
1993	N3	14	1

1984

1991

1994	N3	11	3
1995	N3	7	2
1996	N3	12	2
1997	N3	13	2
1998	N3	8	3

1998

An attractive reworking of the claret and blue theme in the 1990s.

SHEFFIELD UNITED

United were Sheffield's football babies, the Wednesday and Sheffield FC being well established by the time the Blades were formed in 1889. In fact, the club started only when the Wednesday left Bramall Lane and Sir Charles Clegg wanted a good team to play on the ground. The red and white stripes were an obvious alternative to their main rivals' strip and they were soon to be as famous.

At first, no major league was interested in the club, but after a couple of seasons in the Midland League, United were finally elected into the Football League. There was instant promotion to the top flight and this began a golden era for both the Blades and the city in general.

Between 1897 and 1902 the team appeared in three FA Cup finals, winning two against Derby and Southampton, and in the League had a title win and two runners-up spots within the space of four seasons. Stars of this period included arch tackler 'Nudger' Needham and the legendary 22-stone goalkeeper 'Fatty' Foulkes.

Although Wednesday began to take over as Sheffield's senior club, the Blades had more glory days to come, and just before the First World War, a third Cup triumph was earned in a 3-0 win over Chelsea.

Between the Wars inconsistency in the League eventually led to relegation in the late 1930s, but the Cup still proved to be an achievable goal. In 1925 Cardiff were beaten 1-0 in the final and the same score resulted in a loss against Arsenal, 11 years later.

Since the Second World War, United have had a variable history, many spells in all divisions being matched only by changes in the style of the strip. There were broad stripes, narrow stripes, plus irregular versions and even red shorts, but none inspired any great and lasting success. During the last half century, the red and white shirts have been worn by such gifted players as Jimmy Hagan, Tony Currie, Mick Jones, Alan Hodgkinson and the Shaws (Joe and Graham). Yet only occasionally has even a reasonable first division position been achieved.

At least in the 1990s, a battling new version of the Blades had laid the ghosts of the fourth division experience and the teams of Dave Bassett, and later Howard Kendall, sought to find a permanent spot in the top flight. The pressure was on, particularly as Wednesday were enjoying their best period for some years too!

Sheffield United's kit at the end of the 19th century, by which time they had already won the FA Cup and the League title.

United (founded 1889) records and strips

Nearly 100 years after the glory days, a smart three-colour striped shirt suggested signs of renewed success.

Year	Division and position		Cup round reached
1890			2
1891			1
1892			2
1893	2	2P	2
1894	1	10	1
1895	1	6	2

1889-1914

Year	Division	Position	Cup round reached
1896	1	12	2
1897	1	2	1
1898	1	1C	1
1899	1	16	W
1900	1	2	qf
1901	1	14	F
1902	1	10	W
1903	1	4	2
1904	1	7	qf
1905	1	6	1
1906	1	13	2
1907	1	4	1
1908	1	17	1

1924

1935

Year	Division	Position	Cup round reached
1909	1	12	1
1910	1	6	1
1911	1	9	1
1912	1	14	1
1913	1	13	1
1914	1	10	sf
1915	1	6	W
1920	1	14	2
1921	1	20	1
1922	1	11	1
1923	1	10	sf
1924	1	5	1

1962

Year	Division	Position	Cup round reached
1925	1	14	W
1926	1	5	4
1927	1	8	3
1928	1	13	sf
1929	1	11	3
1930	1	20	4
1931	1	15	5
1932	1	7	4
1933	1	10	4
1934	1	22R	3
1935	2	11	4
1936	2	3	F
1937	2	7	4
1938	2	3	4
1939	2	2P	5
1946			4
1947	1	6	qf

Year	Division	Position	Cup round reached
1948	1	12	3
1949	1	22R	4
1950	2	3	4
1951	2	8	4
1952	2	11	qf
1953	2	1P	4
1954	1	20	3
1955	1	13	3
1956	1	22R	5

1975

Year	Division	Position	Cup round reached
1957	2	7	3
1958	2	6	5
1959	2	3	qf
1960	2	4	qf
1961	2	2P	sf

1982

Year	Division	Position	Cup round reached
1962	1	5	qf
1963	1	10	5
1964	1	12	4
1965	1	19	4
1966	1	9	4
1967	1	10	5
1968	1	21R	qf
1969	2	9	3
1970	2	6	4
1971	2	2P	3
1972	1	10	3

1992

Year	Division	Position	Cup round reached
1973	1	14	4
1974	1	13	3
1975	1	6	4
1976	1	22R	3
1977	2	11	3
1978	2	12	3
1979	2	20R	3
1980	3	12	2
1981	3	21R	2
1982	4	1P	1
1983	3	11	3
1984	3	3P	3

1998

Year	Division	Position	Cup round reached
1985	2	18	3
1986	2	7	4
1987	2	9	4
1988	2	21R	4
1989	3	2P	5
1990	2	2P	qf
1991	1	13	3
1992	1	9	5
1993	Pr	19	sf
1994	Pr	20R	3
1995	N1	8	3
1996	N1	9	4
1997	N1	5	3
1998	N1	6	sf

SHEFFIELD WEDNESDAY

Wednesday are an old club, founded in 1867 by a group of cricketers looking for winter exercise. At the time there were at least a dozen good clubs in Sheffield. so there was never a shortage of matches and this early high-quality competition increased the rate of development.

Wednesday's second great period came in the early 1930s with two League titles and a Wembley win.

For the first two decades the players wore blue shirts trimmed with white, changing to a striking quartered design in 1887, but by the time The Wednesday, as they were then called, were elected into the Football League, the first of the famous blue and white stripes had been introduced. It was an exciting time for the club, every season producing a long FA Cup run, including a losing final against Blackburn and their first trophy in 1896, secured in a 2-1 win over Wolves.

By the turn of the century, neighbours United had taken both national trophies but this only spurred Wednesday to reach for even greater successes themselves. During a five-year spell, the Owls won two consecutive League championships, and reached two more Cup semi-finals followed by another Cup win over Everton.

The new nickname resulted from the club buying the Owlerton ground in Hillsborough, which has proved a wonderful, well respected stadium for the whole of the 20th century.

Between the two World Wars there were two spells in the second division, but sandwiched in between was a second golden era. Again Wednesday took two consecutive League titles, and this time followed them up with four third-place spots in five years, the last one accompanying a third Cup win, 4-2 against West Bromwich Albion.

Sadly, this coincided with the beginning of a long drought for the club. After the War, the Owls acquired the reputation of a yo-yo club, as relegation repeatedly followed promotion.

In the early 1960s, a great team was assembled around stars such as Peter Swan, Tony Kay and 'Bronco' Lane. There were several close misses in the League, but following a bribery scandal involving the three 'heroes', and a subsequent defeat in the 1966 FA Cup final against Everton, morale dipped and the club drifted down through the divisions. A new strip of blue shirts with white sleeves was tried, but it provided no reprieve from the gloom of the time, as was also the case of a return to the stripes.

It took two managers of great character and talent to return Wednesday to a hint of former glories. First Jack Charlton and then Howard Wilkinson shook the sleeping giant by the scruff of the neck and the Owls were back in the first division. There was a hiccup relegation year, but under the new manager Trevor Francis the team not only became a League force again, but provided great excitement in both the FA and League Cup competitions. After the departures of Francis and later David Pleat there was need of further consolidation, though now the club's potential looks likely to be fulfilled.

Wednesday (founded 1867) records and strips

	Division and position		Cup round reached
1881			4
1882			sf
1883			4
1884			2

	Division and position		Cup round reached
1904	1	1C	sf
1905	1	9	sf
1906	1	3	qf
1907	1	13	W
1908	1	5	1
1909	1	5	3
1910	1	11	1
1911	1	0	1
1912	1	5	1
1913	1	3	3
1914	1	18	qf
1915	1	7	3
1920	1	22R	1
1921	2	10	2
1922	2	10	1
1923	2	8	3

	Division and position		Cup round reached
1938	2	17	3
1939	2	3	5
1946			5
1947	2	20	5
1948	2	4	4
1949	2	8	4
1950	2	2P	3
1951	1	21R	3
1952	2	1P	3
1953	1	18	3
1954	1	19	sf
1955	1	22R	4

1992-1993

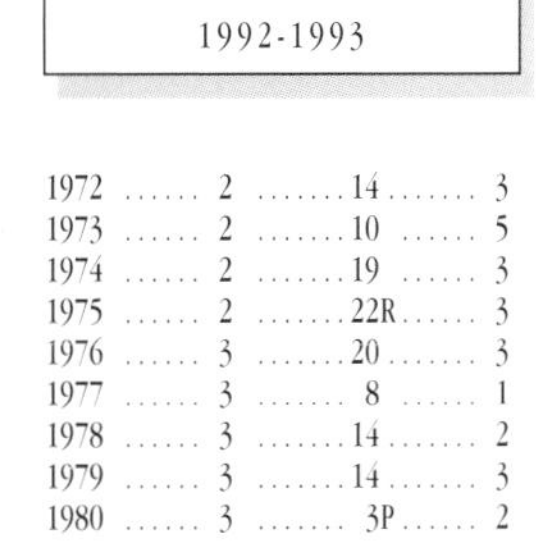

	Division and position		Cup round reached
1972	2	14	3
1973	2	10	5
1974	2	19	3
1975	2	22R	3
1976	3	20	3
1977	3	8	1
1978	3	14	2
1979	3	14	3
1980	3	3P	2

1872-1935

1969-1971

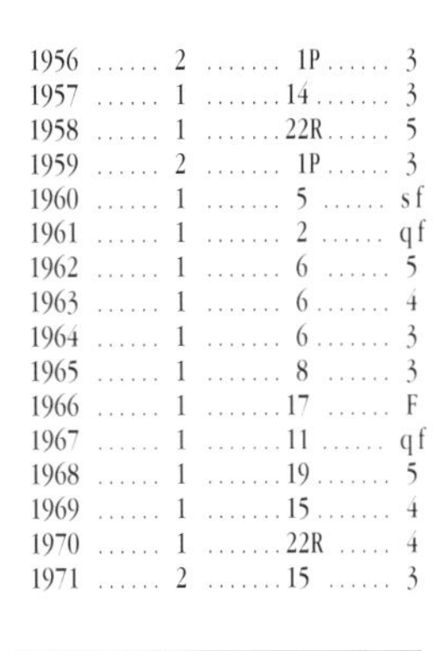

	Division and position		Cup round reached
1956	2	1P	3
1957	1	14	3
1958	1	22R	5
1959	2	1P	3
1960	1	5	sf
1961	1	2	qf
1962	1	6	5
1963	1	6	4
1964	1	6	3
1965	1	8	3
1966	1	17	F
1967	1	11	qf
1968	1	19	5
1969	1	15	4
1970	1	22R	4
1971	2	15	3

1998

1936-1955

1956-1963

1987-1989

	Division and position		Cup round reached
1981	2	10	3
1982	2	4	3
1983	2	6	sf
1984	2	2P	6
1985	1	8	5
1986	1	5	sf
1987	1	13	qf
1988	1	11	3
1989	1	15	4
1990	1	18R	4
1991	2	3P	5
1992	1	3	4
1993	Pr	7	F
1994	Pr	7	4
1995	Pr	13	4
1996	Pr	15	3
1997	Pr.	7	6
1998	Pr.	16	4

	Division and position		Cup round reached
1885			3
1886			
1887			
1888			qf
1889			qf
1890			F
1891			qf
1892			qf
1893	1	12	qf
1894	1	12	sf
1895	1	8	sf
1896	1	7	W
1897	1	6	1
1898	1	5	2
1899	1	18R	1
1900	2	1P	2
1901	1	8	1
1902	1	9	1
1903	1	1C	1

	Division and position		Cup round reached
1924	2	8	2
1925	2	14	2
1926	2	1P	3
1927	1	16	4
1928	1	14	5
1929	1	1C	4
1930	1	1C	sf
1931	1	3	4
1932	1	3	5
1933	1	3	3
1934	1	11	5
1935	1	3	W
1936	1	20	4
1937	1	22R	4

The blue pinstripes marked a return to the first division in 1987.

SHREWSBURY TOWN

Although the Shrews are relatively new to the Football League, they were in fact formed in 1886. However, football in Shrewsbury goes back even further. The boys of the famous public school in the town were playing at least half a century earlier and it was the ex-scholars who eventually formed the first club.

It was also from the school that the Town acquired their blue colours, and these were worn proudly for many years as the club progressed through local football to the Birmingham League and eventually on to the Midland League.

By the 1930s, Shrewsbury Town were sufficiently successful to apply regularly for Football League membership, but could never quite manage to collect enough votes.

After the Second World War, the extension of the third divisions was the opportunity for the club to break through into League football. At first life was a struggle and in many seasons they finished at the wrong end of the table. Not surprisingly the Town became founder members of the fourth division, but by this stage Arthur Rowley, the player-manager, provided the inspiration for a change of fortune. Rowley, a goal-scoring folk hero outside of division one, inspired instant promotion and the following season Shrewsbury were only one place off the second division.

In 1968 Rowley's team came even closer, eventually ending one point short. After this the big man called it a day and the momentum ended. In the 1970s the addition of amber to the strip did not help, as fourth division football returned to Gay Meadow. There was a quick promotion, but prospects remained limited until the arrival of manager Graham Turner. Within 12 months, he led them into the second division for the first time as well as achieving a wonderful run to the quarter-final of the FA Cup.

Shrewsbury looked the part, with high finishes in the League, another quarter-final Cup appearance and a striking shirt, made up of bold amber and blue stripes. However, even the most loyal of Salop's fans must have realised that it could not last, and when Turner left then so did the club's main hope for the future.

Strangely, as the quality faded, so did the club's colours; amber became yellow, which eventually became white. The blue and white, although traditional, only served to see the team drop back into the basement. In the early 1990s they were fighting their way back, but a club with such limited resources needed a manager with the quality of Rowley or Turner to take on the big boys again.

The bold amber and blue kit which marked Shrewsbury's brave fight in the second division.

Shrewsbury (founded 1886) records and strips

Year	Division	Position	Cup round
1963	3	15	3
1964	3	11	1
1965	3	16	5
1966	3	10	5
1967	3	6	3
1968	3	3	3
1969	3	17	1
1970	3	15	2

1975

1989

1886-1914

Year	Division	Position	Cup round
1978	3	11	3
1979	3	1P	qf
1980	2	13	3
1981	2	14	4
1982	2	18	qf
1983	2	9	4
1984	2	8	5
1985	2	8	3
1986	2	17	3

Year	Division	Position	Cup round
1994	N3	1P	2
1995	N2	18	1
1996	N2	18	4

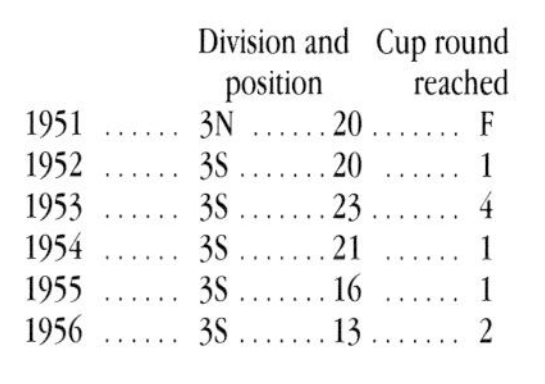

Year	Division and position		Cup round reached
1951	3N	20	F
1952	3S	20	1
1953	3S	23	4
1954	3S	21	1
1955	3S	16	1
1956	3S	13	2

1995

1960

1980

Year	Division	Position	Cup round
1997	N2	22R	1
1998	N3	13	1

1933

Year	Division	Position	Cup round
1971	3	13	2
1972	3	12	3
1973	3	15	2
1974	3	22R	1
1975	4	2P	1
1976	3	9	3
1977	3	10	3

Year	Division	Position	Cup round
1987	2	18	3
1988	2	18	4
1989	2	22R	3
1990	3	11	1
1991	3	18	5
1992	3	22R	1
1993	N3	9	2

1998

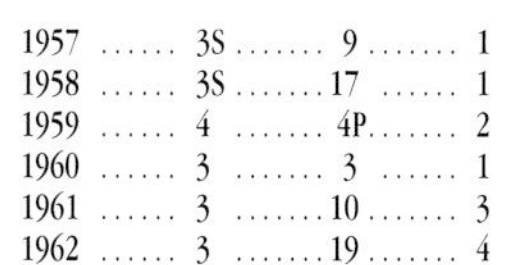

Year	Division	Position	Cup round
1957	3S	9	1
1958	3S	17	1
1959	4	4P	2
1960	3	3	1
1961	3	10	3
1962	3	19	4

Details of the 1981 strip with its broad stripes.

SOUTHAMPTON

In 1885 the Reverend A.B. Sole formed a club for the 'active recreation' of the members of the Young Men's Association of St Mary's Church, and so the Saints began their long climb to the heights of English football.

The team sported some fine, striking outfits in the early years. Although always in red and white, the shirt pattern changed from a sash to quarters and by 1895 it was halves. By this time the club's links with the church had diminished and Southampton had begun to employ professionals in an attempt to succeed in the Southern League.

Whether it was because many of these professionals were from Stoke is not certain, but it was at this stage that the jerseys finally included the stripes which were to find fame in the next century. By 1902, although still competing in the Southern League, the Saints had already played in their second FA Cup final. The two defeats by Bury and Sheffield United were obviously disappointing, but at the time nobody at the Dell expected to have such a long wait for the trophy to come to Southampton.

There were several more good campaigns, plus Southern League success, before the club gained admission to the third division (south) in 1920. Successes continued there, too, with promotion in the second season, but despite several near things the only future highlights before the Second World War were two more Cup semi-final appearances.

After the War, all the early promise, with the presence of talents such as Alf Ramsey and Charlie Wayman, suddenly drained away with a surprise relegation and it was not until the 1960s, under the guidance of Ted Bates, that the club's potential was finally realised. Derek Reeve's and George O'Brien's goal-scoring exploits were followed by those of international stars such as Ron Davies, Martin Chivers, Mick Channon and Terry Paine. The Saints moved from the third to the first division and probably only a leaky defence prevented a major honour coming to the Dell.

Strangely enough, it was during another sad collapse in the mid-1970s that the Saints finally made their Cup breakthrough. As second division 'minnows' Southampton shocked a star-studded Manchester United, Bobby Stokes' single goal winning the day. Two seasons later, they were back in the first division and, wearing a variety of unusual red and white shirts, have often impressed with their stylish play. Southampton's finest ever season probably came in 1984 when they were runners-up to the great Liverpool team in the League, and were pipped by the eventual winners, Everton, in the semi-final of the FA Cup.

Thereafter, limited resources prevented such heights being regularly repeated, but the Saints continued to create teams which produce good football and it would come as no great surprise if more trophies were to be paraded around the town.

In 1984 the Saints almost joined the select band of clubs to win the League and FA Cup double.

Southampton (founded 1885) records and strips

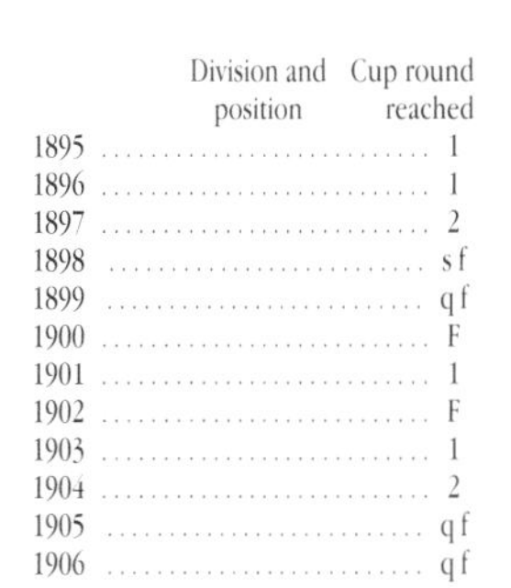

1885-1915

	Division and position		Cup round reached
1895			1
1896			1
1897			2
1898			sf
1899			qf
1900			F
1901			1
1902			F
1903			1
1904			2
1905			qf
1906			qf
1907			2
1908			sf
1909			1
1910			2
1911			1
1912			1
1913			1
1914			1
1915			3
1920			1
1921	3	2	3
1922	3S	1P	2
1923	2	11	qf
1924	2	5	3
1925	2	7	sf
1926	2	14	3
1927	2	13	sf
1928	2	17	3
1929	2	4	3
1930	2	7	3
1931	2	9	3
1932	2	14	3
1933	2	12	3
1934	2	14	3
1935	2	19	4
1936	2	17	3
1937	2	18	3
1938	2	15	3
1939	2	18	3
1946			4
1947	2	14	4
1948	2	3	qf
1949	2	3	3
1950	2	4	3
1951	2	12	3
1952	2	13	3
1953	2	21R	5
1954	3S	6	1
1955	3S	3	2
1956	3S	14	2
1957	3S	4	3
1958	3S	6	2
1959	3	14	3
1960	3	1P	4
1961	2	8	4
1962	2	6	3
1963	2	13	sf
1964	2	5	3
1965	2	4	4
1966	2	2P	3
1967	1	19	4
1968	1	15	4
1969	1	7	4
1970	1	11	4
1971	1	7	5
1972	1	19	3
1973	1	13	3
1974	1	20R	5
1975	2	13	3
1976	2	6	W
1977	2	9	5
1978	2	2P	4
1979	1	14	qf
1980	1	8	3
1981	1	6	5
1982	1	7	3
1983	1	12	3
1984	1	2	sf
1985	1	5	5
1986	1	14	sf
1987	1	12	3
1988	1	12	4
1989	1	13	3
1990	1	7	5
1991	1	14	5
1992	1	16	qf
1993	Pr	18	3
1994	Pr	18	3
1995	Pr	10	5
1996	Pr	17	6
1997	Pr.	16	3
1998	Pr.	12	3

1928-1938

1963-1973

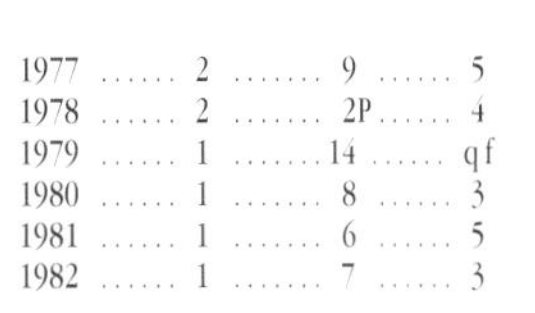

1976-1980

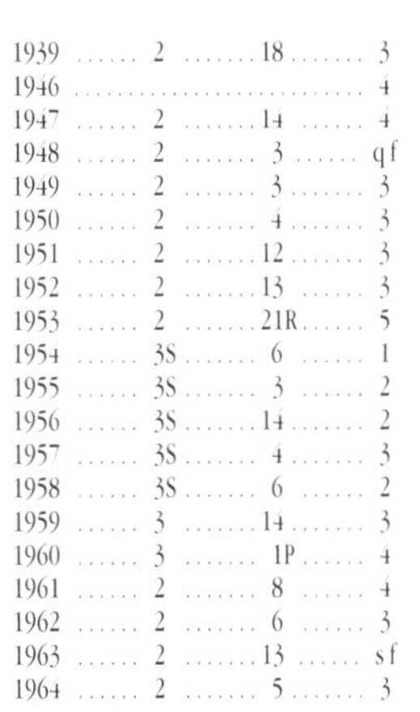

1983-1984

1987-1990

1998

Southampton are always happy to dabble with the latest strip innovations: the narrow hooped stockings of the 1960s remain unique to the Saints.

SOUTHEND UNITED

At the turn of the century, there were several good amateur teams playing football in Southend. Probably the best was Southend Athletic, who wore red shirts and were located in the south end of Prittlewell. However, none of them possessed the resources to develop into a big enough club to represent the area. Thus, using Roots Hall on the other side of Prittlewell as a base, Athletic amalgamated with many of their rivals to become Southend United in 1906.

The new club chose blue and white to differentiate themselves from the earlier Athletic and under the inspirational leadership of Bob Jack, they entered the Southern League.

By successfully remaining in the senior section, United were eventually elected into the third division when the Football League expanded in 1920. The early years were often a struggle, the only highlight being a fifth-round FA Cup appearance in 1926, and it was not until the beginning of the 1930s that Southend suggested better times for the fans, with two successive pushes for promotion. Sadly, the club didn't have the resources to continue to challenge and the Blues returned to mid-table anonymity until after the Second World War.

Although the post-War fans crowded into Roots Hall to see idols such as Sandy Anderson and Northern Ireland international Sammy McCrory, and playing standards certainly improved, the club still sought the missing element which would bring about promotion.

A change of strip was tried in 1960 – an all-white, Real Madrid-style trimmed with blue – but it was the return to the blue shirts later in the decade which witnessed the first change. Unfortunately the move was the wrong way and for the next two decades United became a bit of a yo-yo side, regularly commuting between the bottom two divisions.

The inconsistency was not only confined to the League results, for there were more changes to the club's outfit. Blue shirts became white with blue sleeves. Then the blue returned, trimmed with red, only to be replaced in the mid-1980s by a striking amber trim. By 1984 the smart new presentation was reflected in the playing standards. Southend completed yet another escape from the fourth division, but this time it was not accompanied by an instant collapse. In fact, Roots Hall witnessed an astonishing change of fortune when the club achieved promotion again and proceeded to take on the second division giants with great confidence.

Subsequently the team, clad in all-blue, found life more difficult, but the fans still loved the 'big time' and for a while enjoyed the regular visits from the television cameras before a double relegation undid all the good work.

Southend wore a simple but extremely smart kit on reaching the second division for the first time in 1991.

Southend (founded 1906) records and strips

	Division and position		Cup round reached
1910			2
1911			1
1912			q
1913			1

1905-1921

1914			1
1915			2
1920			1
1921	3	17	3
1922	3S	22	2
1923	3S	15	q

1928-1937

1924	3S	19	2
1925	3S	10	q
1926	3S	11	5
1927	3S	19	2
1928	3S	7	2
1929	3S	12	1
1930	3S	11	2
1931	3S	5	1
1932	3S	3	2
1933	3S	13	4

1938-1955

1934	3S	16	3
1935	3S	21	3
1936	3S	18	3
1937	3S	10	2
1938	3S	12	3

1959-1960

1939	3S	12	1
1946			1
1947	3S	8	3
1948	3S	9	1
1949	3S	18	4
1950	3S	3	3

1981

1951	3S	7	1
1952	3S	9	5
1953	3S	8	1
1954	3S	16	2
1955	3S	10	3

1985

1956	3S	4	4
1957	3S	7	4
1958	3S	7	3
1959	3	8	1
1960	3	12	2
1961	3	20	2
1962	3	16	1
1963	3	8	2
1964	3	14	1
1965	3	12	1
1966	3	21R	3
1967	4	6	1
1968	4	6	1
1969	4	7	4
1970	4	17	1
1971	4	18	3
1972	4	2P	2
1973	3	14	1
1974	3	12	3

1992

1975	3	18	3
1976	3	23R	5
1977	4	10	3
1978	4	2P	3
1979	3	13	3
1980	3	22R	2
1981	4	1P	1

1996

1982	3	7	1
1983	3	15	3
1984	3	22R	1
1985	4	20	1
1986	4	9	1
1987	4	3P	2
1988	3	17	1
1989	3	21R	1
1990	4	3P	1
1991	3	2P	1
1992	2	12	3
1993	N1	18	5
1994	N1	15	3
1995	N1	13	3
1996	N1	14	3
1997	N1	24R	3
1998	N2	24R	2

1998

The first introduction of the amber elements came in 1985 in the form of a chestband.

STOCKPORT COUNTY

Stockport is situated in a highly populated part of north Cheshire and should always have been able to attract large crowds. Sadly for the club, most of the mass movement of people on a Saturday afternoon has passed Edgeley Park by on the way to see one of the big Manchester clubs. Thus County have always had to struggle against the odds but, for the first 50 years in particular, the club had a reasonable amount of success.

It was founded in 1883 as Heaton Norris Rovers, and it took a few amalgamations and a change in Stockport's civic status before the club's current name was adopted. After spells in the Football Combination and the Lancashire League, County were elected to the second division of the Football League in 1900, but life there was often difficult. Years of constant re-election were followed by a spell when the players received no wages. But instead of quitting, they assumed a managerial role, picked their own teams and shared the gate money!

Progress in the years leading up to the First World War was non-existent, the club even failing to obtain re-election for one year. Much was the same afterwards and in 1921 relegation to the new third division (north) followed. For a while it looked as if Stockport's fortunes had changed as the broad blue and white striped shirted team won that first divisional title. But four year later, even with England's Harry Hardy in goal, they fell back again.

County spent the next years battling gamely, trying to regain their second division status. Now clad in all-blue shirts, they failed only by the odd point on several occasions before finally being promoted for just one season before the Second World War.

By the 1950s, Neil Franklin ended his career playing alongside bustling centre-forward Jack Conner as the club continued to be one of the more impressive in the division. The players were now wearing white shirts and black shorts, but on the arrival of the 1960s and a long stay in the fourth division, County had decided to replace the black with blue again. Indeed, in one brief highlight during this period, the 1966/67 promotion campaign, the white shirts were adorned with a blue chestband. This was a time in which many gimmicky attempts were made to attract support. Dancing girls and catchy slogans provided lots of publicity, but did not really impress the genuine fans.

By 1970 the club were back in the basement and the next two decades provided little more of note than several changes of strip. An all-white outfit was eventually given more blue until Stockport resembled the Argentinian national squad. However, in the 1990s, under the astute management of Danny Bergara, there was a great revival. Following promotion in 1991, there were many exciting seasons battling to regain the club's long lost second flight status before finally achieving it in 1997. The new shirts, a combination of stripes and solid blue looked well at this level.

After years struggling in the basement, the 1990s-style Stockport had finally regained that long lost second division status.

Stockport (founded 1883) records and strips

	Division and	position	Cup round reached
1901	2	17	q
1902	2	17	p
1903	2	17	q

1895-1907

1904	2	16L	p
1905			p
1906	2	10	1
1907	2	12	1

1920

1908	2	13	1
1909	2	18	2
1910	2	13	2
1911	2	17	p
1912	2	16	1
1913	2	19	1
1914	2	12	p
1915	2	14	1
1920	2	16	1
1921	2	22R	3
1922	3N	1P	1
1923	2	20	p

1931

1924	2	13	p
1925	2	19	2
1926	2	22R	3
1927	3N	6	1
1928	3N	3	2
1929	3N	2	3
1930	3N	2	3
1931	3N	7	2
1932	3N	12	1
1933	3N	3	2
1934	3N	3	2
1935	3N	7	5
1936	3N	5	1
1937	3N	1P	1
1938	2	22R	3

1952

1939	3N	9	4
1946			1
1947	3N	4	3
1948	3N	17	4
1949	3N	8	3
1950	3N	10	5
1951	3N	10	4
1952	3N	3	1
1953	3N	11	3
1954	3N	10	3
1955	3N	9	1
1956	3N	7	1
1957	3N	5	1
1958	3N	9	4
1959	3	21R	3
1960	4	10	2
1961	4	13	4
1962	4	16	1
1963	4	19	1

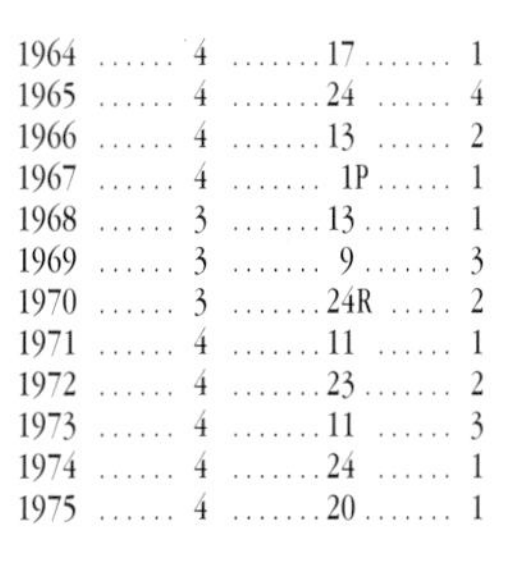

1964	4	17	1
1965	4	24	4
1966	4	13	2
1967	4	1P	1
1968	3	13	1
1969	3	9	3
1970	3	24R	2
1971	4	11	1
1972	4	23	2
1973	4	11	3
1974	4	24	1
1975	4	20	1

1967

1976	4	21	1
1977	4	14	1
1978	4	18	2
1979	4	17	3
1980	4	16	1
1981	4	20	1
1982	4	18	2
1983	4	16	1
1984	4	22	1
1985	4	22	1
1986	4	11	1
1987	4	19	1
1988	4	20	3
1989	4	20	1

1980

1992

1990	4	4	1
1991	4	2P	1
1992	3	5	2
1993	N2	6	3
1994	N2	4	4
1995	N2	11	1

1998

1996	N2	9	3
1997	N2	2P	4
1998	N1	8	4

During the 'black and white' era, the 1960 team wore strange, irregularly striped stockings.

STOKE CITY

For over 85 years many famous players, including the great Stanley Matthews, have proudly worn the red and white stripes of Stoke. To many clubs that would be a lifetime in itself, but the Potters had already existed for over 40 years by 1908, and in that time had worn many contrasting colours.

The club's first trophy after 109 years came in the 1972 League Cup Final.

It was a group of Old Carthusians who were employed by the local railway company who formed the first club. Unusually, they did not use their old school colours, but sported an exciting strip of claret and blue stripes with claret knickerbockers! Later, in the 1870s when the team began winning county competitions, there was a complete switch of style to narrow sky blue and black hoops, followed in turn by another radical change to narrow red and white stripes and black shorts three years later.

In 1883 Stoke acquired the Victoria Ground and five years later were founder members of the Football League. Of course, this event signalled yet another change and those early years of struggle were tackled in an all-claret shirt. There was one final flirtation with the claret and blue stripes before the now traditional strip was introduced in 1908.

Sadly, this coincided with bankruptcy and resignation from the League. Although Stoke enjoyed many stirring FA Cup runs, the League competition even in the second division proved too strong. It was not until after the First World War that the Potters returned to the League, this time in the second division, but they had to wait until the mid-1930s before a regular place in the top flight was re-established.

In the first year after the Second World War a highly promising team missed the League title by only two points, but sadly this squad was soon broken up as Matthews and Neil Franklin were sold. Without them the Potters were not the same force and it was back to the second flight until the early 1960s.

Manager Tony Waddington then broke all the rules by signing a whole string of 'old men' to face a long exhausting promotion battle. Matthews was re-signed, followed by Jimmy McIlroy and Dennis Viollet. The crowds poured back into the Victoria Ground and the veterans turned up trumps and took the second division championship. Although he also made full use of many talented youngsters, Waddington continued to sign seasoned campaigners and finally broke the club's trophy duck with the 1972 League Cup final win over Chelsea, with great contributions from George Eastham, Peter Dobing and Gordon Banks.

Despite the presence of Jimmy Greenhoff and Peter Shilton the momentum faded and slowly the Potters drifted back into mediocrity. Even playing around with the stripes could not halt the decline.

Happily the arrival of manager Lou Macari seemed to have blown the cobwebs off the old club and the humiliation of the third division ended. They reached the play-offs for the Premiership in 1996, but sadly went down again two years later.

Stoke (founded 1863) records and strips

1870-1908

1967-1972

1983-1985

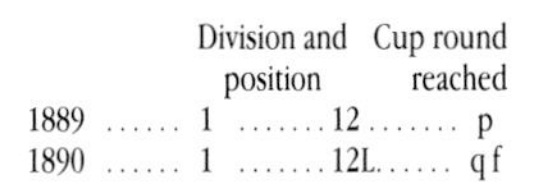

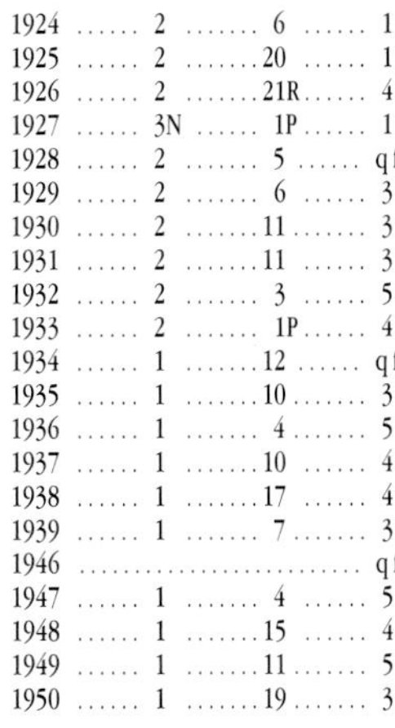

1908-1939

1957-1964

1975-1977

1998

	Division and	position	Cup round reached
1889	1	12	p
1890	1	12L	qf
1891			qf
1892	1	13	qf
1893	1	7	1
1894	1	11	2
1895	1	14	2
1896	1	6	qf
1897	1	13	2
1898	1	16	2
1899	1	12	sf
1900	1	9	1
1901	1	16	1
1902	1	16	qf
1903	1	6	qf
1904	1	16	1
1905	1	12	2
1906	1	10	2
1907	1	20R	1
1908	2	10	qf
1909			1
1910			1
1911			1
1912			p
1913			1
1914			1
1915			p
1920	2	10	1
1921	2	20	1
1922	2	2P	3
1923	1	21R	2
1924	2	6	1
1925	2	20	1
1926	2	21R	4
1927	3N	1P	1
1928	2	5	qf
1929	2	6	3
1930	2	11	3
1931	2	11	3
1932	2	3	5
1933	2	1P	4
1934	1	12	qf
1935	1	10	3
1936	1	4	5
1937	1	10	4
1938	1	17	4
1939	1	7	3
1946			qf
1947	1	4	5
1948	1	15	4
1949	1	11	5
1950	1	19	3
1951	1	13	5
1952	1	20	4
1953	1	21R	4
1954	2	11	4
1955	2	5	3
1956	2	13	5
1957	2	5	3
1958	2	11	5
1959	2	5	4
1960	2	17	3
1961	2	18	5
1962	2	8	4
1963	2	1P	3
1964	1	17	5
1965	1	11	4
1966	1	10	3
1967	1	12	3
1968	1	18	4
1969	1	19	5
1970	1	9	4
1971	1	13	sf
1972	1	17	sf
1973	1	15	3
1974	1	5	3
1975	1	5	3
1976	1	12	5
1977	1	21R	3
1978	2	7	3
1979	2	3P	3
1980	1	18	3
1981	1	11	3
1982	1	18	3
1983	1	13	4
1984	1	18	3
1985	1	22R	3
1986	2	10	3
1987	2	8	5
1988	2	11	3
1989	2	13	4
1990	2	24R	3
1991	3	14	2
1992	3	4	1
1993	N2	1P	1
1994	N1	10	4
1995	N1	11	3
1996	N1	4	3
1997	N1	12	3
1998	N1	23R	3

The last shirt worn by the club in the first division, a rare combination of pin stripes and solid red sleeves.

SUNDERLAND

The club's history started in 1879 when the Sunderland and District Teachers Association FC was formed to 'provide recreation and amusement' for its members. Those early players wore all-blue, but a general lack of success encouraged the team to adopt a red and white halved shirt in the hope that it might inspire some progress.

'The team of all talents' had by 1895 won three League championships in four years.

Sunderland, as they became in 1880, now had serious ambitions, encouraging Scottish professionals to settle in the area and approaching the newly formed Football League for membership. At first there was resistance from the League because of the geographical isolation, but eventually it relented and Sunderland replaced Stoke City in 1890.

The impact of the new club in the League was phenomenal. After a year of consolidation and now sporting the famous red and white stripes, Sunderland proceeded to dominate the English soccer scene for the next decade. In the first four years, the Wearsiders claimed three League titles and made three FA Cup semi-final appearances. They became known as the team of all talents, such was there all-round strength, but even when the side broke up, Sunderland were still strong enough to take two more titles before the First World War. The second in 1913 was almost a 'double', only the equally strong Aston Villa preventing their own earlier feat being repeated. Charles Buchan's men lost the Cup final by a single goal.

After the War, although Sunderland regularly challenged for honours, no more trophies came to Roker Park until the late 1930s. That great team, starring Raich Carter, Bobby Gurney and Patsy Gallacher, easily took the 1936 League title after being pipped by mighty Arsenal the previous year. The following season the FA Cup was paraded around the town after a convincing 3-1 win over Preston and more successes seemed likely when the Second World War interrupted the good run.

On the resumption of League competition, most of the team had gone and the club's attempt at buying success never really worked. Players such as Len Shackleton, Trevor Ford and later Brian Clough only occasionally provided a glimmer of hope. Worse was to follow, with relegation to the second division; white shorts were introduced, but after one promotion there came another drop.

Bob Stokoe reintroduced the old-style kit, and thanks to the heroics of Jim Montgomery, Sunderland shocked Leeds United by winning the 1973 FA Cup final by a single goal. However, although this team also returned to division one, yet again there was no real consolidation. There were to be more fancy outfits than practical planning. Even after the brave Cup failure against Liverpool at Wembley in 1992, the club looked more likely to spend more time in the League's lower reaches – until the arrival of Peter Reid.

Instant promotion was the result. Sadly this was followed by instant relegation. The club missed returning to the Premiership in 1998 only by losing a penalty shoot-out to Charlton in the play-off final.

Sunderland (founded 1879) records and strips

Year	Division	Position	Cup round reached
1890			1
1891	1	7	qf
1892	1	1C	sf
1893	1	1C	sf
1894	1	2	2
1895	1	1C	sf
1896	1	5	2
1897	1	15	2
1898	1	2	1
1899	1	7	2
1900	1	3	2
1901	1	2	1
1902	1	1C	2
1903	1	3	1
1904	1	6	1
1905	1	5	1
1906	1	14	3
1907	1	10	3
1908	1	16	1
1909	1	3	qf
1910	1	8	3
1911	1	3	1
1912	1	8	3
1913	1	1C	F
1914	1	7	qf
1915	1	8	1
1920	1	5	3
1921	1	12	1
1922	1	12	1
1923	1	2	2
1924	1	3	1
1925	1	7	2
1926	1	3	5
1927	1	3	3
1928	1	15	4
1929	1	4	3
1930	1	9	5
1931	1	11	sf
1932	1	13	4
1933	1	12	qf
1934	1	6	4
1935	1	2	4
1936	1	1C	3
1937	1	8	W
1938	1	8	sf
1939	1	16	5
1946			5
1947	1	9	3
1948	1	20	3
1949	1	8	4
1950	1	3	4
1951	1	12	qf
1952	1	12	3
1953	1	9	4
1954	1	18	3
1955	1	4	sf
1956	1	9	sf
1957	1	20	4
1958	1	21R	3
1959	2	15	3
1960	2	16	3
1961	2	6	qf
1962	2	3	4
1963	2	3	5
1964	2	2P	qf
1965	1	15	4
1966	1	19	3
1967	1	17	5
1968	1	16	3
1969	1	17	3
1970	1	21R	3
1971	2	13	3
1972	2	5	4
1973	2	6	W
1974	2	6	3
1975	2	4	4
1976	2	1P	qf
1977	1	20R	3
1978	2	6	3
1979	2	4	4
1980	2	2P	3
1981	1	17	3
1982	1	19	4
1983	1	16	3
1984	1	13	4
1985	1	21R	3
1986	2	18	4
1987	2	20R	3
1988	3	1P	3
1989	2	11	3
1990	2	6P(pl)	3
1991	1	19R	3
1992	2	18	F
1993	N1	21	4
1994	N1	12	4
1995	N1	20	4
1996	N1	1P	3
1997	Pr.	18R	3
1998	N1	3	4

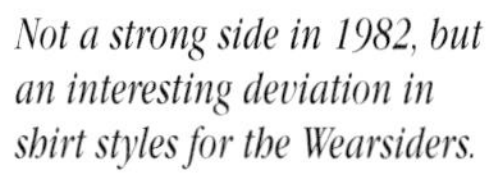

Not a strong side in 1982, but an interesting deviation in shirt styles for the Wearsiders.

1879-1927

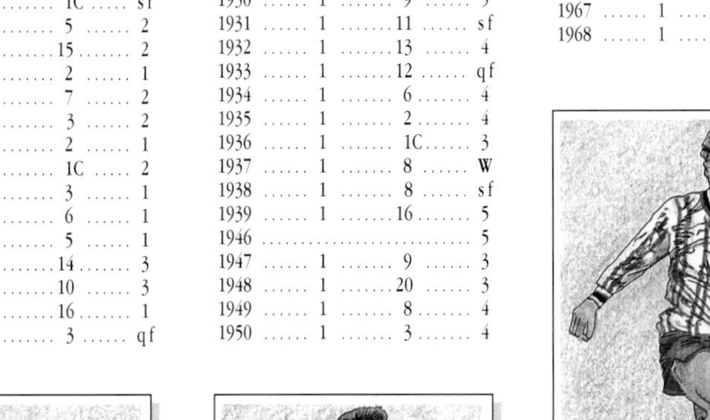

1972-1981

1995-1996

1981-1983

1928-1939

1961-1972

1998

SWANSEA CITY

'The Welsh Real Madrid' looked the part when the club finished sixth in the first division in 1982.

Although rugby union has dominated the sports world in South Wales – and in Swansea there was a particularly strong club – it seems strange that the fledgling soccer club should have adopted the same all-white strip as their rivals in the other code. However, that was the decision back in 1900. Soon the enthusiastic Swans were joined by others in the area and a healthy local league was established.

Twelve years later, following a public meeting the present club was founed and after the First World War, Swansea Town (City was introduced only when Swansea was later granted city status) were elected to the third division. Probably inspired by the success of Cardiff City, the Swans pushed hard for promotion themselves. In 1925 they were well rewarded, going up in style, and following up with a season which saw an FA Cup semi-final plus a brave attempt to go one stage further in the League.

The following seasons were less dramatic, other than ensuring that the club avoided relegation, but after the Second World War Swansea found it difficult to reorganise, and did, in fact, drop into the third division. Eventually, led by manager Billy McCandless, Swansea teams which included Ivor and Len Allchurch, Cliff Jones, Terry Medwin and Mel Charles regularly threatened to win through to the first division. But financial limitations demanded that all these stars ultimately had to be sold.

At this stage black shorts had been introduced, as they had in the 1930s, but the all-white tradition was strong, and returned with the swan image literally copied down to the inclusion of the occasional orange trim.

After an exciting 1964 FA Cup semi-final season, which included an almost unbelievable win at Anfield, there was a gradual decline and for the next 13 years the club see-sawed between the bottom two divisions. The City (from 1970) were languishing in division four when ex-Liverpool hero John Toshack took over. The big Welshman had obviously had his ear to keyhole of the Anfield boot room because his professionalism and organisational skills, plus his contacts at the higher levels, provided an instant transformation at Vetch Field.

It took just four years to take the three promotional steps to the first division, and in that first season in the top flight Swansea made a bold effort to take the title itself. Eventually they slipped back to sixth place, but in their stylish black-trimmed all-white strip they impressed many people. It was, however, much too sudden to last, and sadly it only took four more years to slip all the way back.

The 1990s brought some renewed optimism when the Swans were once more on the fringe of promotion to the second flight, but soccer in this area still has to fight to match the success of the rugby code.

By 1998 even the efforts of another ex-Liverpool favourite Jan Molby, as player-manager, had failed to halt another dramatic decline.

Swansea (founded 1912) records and strips

	Division and position		Cup round reached
1921	3	5	2
1922	3S	10	3

1910

	Division and position		Cup round reached
1923	3S	3	p
1924	3S	4	2
1925	3S	1P	2
1926	2	5	sf
1927	2	12	qf
1928	2	6	3
1929	2	19	4
1930	2	15	3

1925

	Division and position		Cup round reached
1931	2	20	3
1932	2	15	3

1933

	Division and position		Cup round reached
1933	2	10	3
1934	2	19	5
1935	2	17	4
1936	2	13	3
1937	2	16	5

1955

	Division and position		Cup round reached
1938	2	18	3
1939	2	19	3
1946			3
1947	2	21R	4
1948	3S	5	3
1949	3S	1P	2
1950	2	8	4
1951	2	18	3
1952	2	19	5
1953	2	11	3
1954	2	20	4
1955	2	10	5
1956	2	10	3

	Division and position		Cup round reached
1957	2	10	3
1958	2	19	3
1959	2	11	3
1960	2	12	4
1961	2	7	5
1962	2	20	3
1963	2	15	4
1964	2	19	sf
1965	2	22R	5

1964

	Division and position		Cup round reached
1966	3	17	1
1967	3	21R	2
1968	4	15	4
1969	4	10	3
1970	4	3P	3
1971	3	11	4
1972	3	13	4
1973	3	23R	1
1974	4	14	1
1975	4	22	1
1976	4	11	1
1977	4	5	1
1978	4	3P	3

1971

	Division and position		Cup round reached
1979	3	3P	3
1980	2	12	5

1982

	Division and position		Cup round reached
1981	2	3P	3
1982	1	6	3
1983	1	21R	3
1984	2	21R	3

1998

	Division and position		Cup round reached
1985	3	20	1
1986	3	24R	2
1987	4	12	4
1988	4	6P(pl)	2
1989	3	12	2
1990	3	17	3
1991	3	20	3
1992	3	19	2
1993	N2	5	4
1994	N2	13	1
1995	N2	10	4
1996	N2	22R	1
1997	N3	5	1
1998	N3	20	1

Just as tangerine belongs to Blackpool, then the all-white really belongs to Swansea, despite what they say at Elland Road.

SWINDON TOWN

Despite being located in something of a footballing backwater, Swindon Town have continued to overcome the problems of limited resources, occasionally achieving undreamed-of success.

Founded in 1881 by the Rev. W Pitt, the club soon thrived as the town became the centre of Wiltshire football, and by the end of the century professionals were being taken on as the Railwaymen's ambitions grew. These players wore either the white or bright green jerseys favoured at that time, but in 1904 the club's colours were changed to red with white shorts, a combination which has remained until today.

Swindon had just gone through a bad time and only devoted clubmen such as Sam Allen saved them from extinction. The red shirts were a symbol of new hope, and from then things improved dramatically. In 1910 and 1912 the Railwaymen reached FA Cup semi-finals and it was only the onset of war which prevented greater successes.

The club became founder members of the third division and throughout the 1920s were one of the dominant forces. Standards slipped in the next decade but the team was usually a match for most clubs on its day.

After the Second World War, things continued very much in the same vein until the early 1960s. Manager Bert Head assembled a bright young team, including Don Rogers and Mike Summerbee. Many came through the youth scheme, based on that at Manchester United, and this was not the only similarity between the clubs. Swindon would happily echo all the sartorial changes made by the Old Trafford club during this period.

At the end of the decade, the Robins even repeated United's tradition of success at Wembley when they defeated Arsenal 3-1 in an exciting League Cup final. In the same season a second promotion campaign was completed with the club surviving twice as long as after a previous rise four years earlier. Despite these successes there had been many changes of staff at the club, stars being sold to balance the books. The only form of continuity at the club was the presence of John Trollope, who during 20 years as the fans' favourite clocked up over 750 first-team appearances.

In 1985 the Wiltshire club were depressed members of the fourth division when Lou Macari was engaged as manager to change their fortunes. This he did in dramatic style as he took Swindon back to the second division. When he moved on, Ossie Ardiles continued the improvement until it looked as if first division status had finally been achieved in 1990 via the play-off. Sadly for the Robins, earlier financial irregularities were punished by the League's decision to keep them down.

Normally, that would have spelt the end for such a positive period, but the appointment of Glen Hoddle as player-manager brought renewed impetus and in 1993 Swindon ascended to Premier League status. Alas, Hoddle went and the club, probably overstretched, suffered two consecutive relegations. Hopefully, Steve McMahon's managerial enthusiasm will lead them all the way back.

In 1969 Swindon were promoted and became League Cup winners.

Swindon (founded 1881) records and strips

1881-1936

1972-1975

1993

1962-1972

1998

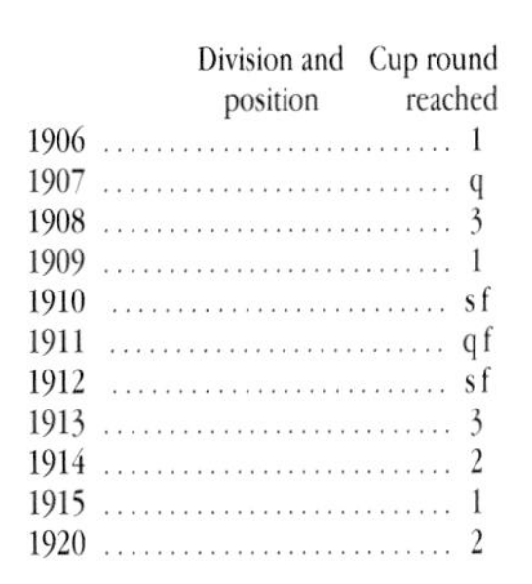

1937-1955

1989

Year	Division and position		Cup round reached
1906			1
1907			q
1908			3
1909			1
1910			sf
1911			qf
1912			sf
1913			3
1914			2
1915			1
1920			2
1921	3	4	2
1922	3S	6	2
1923	3S	9	1
1924	3S	6	qf
1925	3S	4	1
1926	3S	6	4
1927	3S	5	1
1928	3S	6	4
1929	3S	10	5
1930	3S	14	4
1931	3S	12	1
1932	3S	17	1
1933	3S	22	3
1934	3S	8	3
1935	3S	16	4
1936	3S	19	1
1937	3S	13	2
1938	3S	8	4
1939	3S	9	2
1946			1
1947	3S	4	2
1948	3S	16	5
1949	3S	4	3
1950	3S	14	2
1951	3S	17	2
1952	3S	16	5
1953	3S	18	3
1954	3S	19	2
1955	3S	21	1
1956	3S	24	4
1957	3S	23	2
1958	3S	4	1
1959	3	15	2
1960	3	16	1
1961	3	16	2
1962	3	19	1
1963	3	2P	4
1964	2	14	5
1965	2	21R	3
1966	3	7	3
1967	3	8	5
1968	3	9	4
1969	3	2P	3
1970	2	5	qf
1971	2	12	4
1972	2	11	3
1973	2	16	4
1974	2	22R	3
1975	3	4	4
1976	3	19	3
1977	3	11	4
1978	3	10	3
1979	3	5	4
1980	3	10	4
1981	3	17	2
1982	3	22R	3
1983	4	8	4
1984	4	15	4
1985	4	8	1
1986	4	1P	1
1987	3	3P	4
1988	2	12	4
1989	2	6	4
1990	2	4	3
1991	2	21	3
1992	2	8	5
1993	N1	5P(pl)	3
1994	Pr	22R	3
1995	N1	21R	4
1996	N2	1P	5
1997	N1	19	3
1998	N1	18	3

One of Swindon's many Manchester United look-alikes was the black, red and white stockings of 1973.

TORQUAY UNITED

Unlike France's Cote d'Azur, the English 'Riviera' has never boasted a club to take on the might of the land. In fact, in the 19th century there was little interest in the game at all in the Devon seaside resort and it was not until 1898 that the professional club's predecessor was formed. There were lots of minor clubs in the area at this stage, and two, Torquay Town and Babbacombe, who were the most ambitious, amalgamated to form Torquay United in 1921 in an effort to impress the football authorities.

The new club took black and white stripes as their colours, and after several seasons of steady improvement in the Southern League, the 'Magpies' were eventually elected into the Football League in 1927. The first season was a portent of what was to come, the club finishing bottom of the third division (south) and having to apply for re-election. However, the other clubs supported them well, and although United continued to struggle, no further application was required before the Second World War.

Just before the outbreak of hostilities, the striped shirts were exchanged for plain white and these were retained in peacetime when playing standards improved slightly.

In 1954 it was decided that the club should echo more directly the town's image – i.e. the sea and sand enjoyed by tourists, and the new gold silk shirts with blue sleeves became an instant success with the fans. It was soon obvious that players were impressed, too. After two earlier near misses, in 1957 only the superior goal average of Alf Ramsey's Ipswich prevented promotion to the second division. Sadly, the next season even the goal-scoring feats of Sammy Collins could not prevent a slip into the fourth division.

United suffered the frustrations of a series of yo-yo seasons before promotion to division three in 1966 signalled a golden period in many senses of the word. The strip was all-gold with blue trimmings, and the team again was just denied a place in division two on several occasions. Four and three points respectively, during two of these years, could have changed Torquay's history.

Once again even a major goal-scorer failed to maintain the momentum, and the efforts of Robin Stubbs could not prevent another fall into the fourth division. Torquay have tried to re-evaluate their approach on several occasions. The strip has varied between a return to white shirts and a subsequent reintroduction of the gold and blue, but with no great effect.

Since the mid-1980s, the club's geographical and resulting cash crises have usually found United at or near the foot of the lowest level. Despite bravely sporting a striped shirt incorporating all the traditional colours, Torquay faced a fight for their very existence as the 1990s progressed, although in 1998 there were some signs of improvement.

In the late 1960s, Torquay went close to promotion to the second division on several occasions.

Torquay (founded 1898) records and strips

	Division and position		Cup round reached
1928	3S	22	Sc
1929	3S	18	2

1898-1937

1930	3S	19	1
1931	3S	11	3
1932	3S	19	1
1933	3S	10	2
1934	3S	20	2

1938-1954

1935	3S	10	2
1936	3S	10	2
1937	3S	20	1
1938	3S	20	1
1939	3S	19	2
1946			1
1947	3S	11	1
1948	3S	18	3
1949	3S	9	4
1950	3S	5	2
1951	3S	20	1
1952	3S	11	2

1953	3S	12	1
1954	3S	13	1
1955	3S	8	4
1956	3S	5	3
1957	3S	2	3

1954-1958

1958	3S	21	2
1959	4	12	3
1960	4	3P	2
1961	3	12	2
1962	3	21R	2
1963	4	6	2
1964	4	6	2
1965	4	11	3
1966	4	3P	1

1969

1967	3	7	1
1968	3	4	1
1969	3	6	2
1970	3	13	1
1971	3	10	4
1972	3	23R	3
1973	4	18	2
1974	4	16	1
1975	4	14	1
1976	4	9	1
1977	4	16	1
1978	4	9	1
1979	4	11	3
1980	4	9	2
1981	4	17	3
1982	4	15	1
1983	4	12	4

1984	4	9	1
1985	4	24	2
1986	4	24	2
1987	4	23	1
1988	4	5	3
1989	4	14	3
1990	4	15	4
1991	4	7	1
1992	4	23	2
1993	N3	19	1

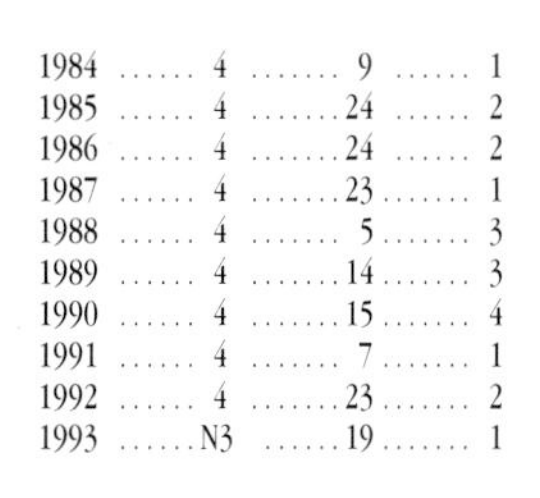

This 1990s shirt incorporates all the earlier colour schemes.

1976

1992

1994	N3	6	2
1995	N3	13	2
1996	N3	24	2
1997	N3	21	1

1998	N3	5	2

1987

1998

TOTTENHAM HOTSPUR

It's hard to believe that the great lilywhite teams of the 20th century could have made such a slow, humble start to their club's history. In 1882 a cricket club from nearby Percy Park called itself Hotspur after Henry Percy, who was renowned for his valour in battle, and within a few months started a football section to occupy the winter months. Nobody in north-east London would dare to admit now but this early team, for a while, wore the same blue and red shirts as their counterparts at Arsenal!

This early club lapsed but was quickly re-formed and, now clad in chocolate and amber halves, continued to upgrade standards until finally engaging professionals just before the turn of the century. Spurs entered the Southern League and it was from this base that they shocked the northern giants by winning the 1901 Cup final against Sheffield United, becoming the only non-League side to win the Cup since the League was formed.

It was at this time that the famous white shirts were introduced but it was another eight years before Tottenham were finally accepted into the Football League. Of course, a club of Spurs' standing just had to obtain instant promotion, but then, strangely, they struggled. Indeed, it was only after a temporary relegation that things improved. In 1921 a single goal versus Wolves resulted in a second Cup win, which was followed by a League runners-up spot. However, even then, before the Second World War there were more seasons spent in the second division than the first.

On the resumption of peacetime football, the club's history and fortunes took a huge upturn. Manager Arthur Rowe devised the 'push and run' style and employing such talent as Alf Ramsey, Ron Burgess and Eddie Baily, proceeded not just to take Spurs back to the first division but to win the title itself the following year.

A decade later a member of this side, Bill Nicholson became the manager and assembled one of the finest teams in the history of the game. The League and FA Cup double-winning team was the complete combination, featuring a tough defence, creative midfield and an attack which seemed to be able to score at will. Once this team began to break up Spurs were never quite the same League force again, despite several near things. However, in the cup competitions the club became the most successful in the country.

When Jimmy Greaves arrived he picked up two FA Cup winner's medals and a Cup Winners' Cup gong against Atletico Madrid in 1963. In the 1970s came League Cup (twice) and UEFA Cup wins and, a decade later, a further UEFA Cup, two FA Cups plus one runners-up spot. Even in the bleak early 1990s, in which the club was almost faced with extinction, Terry Venables still managed to inspire an eighth FA Cup victory.

As Spurs seem capable of winning at least one major trophy in a year ending in the number one, they could hope to begin the next millenium with success. But, of course they are looking for more glory nights before that happened.

The famous 'double' strip of 1961.

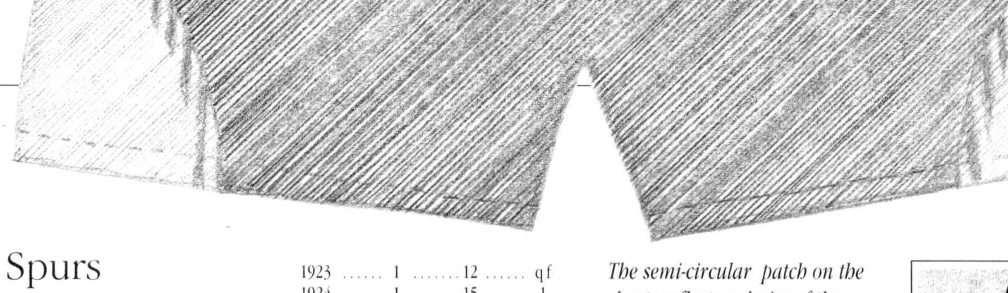

Spurs (founded 1882) records and strips

1923	1	12	qf
1924	1	15	1
1925	1	12	3
1926	1	15	4
1927	1	13	3
1928	1	21R	5
1929	2	10	3

The semi-circular patch on the shorts reflects a desire of the 1990s club to regain some of the old individuality.

1987

1988	1	13	4
1989	1	6	3
1990	1	3	3
1991	1	10	**W**

1882-1896

1959-1963

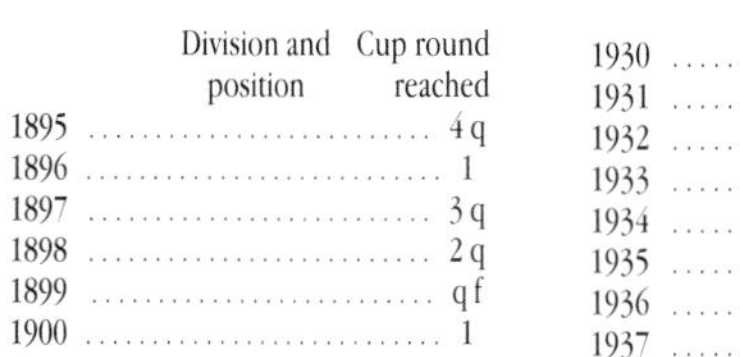

	Division and position		Cup round reached
1895			4q
1896			1
1897			3q
1898			2q
1899			qf
1900			1

1930	2	12	3
1931	2	3	4
1932	2	8	3
1933	2	2P	4
1934	1	3	5
1935	1	22R	5
1936	2	5	qf
1937	2	10	qf

1962	1	3	**W**
1963	1	2	3
1964	1	4	3
1965	1	6	5
1966	1	8	5
1967	1	3	**W**
1968	1	7	5
1969	1	6	qf
1970	1	11	4
1971	1	3	qf
1972	1	6	qf

1992

1992	1	15	3
1993	Pr	8	sf
1994	Pr	15	4
1995	Pr	7	sf
1996	Pr	8	5
1997	Pr.	10	3
1998	Pr.	14	4

1896-1957

1965-1974

1901			**W**
1902			1
1903			qf
1904			qf
1905			2
1906			3
1907			3
1908			1
1909	2	2P	3
1910	1	15	3
1911	1	15	2
1912	1	12	1
1913	1	17	2
1914	1	17	2
1915	1	20R	2
1920	2	1P	qf
1921	1	6	**W**
1922	1	2	sf

1938	2	5	qf
1939	2	8	4
1946			3
1947	2	6	3
1948	2	8	sf
1949	2	5	3
1950	2	1P	5
1951	1	1C	3
1952	1	2	4
1953	1	10	sf
1954	1	16	qf
1955	1	16	5
1956	1	18	sf
1957	1	2	5
1958	1	3	4
1959	1	18	5
1960	1	3	5
1961	1	1C	**W**

1973	1	8	4
1974	1	11	3
1975	1	19	3
1976	1	9	3
1977	1	22R	3
1978	2	3P	3
1979	1	11	qf
1980	1	14	qf
1981	1	10	**W**
1982	1	4	**W**
1983	1	4	5
1984	1	8	4
1985	1	3	4
1986	1	10	5
1987	1	3	F

1998

TRANMERE ROVERS

Not a lot is known about the early years of the club. From the formation in 1883, by some local cricketers, it was over eight years before they took part in regular league competitions. In the first five years, both as Belmont and Tranmere Rovers, the team sported blue shirts, but by 1889, in an effort to improve performances, it was decided to wear maroon and orange halved jerseys 'to dazzle their opponents'. It obviously worked as the Rovers had won the Liverpool Shield four times by 1905.

Perhaps opponents had complained about some unfair advantage, because by this time the blue shirts and white shorts had been reintroduced, and in some form or other this combination has remained ever since.

Tranmere's progress improved over the years, so that when the third division (north) was formed the club became founder members. Now wearing royal blue shirts, Rovers overcame early difficulties to become one of the stronger teams in their flight and in 1938 were promoted to division two. Sadly, they were out of their depth at that level and when the League recommenced after the Second World War, they were back in the third division.

In the past, the club had had to sell its starlets to survive, the proximity of the two Liverpool clubs taking much of their own potential support. In this way 'Dixie' Dean and 'Pongo' Waring had been lost. But in the 1940s and 1950s one man remained to create a unique record. Harold Bell played in 401 consecutive League matches (plus 58 Cup ties) and went on to record 595 appearances altogether.

Three years after Bell had retired in 1959, new manager Dave Russell, inspired by Real Madrid, proceeded to change the club's outfit. He put it in simple terms. 'Liverpool are red, Everton are blue and now Tranmere are all-white".

Obviously, it would take much more than a change of club colours to overcome the dominance of the two clubs on the other side of the Mersey. Both Liverpool clubs were beginning an outstanding period and further fiddling with blue trimmings over the next two decades could do nothing to change Tranmere's constant see-sawing between the bottom two divisions.

For a while, manager Bryan Hamilton reintroduced the old blue-shirted style; however, with Rovers still in the fourth division, when the Peter Johnson-John King combination took over in 1987 the all-white strip returned because it was associated with a period of relative success. It was an inspired symbolic move. The club's status has changed beyond recognition. Promotion to the third division was followed by two successful Wembley appearances, first the Leyland Daf Cup final, then a play-off final for promotion to division two.

The club consolidated at their new exalted level and with experienced internationals such as John Aldridge – later as player/manager – still dreamed of going all the way to the Premier League.

The 1990s Tranmere side was the most successful ever in the club's history.

Tranmere (founded 1883) records and strips

1884-1921

1979-1981

1989-1993

1921-1957

1971-1977

1984-1985

1998

	Division and	position	Cup round reached
1922	3N	18	q
1923	3N	16	q
1924	3N	12	p
1925	3N	21	p
1926	3N	7	p
1927	3N	9	1
1928	3N	5	3
1929	3N	7	2
1930	3N	12	1
1931	3N	3	1
1932	3N	4	3
1933	3N	11	4
1934	3N	7	4f
1935	3N	6	2
1936	3N	3	4
1937	3N	19	1
1938	3N	1P	3
1939	2	22R	3
1946			2
1947	3N	10	1
1948	3N	18	2
1949	3N	11	1
1950	3N	5	2
1951	3N	4	2
1952	3N	11	4
1953	3N	12	3
1954	3N	14	3
1955	3N	19	1
1956	3N	16	2
1957	3N	23	1
1958	3N	11	3
1959	3	7	2
1960	3	20	1
1961	3	21R	2
1962	4	15	1
1963	4	8	3
1964	4	7	1
1965	4	5	1
1966	4	5	1
1967	4	4P	2
1968	3	9	5
1969	3	7	1
1970	3	16	4
1971	3	18	1
1972	3	19	4
1973	3	10	2
1974	3	16	2
1975	3	22R	3
1976	4	4P	1
1977	3	14	1
1978	3	12	1
1979	3	23R	2
1980	4	15	2
1981	4	21	2
1982	4	11	1
1983	4	19	3
1984	4	10	1
1985	4	6	2
1986	4	19	2
1987	4	20	2
1988	4	14	1
1989	4	2P	3
1990	3	4	1
1991	3	5P(pl)	2
1992	2	14	3
1993	N1	4	4
1994	N1	5	3
1995	N1	5	4
1996	N1	13	3
1997	N1	11	3
1998	N1	14	5

The dazzling early maroon and orange jerseys contrast greatly with the smart, plain white shirts of recent seasons.

WALSALL

In a long and complicated early history, the Walsall club had many forms. At different times, Walsall Town and Walsall Swifts were the local dominant force and in 1888, in an attempt to improve their status, the two clubs amalgamated. It was as Walsall Town Swifts that the club joined the second division of the League five years later.

During this period various strips were worn in red and white. Halves followed the original striped shirts, and a later all-red shirt was adorned with a white yoke. Whether these changes unsettled the Saddlers is not certain, but after three seasons they failed to be re-elected. After a gap of one year, and now called Walsall FC, the club returned but again for only five seasons.

By 1921 Walsall regained their League status as founder members of the third division (north), but despite early promise, struggled until 1933. Now sporting a claret and blue strip and attempting to emulate midland neighbours Aston Villa, the club twice went close in promotion chases, but probably earned a more lasting fame by beating the mighty Arsenal in the FA Cup.

Although these heady days did not last, two more good seasons immediately after the Second World War suggested a permanent improvement was imminent. In fact, the red and white hoops of this team had long since changed by the time real success arrived. In 1960, red-shirted forwards such as Tony Richards and Colin Taylor ran riot in the fourth division, scoring 102 goals, and in the following season failed to equal that total by only four goals as they were promoted for the second year running.

In the rarefied atmosphere of the second division, the Saddlers lasted only two seasons, but back in the third division still managed to continue to discover fine forwards such as Allan Clarke. Sadly, as financial pressures obliged many of these potential stars to be sold off, no further promotions looked possible.

White shirts came and went, the red shirts returned, but there was still no evidence of success on the pitch. It took a change of control at board level to effect a move in the right direction and in the club's centenary year the Saddlers were back in the second division. At the start of that 1988/89 season, clad in a smart all-white kit and with ambitions to build a smart new stadium, the Saddlers must have been full of optimism. But instead of consolidating their position, they experienced a traumatic drop back to the fourth division.

Whether it was the grand plan which distracted the players from their task or just bad luck, was uncertain. But come the 1990s at least Walsall had their new ground , the purpose-built Bescot Stadium, and were in the first stages of trying to improve their League position again.

The fine Walsall team of 1960 progressed from the fourth to the second division in two seasons.

Walsall (founded 1888) records and strips

	Division and position		Cup round reached
1893	2	12	p
1894	2	10	p
1895	2	14L	q
1896			p
1897	2	12	p
1898	2	10	1
1899	2	6	p
1900	2	12	1
1901	2	16L	p
1922	3N	8	1
1923	3N	3	p
1924	3N	17	p
1925	3N	19	p
1926	3N	21	1
1927	3N	14	3
1928	3S	18	1
1929	3S	14	3
1930	3S	17	4
1931	3S	17	3
1932	3N	16	1
1933	3N	5	4
1934	3N	4	2
1935	3N	14	3
1936	3N	10	3
1937	3S	17	4
1938	3S	21	2
1939	3S	21	5
1946			1
1947	3S	5	3
1948	3S	3	3
1949	3S	14	4
1950	3S	19	1
1951	3S	15	1
1952	3S	24	1
1953	3S	24	1
1954	3S	24	3
1955	3S	23	3
1956	3S	20	3
1957	3S	15	1
1958	3S	20	1
1959	4	6	1
1960	4	1P	2
1961	3	2P	1
1962	2	14	4
1963	2	21R	3
1964	3	19	1
1965	3	19	1
1966	3	9	4
1967	3	12	3
1968	3	7	4
1969	3	13	3
1970	3	12	3
1971	3	20	2
1972	3	9	4
1973	3	17	2
1974	3	15	2
1975	3	8	5
1976	3	7	1
1977	3	15	3
1978	3	6	5
1979	3	22R	1
1980	4	2P	2
1981	3	20	2
1982	3	20	2
1983	3	10	3
1984	3	6	1
1985	3	11	3
1986	3	6	3
1987	3	8	5
1988	3	3P	2
1989	2	24R	3
1990	3	24R	3
1991	4	16	2
1992	4	15	1
1993	N3	5	1
1994	N3	10	2
1995	N3	2P	3
1996	N2	11	4
1997	N2	12	1
1998	N2	19	4

1966-1972

1988

1888-1939

1980

1998

1947

1959-1960

The irregular hooped tops of the 1960 stockings were a one-off at the time.

WATFORD

Football in Watford goes back as far as 1865 when Hertfordshire Rangers dominated the local scene. Captain RC Barker played in goal for England versus Scotland, and the Rangers' FA Cup exploits were responsible for encouraging other clubs to develop in the area. One such club, Watford Rovers, eventually decided to amalgamate with the Rangers in 1891 and Watford FC were born.

The Elton John - Graham Taylor inspired team reached the FA Cup final a year after being runners-up in the League.

The new club's first strip was a dazzling red, yellow and green hooped special.

It was probably an attempt to include all the previous colours and it was sufficiently impressive to see Watford enter the Southern League. But later, with the backing of the council and inspired by the famous player-manager John Goodall, it was in white shirts that the team played until the First World War.

Yet another strip change had taken place by the time the Hornets entered the third division, with other Southern League clubs in 1920. But the black and white stripes enjoyed only mixed success until the fickle board proposed another change of colours in 1927. At least the new royal blue shirts were retained for another two decades and by the late 1930s Watford had a team consistently challenging for promotion. In 1938 they were just three tantalising points short of second division experience.

After the Second World War the blue became turquoise, a colour probably unique to the Hertfordshire club, but playing standards had slumped, and by 1959 Watford had become founder members of the fourth division. However, the 1960s proved to be a watershed in the club's history and it started with the pairing of former Arsenal star Cliff Holton with Dennis Uphill. Their 72 goals turned a mediocre start to the 1960 season into a glorious promotion year, and during the rest of the decade Watford illustrated the capacity to improve further. The new gold-shirted heroes constantly impressed, twice missing promotion only on the final day, but eventually Ken Furphy's men won through in 1969.

It was generally believed that with talent such as Pat Jennings and Tony Currie around, the club could cope at this higher level, but despite an FA Cup semi-final appearance at the end of a run which saw the defeat of mighty Liverpool in 1970, the following decade provided many traumas. However, In 1977 Watford were wallowing in the fourth division doldrums when the club witnessed a fairy-tale turn-around. Millionaire pop star Elton John became chairman, took on a promising manager in Graham Taylor, and the two of them, with later help from Bertie Mee, proceeded to illustrate to the football world just how to run a football club.

Consecutive promotions followed by three seasons of consolidation in the second division eventually resulted in top flight football coming to Watford. New young stars such as John Barnes, Mo Johnson, Luther Blissett and Nigel Callaghan showed no sign of being overawed among the elite. They eventually finished as runners-up and the following season reached their first FA Cup final, losing 2-0 to Everton.

Later seasons proved less easy and when the management team broke up and the financial backing diminished the Hornets slipped back into the third flight. But the fine structure of the club remained and the eventual return of Taylor and John promised yet another rise in fortune.

Early signs were very promising, and in 1998 the club returned to the Second flight.

Watford (founded 1891) records and strips

Year	Division and position		Cup round reached
1906			2
1907			1
1908			1

Year	Division	Position	Cup round reached
1932	3S	11	qf
1933	3S	11	3
1934	3S	15	1f
1935	3S	6	2
1936	3S	5	4
1937	3S	4	1
1938	3S	4	3
1939	3S	4	3
1946			4
1947	3S	16	2
1948	3S	15	1
1949	3S	17	1
1950	3S	6	4
1951	3S	23	1
1952	3S	21	2
1953	3S	10	2
1954	3S	4	1

1963-1972

1991-1993

1899-1947

Year	Division	Position	Cup round reached
1973	3	19	3
1974	3	7	2
1975	3	23R	1

Year	Division	Position	Cup round reached
1988	1	20R	qf
1989	2	4	5
1990	2	15	4

1983-1986

1998

Year	Division	Position	Cup round reached
1909			1
1910			1
1911			1
1912			1
1913			p
1914			p

Year	Division	Position	Cup round reached
1955	3S	7	3
1956	3S	20	2
1957	3S	11	2
1958	3S	16	1
1959	4	15	2

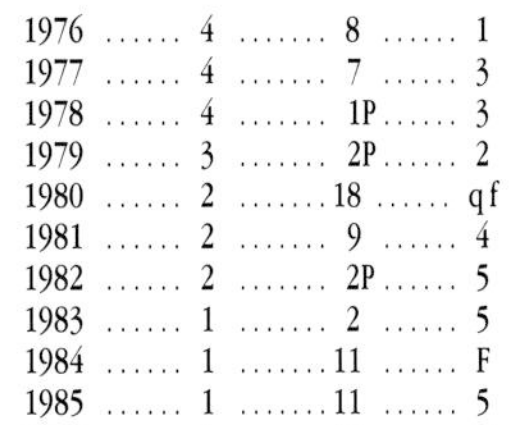

Year	Division	Position	Cup round reached
1976	4	8	1
1977	4	7	3
1978	4	1P	3
1979	3	2P	2
1980	2	18	qf
1981	2	9	4
1982	2	2P	5
1983	1	2	5
1984	1	11	F
1985	1	11	5
1986	1	12	6
1987	1	9	sf

Year	Division	Position	Cup round reached
1991	2	20	3
1992	2	10	3
1993	N1	16	3
1994	N1	19	3
1995	N1	7	5
1996	N1	23R	3
1997	N2	13	4
1998	N2	1P	3

1948-1959

1959-1963

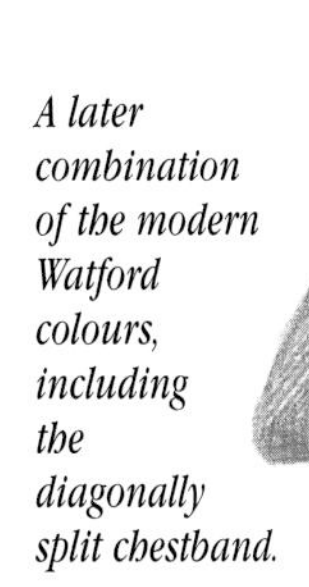

A later combination of the modern Watford colours, including the diagonally split chestband.

Year	Division	Position	Cup round reached
1915			p
1920			p
1921	3	6	2
1922	3S	7	2
1923	3S	10	1
1924	3S	20	3
1925	3S	11	1
1926	3S	15	2
1927	3S	21	2
1928	3S	15	1
1929	3S	8	4
1930	3S	15	2
1931	3S	18	5

Year	Division	Position	Cup round reached
1960	4	4P	5
1961	3	4	3
1962	3	17	3
1963	3	17	4
1964	3	3	2
1965	3	9	1
1966	3	12	2
1967	3	3	3
1968	3	6	3
1969	3	1P	4
1970	2	19	sf
1971	2	18	4
1972	2	22R	3

WEST BROMWICH ALBION

When a famous old club such as West Bromwich Albion have worn the same navy blue and white stripes through over a century of football success, it's hard to believe that for the first ten years there was a change of strip nearly every season.

Having been formed by cricketers looking for some sporting action in the winter, the club wore whatever was available locally. Blue and maroon, yellow and white, chocolate and navy, red and white, all combinations were tried, and even after the Albion had already appeared in three consecutive FA Cup finals (winning the third against the mighty Preston North end) the committee still wanted to try something more 'exotic'. During this second ever Football League season (WBA were founder members) this new attire was described as 'scarlet and blue broad striped jerseys and black knickers with scarlet stripes down the side' and not surprisingly attracted wolf-whistles and the nickname of the 'Nigger Minstrels'. The blue and white stripes were hastily reintroduced and have remained ever since.

The Throstles continued to be one of the country's top club sides. A second Cup victory in 1892, over midland rivals Aston Villa, was followed by another final when the Birmingham team got its revenge, 1-0. Strangely, although most Cup runs ended only in the final stages, Albion rarely challenged for League honours, consistency never being strong during the club's history (there were even two spells in the second division). Even then, there was one further Cup runners-up spot before the First World War.

Throughout most of this period the defence had been marshalled by the great Jesse Pennington, and he finally got his just reward when, in 1920, the 'Baggies', as they have been affectionately called, took their only League title. Five years later they were just pipped by Huddersfield when attempting a second championship win, but oddly enough there had been little Cup success during this period.

During the 1930s, the old inconsistency remained, producing a combination of Wembley visits and second division football. However, the 1931 FA Cup final win over Birmingham City must have been sweet.

Since the Second World War, there have been two more splendid Albion sides. The first, created by Vic Buckingham, came within a whisker of the League and FA Cup double in 1954. The goal-scoring feats of Ronnie Allen and Johnny Nicholls secured the Cup win over Preston, but the team, handicapped by injuries, just failed to catch Wolves in the League. After other good results in the League, this team eventually broke up, but the 1960s also proved a successful period. New goal-scoring heroes Jeff Astle and Tony Brown were the inspiration behind a fifth Cup win in 1968. The single-goal victory over Everton was sandwiched between three League Cup finals and the Baggies were an exciting club to watch.

Since then there has been little to stimulate the fans and Albion dropped to the third division for the first time. But manager Ossie Ardiles led them to the new first division in 1993 and despite initial teething problems, the club is now looking to climb even further.

In the 19th century, the Albion were amongst the most feared Cup-fighters in the land.

Albion (founded 1879) records and strips

Year	Division	Position	Cup round reached
1885			qf
1886			F
1887			F

1880-1882

Year	Division	Position	Cup round reached
1888			W
1889	1	6	sf
1890	1	5	1
1891	1	12	sf

1882-1889

Year	Division	Position	Cup round reached
1892	1	12	W
1893	1	8	1
1894	1	8	1
1895	1	16	F
1896	1	13	qf
1897	1	12	2
1898	1	7	qf
1899	1	14	qf
1900	1	13	qf
1901	1	18R	sf
1902	2	1P	1
1903	1	7	1
1904	1	18R	1
1905	2	10	1
1906	2	4	p
1907	2	4	sf
1908	2	5	2
1909	2	3	2
1910	2	11	3
1911	2	1P	2
1912	1	9	F
1913	1	10	1
1914	1	5	3
1915	1	11	1
1920	1	1C	1
1921	1	14	1
1922	1	13	3
1923	1	17	3
1924	1	16	qf
1925	1	2	qf
1926	1	13	4
1927	1	22R	3
1928	2	8	3
1929	2	7	qf
1930	2	6	3
1931	2	2P	W
1932	1	6	3
1933	1	4	4

1889-1933

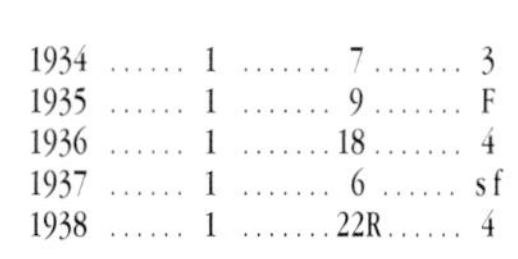

Year	Division	Position	Cup round reached
1934	1	7	3
1935	1	9	F
1936	1	18	4
1937	1	6	sf
1938	1	22R	4

1934-1957

Year	Division	Position	Cup round reached
1939	2	10	4
1946			4
1947	2	7	4
1948	2	6	4
1949	2	2P	qf
1950	1	14	3
1951	1	16	3

1961-1972

Year	Division	Position	Cup round reached
1952	1	13	5
1953	1	4	4
1954	1	2	W
1955	1	17	4
1956	1	13	5
1957	1	11	sf
1958	1	4	qf
1959	1	5	5
1960	1	4	5
1961	1	10	3
1962	1	9	5
1963	1	14	4
1964	1	10	4
1965	1	14	3
1966	1	6	3
1967	1	13	4
1968	1	8	W
1969	1	10	sf
1970	1	16	3
1971	1	17	4
1972	1	16	3
1973	1	22R	5
1974	2	8	5
1975	2	6	4
1976	2	3P	5
1977	1	7	3

1972-1980

Year	Division	Position	Cup round reached
1978	1	6	sf
1979	1	3	5
1980	1	10	3
1981	1	4	4
1982	1	17	sf
1983	1	11	4
1984	1	17	5
1985	1	12	3
1986	1	22R	3
1987	2	15	3
1988	2	20	3
1989	2	9	3
1990	2	20	5
1991	2	23R	3
1992	3	7	2
1993	N2	4P(pl)	3
1994	N1	21	1

1998

Year	Division	Position	Cup round reached
1995	N1	19	3
1996	N1	11	3
1997	N1	16	3
1998	N1	10	4

The white stockings with the unusual positioning of the dark blue hoops were a memorable feature of the last great Cup era.

WEST HAM UNITED

This famous East End club had a relatively late start, being formed in 1900. For 30 years the major team in the area had been Upton Park, but in 1895 a works from Thames Ironworks started playing in local leagues. When, three years later, the club decided to take on professional players, the firm withdrew its support and a new limited company was formed calling itself West Ham United.

The early team had played in red, white and blue, also in an all-Harrovian blue strip in honour of the Ironworks owner's old school. However, the new professional club chose claret and blue as their colours.

For the next two decades, the club successfully built up their resources, buying the Boleyn Ground and taking on well-known players, and when football recommenced after the First World War, the Hammers were considered good enough to be elected to the second division.

And good enough they were. After three close attempts, West Ham were not only promoted, but made history by taking part in the first ever Wembley FA Cup final. Bolton won that day, but it gave the Eastenders a taste of things to come. However, the great times were not immediate; despite the free scoring of forwards such as Vic Watson, it was second division football from 1932 until well after the Second World War.

In the 1950s, Ted Fenton assembled a side which resembled a future managers' who's who. Dave Sexton, John Bond, Malcolm Allison, Frank O'Farrell, Noel Cantwell and Ken Brown were members of a team eventually promoted in 1958. The famous club song of 'I'm Forever Blowing Bubbles' echoed around the ground, and far from the bubble bursting the club went on from strength to strength. Ron Greenwood, the new manager, groomed Bobby Moore, Martin Peters and Geoff Hurst into players capable of bringing the FA Cup and the subsequent European Cup Winners Cup to West Ham, and the same three provided the backbone of England's Wembley win in the World Cup a year later.

Because of the club's attitude of providing entertaining, free-flowing football, sometimes at the expense of sensible efficiency, West Ham have rarely threatened to dominate the League. In knockout competitions, however, it's been very different. There were two more FA Cup wins, the first against second division Fulham and old boy Bobby Moore, and the second five years later, as a second division club themselves, against a strong Arsenal side. The trophies were rewards for great service from Trevor Brooking and Billy Bonds, and this team almost emulated the 1960s heroes, reaching the Cup Winners Cup Final, losing to Anderlecht only after a gallant fight.

Since then the Hammers have gone through a mixed period, experiencing life in both first and second flights, but with Billy Bonds and Harry Redknapp providing continuity and enthusiasm, it seemed that before too long those bubbles would be blown again!

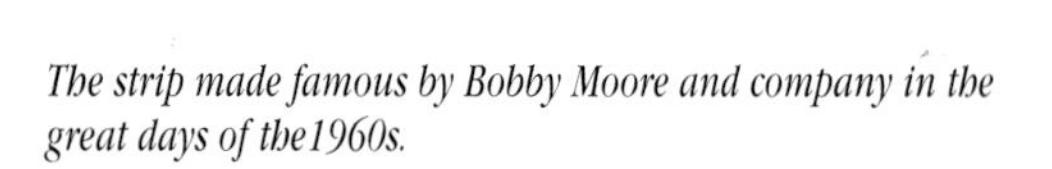

The strip made famous by Bobby Moore and company in the great days of the1960s.

West Ham (founded 1900) records and strips

	Division and position		Cup round reached
1913			2
1914			2

	Division and position		Cup round reached
1937	2	6	3
1938	2	9	3
1939	2	11	5
1946			4
1947	2	11	3
1948	2	6	3
1949	2	7	3
1950	2	19	4
1951	2	13	4
1952	2	12	4
1953	2	14	3
1954	2	13	4
1955	2	8	3
1956	2	16	qf
1957	2	8	4

1962-1975

1995-1996

1900-1929

	Division and position		Cup round reached
1976	1	18	3
1977	1	17	3
1978	1	20R	4
1979	2	5	3
1980	2	7	W
1981	2	1P	3

	Division and position		Cup round reached
1989	1	19R	qf
1990	2	7	3
1991	2	2P	sf
1992	1	22R	5
1993	N1	2P	4
1994	Pr	13	qf

	Division and position		Cup round reached
1915			1
1920	2	7	3
1921	2	5	1
1922	2	4	1
1923	2	2P	F
1924	1	13	2
1925	1	13	3

	Division and position		Cup round reached
1958	2	1P	5
1959	1	6	3
1960	1	14	3
1961	1	16	3
1962	1	8	3
1963	1	12	qf
1964	1	14	W

1976-1980

1998

1937-1956

1957-1961

	Division and position		Cup round reached
1982	1	9	4
1983	1	8	3
1984	1	9	5
1985	1	16	6
1986	1	3	6
1987	1	15	5
1988	1	16	4

	Division and position		Cup round reached
1995	Pr	14	4
1996	Pr	10	4
1997	Pr.	14	3
1998	Pr.	8	qf

1985-1988

The elegant shirt worn by the Hammers in 1986, their best ever League season.

	Division and position		Cup round reached
1926	1	18	3
1927	1	6	4
1928	1	17	4
1929	1	17	qf
1930	1	7	qf
1931	1	18	3
1932	1	22R	4
1933	2	20	sf
1934	2	7	4
1935	2	3	3
1936	2	4	3

	Division and position		Cup round reached
1965	1	9	4
1966	1	12	4
1967	1	16	3
1968	1	12	5
1969	1	8	5
1970	1	17	3
1971	1	20	3
1972	1	14	5
1973	1	6	4
1974	1	18	3
1975	1	13	W

WIGAN ATHLETIC

The striking strip of the late 1980s when Wigan went close to promotion to division two.

After 11 years of battling away in the early days of the third division, Wigan Borough had to call it a day in 1932. There seemed to be little future for senior football in this rugby league town, particularly so with the Manchester and Liverpool giants constantly taking away potential support.

However, some of the people of Wigan had other ideas and the Athletic were born. The Football League status had been lost, but in the north-west, regional leagues were strong. The red and white halved shirted team began life in the Lancashire combination and slowly built up a reputation as a powerful side.

After the Second World War, the Latics changed both their League and their shirts – the local supplier only had blue in stock – and it was Wigan's neighbours to the south who entertained them in the Cheshire League. It was the club's chance to prove their worth against the likes of Altrincham, Macclesfield, Northwich Victoria, Stalybridge Celtic and Hyde United. Wigan were good enough and in 1954 they even took Newcastle United to a third round replay.

By the end of the 1960s the powerful non-League clubs in the area had formed the Northern Premier League. In the following ten seasons, Wigan not only won the championship twice, but ended their stay with the best record of all.

The Latics' non-League era ended in 1978, when they were elected to replace fellow Lancastrians Southport in the senior competition. It was an interesting time, as most of the smaller clubs in the area were struggling but Wigan were on the up. After three impressive opening seasons they were promoted to division three. Stripes had been introduced and there was a positive air of confidence.

After three further years of consolidation, manager Roy Matthias bought in players like Bobby Campbell and Andy Holden, and in twice finishing fourth they went close to reaching the second division. The following season only a massive injury list prevented at least a play-off spot.

It was an exciting time all round. The fans rolled in and the teams wore a variety of unique strips: blue shirts with a white band, white shirts with blue shoulder stripes, and even blue and white diagonal halves.

Despite all the League successes, the Latics' biggest thrill came in 1985 when they won the Freight Rover Trophy, but soon that Wembley triumph seemed a long way away. The pressures of competing for fans in southern Lancashire were proving difficult to overcome and Athletic began to struggle. As shirts became plain blue, then 'Inter Milan' blue and black stripes and even irregular blue and white stripes, Springfield Park regulars desperately hoped for a brighter future.

Wigan (founded 1932) records and strips

	Division and position	Cup round reached
1932 to 1939	Lancashire Construction	
1946	LC	q 2

1966-1969

1932-1934

1947	LC	q 2
1948	LC	q 4
1949	LC	q 1
1950	LC	q 3
1951	LC	q 4
1952	LC	q 4
1953	LC	q 4

1946-1956

1954	LC	3
1955	LC	4
1956	LC	4
1957	LC	W
1958	LC	3
1959	LC	s f
1960	LC	s f
1961	LC	5
1962	CL	q f
1963	CL	4

1964	CL	3
1965	CL	5
1966	CL	3
1967	CL	4
1968	NP	4
1969	NP	5
1970	NP	3

1977-1979

1971	NP	1
1972	NP	1
1973	NP	3
1974	NP	5
1975	NP	5
1976	NP	3

1986

1977	NP		q f
1978	NP		3
1979	4	6	1
1980	4	6	4
1981	4	11	1

The shoulder stripes of the late 1980s, a dashing style to suit the League successes.

1987-1988

1994-1995

1982	4	3P	1
1983	3	18	1
1984	3	15	3
1985	3	16	3

1989

1986	3	4	4
1987	3	4	q f
1988	3	7	2
1989	3	17	1
1990	3	18	3

1991	3	10	3
1992	3	15	3
1993	N2	23R	2
1994	N3	19	3
1995	N3	14	2
1996	N3	10	3
1997	N3	1P	1
1998	N2	11	3

1995-1998

WIMBLEDON

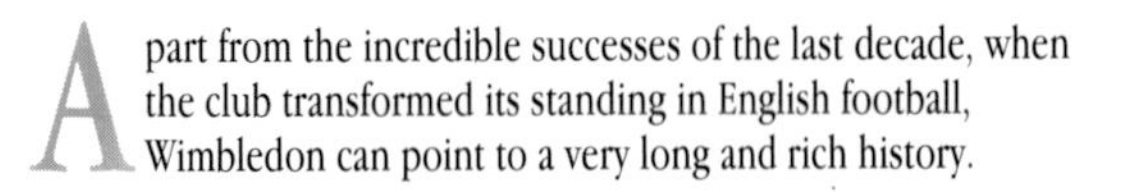

Apart from the incredible successes of the last decade, when the club transformed its standing in English football, Wimbledon can point to a very long and rich history.

Founded in 1889 as Wimbledon Old Centrals, a name taken from a nearby school, they were content to play in local leagues until well into the next century. In 1905 the name was changed to Wimbledon, but it wasn't until Jack Meadows took control and got the club elected into the Athenian League, and then risked a move to the Isthmian League, that the Dons began a long road to success.

The blue and white striped Dons struggled at first, but by the 1930s had become a dominant force. In that decade, wearing all-blue shirts, they won the championship four times, and reached the FA Amateur Cup final in 1935, losing to the then redoubtable Cup stars, Bishop Auckland. That year 18,000 fans turned up to see a tie versus HMS Victory! What the club would do for a following like that now.

After the Second World War there was a quieter spell for Wimbledon, but by the late 1950s another strong side had been put together. In 1959 there was another Isthmian League championship, followed by the club's only Amateur Cup win, 4-2 versus Sutton with Eddie Reynolds scoring all four with his head.

Times were changing and Wimbledon then abandoned the amateur ranks for the semi-professional world of the Southern League. Again the club responded well to new surroundings and won the title three times in the next decade. Wimbledon also shocked the football world by taking all-conquering Leeds United to a FA Cup replay in 1975. Such qualities did not go unnoticed and two years later the Dons replaced Workington in the fourth division.

To celebrate their new status, the team wore an all-white strip, but the ups and downs of the first few years persuaded the club to return to blue, although by now the first of the yellow trims appeared. Manager Dario Gradi left, later to find success at Crewe, and new boy Dave Bassett imposed his simple but highly efficient philosophy on his players. Winning seasons followed, and by 1987 Wimbledon were in the first division.

Everybody felt it wouldn't last – perhaps that's why Bassett left – but surprisingly Bobby Gould continued the momentum and kept the club not only in the first division but often near the top. The astonishing Cup final win against Liverpool proved to all that the collective individual talents of good players such as John Fashanu and Dave Beasant could be even stronger as a whole.

There have been no trophies since then and a move from Plough Lane, the traditional home, to Selhurst Park has proved difficult for the fans. But every year the pundits have been proved wrong and the club was surviving when potentially stronger ones went to the wall.

In 1988 came the culmination of Wimbledon's dream, beating mighty Liverpool in the FA Cup final.

Wimbledon (founded 1889) records and strips

1889 to 1939 Athenian League, Isthmian League

1910

Year	Division	Position	Cup round reached
1946	IL		q1

1935

Year	Division	Position	Cup round reached
1947	IL		q2
1948	IL		1
1949	IL		q4

1954

Year	Division	Position	Cup round reached
1950	IL		q1
1951	IL		q1
1952	IL		p
1953	IL		1
1954	IL		q1
1955	IL		q1
1956	IL		q1
1957	IL		p
1958	IL		p

1960

Year	Division	Position	Cup round reached
1959	IL		p
1960	IL		q2
1961	IL		q2
1962	IL		q2
1963	IL		2
1964	IL		2
1965	SL		q4
1966	SL		2
1967	SL		1
1968	SL		2
1969	SL		q4
1970	SL		1
1971	SL		1
1972	SL		q4
1973	SL		q3
1974	SL		1
1975	SL		4

1978

Year	Division	Position	Cup round reached
1976	SL		2
1977	SL		3
1978	4	13	1
1979	4	3P	3
1980	3	24R	2

1988

Year	Division	Position	Cup round reached
1981	4	4P	4
1982	3	21R	2
1983	4	1P	1
1984	3	2P	2
1985	2	12	5

1990

Year	Division	Position	Cup round reached
1986	2	3P	3
1987	1	6	qf
1988	1	7	W
1989	1	12	qf
1990	1	8	3

1998

Year	Division	Position	Cup round reached
1991	1	7	4
1992	1	13	3
1993	Pr	12	5
1994	Pr	6	5
1995	Pr	9	5
1996	Pr	14	qf
1997	Pr.	8	sf
1998	Pr.	15	5

The yellow yoke of the Cup-winning shirts.

WOLVERHAMPTON WANDERERS

Yet another shock for modern supporters – Wolves playing in red and white striped shirts! Yet back in those early days, when the St Lukes club amalgamated with the local Wanderers to form the Wolves we now know, these were indeed the colours.

This bold outfit links the great times before the War with the Billy Wright years in the 1950s.

However, by the time Wolves became successful enough to become founder members of the League – and then as FA Cup runners-up, were not far off the celebrated double – the famous old gold and black colours were well established. At first the shirts were diagonally halved, but by 1893 and for the next three decades they were striped, either narrow or broad, which in their day were just as famous as another version much later.

In 1893 the first Cup success was achieved with a 1-0 victory over Everton, and although many good League campaigns proved eventually fruitless, the Cup often provided lots of excitement. Another final in 1896, lost to Sheffield Wednesday, was followed by a fourth ten years later. This 3-1 win over Newcastle was as much unexpected as it was appreciated, as the Wolves had been relegated and had thus commenced a long spell in the second division. The next quarter of a century provided no change except for a one-year hiccup in the third division.

However, by the end of the 1930s, Major Frank Buckley was put in charge and improved the team's efficiency to such a degree that the club narrowly missed two consecutive championships. It was therefore an even greater surprise when in the last FA Cup final before the Second World War, Wolves were thrashed 4-1 by Portsmouth.

Buckley had left when football resumed but one of his proteges, Stan Cullis, proved more than equal to the task of continuing the progress. In fact, during the next decade his Wolves team dominated events in a fashion few clubs have managed over the years. With a star line-up including Billy Wright, Bert Williams, Ron Flowers, Roy Swinbourne, Dennis Westcott, Johnny Hancocks, Jimmy Mullen, Peter Broadbent and Bill Shorthouse, the gold-shirted Wanderers won three League championships in six seasons as well as coming close on many other occasions. There was also a fourth FA Cup win in 1960, when Blackburn Rovers were overwhelmed 3-0.

Amazingly, in 1966 Wolves were relegated, but following a fairly speedy return, the 1970s proved to be another period of success. First in 1972, a European trophy was denied Wolverhampton in the UEFA Cup final, ironically by fellow English club Tottenham Hotspur. This near thing was then followed by League Cup final victories over Manchester City and Nottingham Forest.

But by the mid-1980s a sudden, disastrous slide saw Wolves floundering in the fourth division. Three successive relegations left the club financially destitute. It took an almighty effort by highly underrated manager Graham Turner to pull the club around. Later, back in the second flight and now managed by Mark McGhee after a spell from Graham Taylor, a much more ambitious Wolves hoped that the goal-scoring of England international Steve Bull would put the shine back on the old gold shirts.

Wolves (founded 1876) records and strips

1876-1933

1967-1972

1995

Year	Division and position		Cup round reached
1884			2
1885			1
1886			4
1887			3
1888			3
1889	1	3	F
1890	1	4	sf
1891	1	4	qf
1892	1	6	qf
1893	1	11	W
1894	1	9	1
1895	1	11	qf
1896	1	14	F
1897	1	10	2
1898	1	3	2
1899	1	8	2
1900	1	4	2
1901	1	13	qf
1902	1	14	1
1903	1	11	1
1904	1	8	2
1905	1	14	2
1906	1	20R	2
1907	2	6	1
1908	2	9	W
1909	2	7	1
1910	2	8	2
1911	2	9	3
1912	2	5	3
1913	2	10	2
1914	2	9	2
1915	2	4	2
1920	2	19	2
1921	2	15	F
1922	2	17	1
1923	2	22R	2
1924	3N	1P	3
1925	2	6	1
1926	2	4	3
1927	2	15	qf
1928	2	16	4
1929	2	17	3
1930	2	9	3
1931	2	4	qf
1932	2	1P	4
1933	1	20	3
1934	1	15	4
1935	1	17	4
1936	1	15	3
1937	1	5	qf
1938	1	2	4
1939	1	2	F
1946			4
1947	1	3	4
1948	1	5	4
1949	1	6	W
1950	1	2	5
1951	1	14	sf
1952	1	16	4
1953	1	3	3
1954	1	1C	3
1955	1	2	qf
1956	1	3	3
1957	1	6	4
1958	1	1C	qf
1959	1	1C	4
1960	1	2	W
1961	1	3	3
1962	1	18	4
1963	1	5	3
1964	1	16	3
1965	1	21R	qf
1966	2	6	5
1967	2	2P	4
1968	1	17	3
1969	1	16	4
1970	1	13	4
1971	1	4	4
1972	1	9	3
1973	1	5	sf
1974	1	12	3
1975	1	12	3
1976	1	20R	qf
1977	2	1P	qf
1978	1	15	4
1979	1	18	sf
1980	1	6	5
1981	1	18	sf
1982	1	21R	3
1983	2	2P	4
1984	1	22R	3
1985	2	22R	3
1986	3	23R	1
1987	4	4	1
1988	4	1P	3
1989	3	1P	1
1990	2	10	3
1991	2	12	3
1992	2	11	3
1993	N1	11	4
1994	N1	8	qf
1995	N1	4	qf
1996	N1	20	4
1997	N1	3	3
1998	N1	9	sf

1998

1957-1962

1973-1976

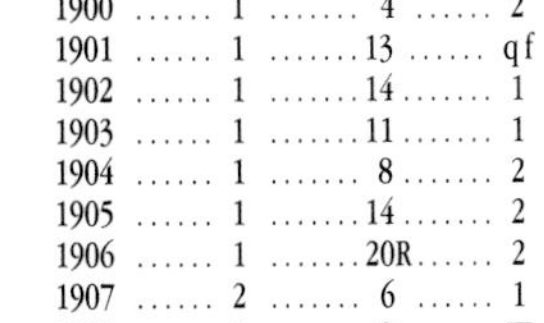

1936-1956

The old gold and black stockings with hoops only on the bottom half.

WREXHAM

Although the North Wales club have had limited success in the League, they share with West Bromwich Albion and Blackpool the distinction of having the greatest number of different team colours down the years. Founded back in 1873, Wrexham appear to have worn a different type of shirt for every decade until the Second World War.

The late 1970s saw Wrexham rise to the giddy heights of the second division.

During the 19th century, while the club progressed through the non-League system and began to challenge for the English FA Cup, the strips changed from red and black hoops to dark and light blue halves until finally alternating blue with white sleeves and stripes in the same colour combination.

For the new century, green shirts were the vogue when Wrexham were a force in the Birmingham and District League. They were still in this league just after the First World War, but were now sporting red shirts, and it must have come as a surprise, when they joined the Football League in 1921, that they didn't change the strip for the occasion. However, as the first four seasons provided no huge success, yet another change did follow. Blue jerseys returned but this time with a bold, striking white hoop across the body and sleeves.

Performances improved but obviously not enough to impress the management and all-blue arrived in 1932. This time there was an immediate response as Wrexham missed promotion by just two points.

After the Second World War, the red shirts reappeared and have remained ever since. Probably the club felt a need for continuity, and in the 1950s Wrexham were one of the strongest teams in the third division (north). Sadly the next decade provided gloomy fare for the Robins' fans, with many seasons spent in the fourth.

Eventually a group of youngsters matured into a team of some talent, with Arfon Griffths a shining star. For a while, not all the fans in North Wales trooped off to Manchester or Liverpool every week, and with promotion achieved, they were entertained by a good third division side. Griffiths became manager and in an exciting season in 1978, led the club not only to the quarter-finals of the FA Cup and the League Cup, but also to the second division.

It was never easy at this level, but Dixie McNeil continued to score regularly and Joey Jones was a rock for both Wrexham and Wales. When the end came, it was quick and painful, and within two seasons the Robins were back in the fourth division.

With limited resources, there was little hope for immediate improvement. As usual, the chief area for optimism was the Welsh Cup. As the fortunes of all Welsh clubs were low at this stage, there was always a good chance of success, and over the years the European Cup Winners' Cup has provided many exciting nights at the Racecourse Ground.

Happily, in 1992 a historic win over Arsenal in the FA Cup gave the club new heart, and promotion to the new second division in 1993 provided even further grounds for optimism.

Wrexham (founded 1873) records and strips

1873-1919

	Division and position		Cup round reached
1922	3N	12	2
1923	3N	10	3
1924	3N	16	2
1925	3N	16	qf
1926	3N	19	1
1927	3N	13	2
1928	3N	11	4
1929	3N	3	1
1930	3N	17	4
1931	3N	4	3
1932	3N	10	1
1933	3N	2	2
1934	3N	6	1
1935	3N	18	2
1936	3N	18	1
1937	3N	8	3
1938	3N	10	2
1939	3N	4	1
1946			3
1947	3N	7	2
1948	3N	3	2
1949	3N	9	1
1950	3N	20	2
1951	3N	14	2
1952	3N	18	2
1953	3N	3	3
1954	3N	8	3
1955	3N	18	2
1956	3N	14	1
1957	3N	12	4
1958	3N	12	1
1959	3	18	1
1960	3	23R	3
1961	4	16	1
1962	4	3P	3
1963	3	9	3
1964	3	23R	2
1965	4	14	2
1966	4	24	2
1967	4	7	2
1968	4	8	1
1969	4	9	2
1970	4	2P	4
1971	3	9	1
1972	3	16	3
1973	3	12	2
1974	3	4	qf
1975	3	13	1
1976	3	6	1
1977	3	5	4
1978	3	1P	qf
1979	2	15	4
1980	2	16	5
1981	2	16	5
1982	2	21R	4
1983	3	22R	2
1984	4	20	1
1985	4	15	1
1986	4	13	2
1987	4	9	3
1988	4	11	2
1989	4	7	1
1990	4	21	1
1991	4	24	1
1992	4	14	4
1993	N3	2P	1
1994	N2	12	1
1995	N2	13	4
1996	N2	8	3
1997	N2	8	6
1998	N2	7	3

1919-1957

1963-1970

1998

1981

1993

The white-banded blue shirts almost saw an earlier Wrexham team into the second division.

WYCOMBE WANDERERS

The League's relative newcomer is another club with a long and rich history going back as far as 1884. Wycombe's attitudes in those early days were very casual, playing only friendlies and usually waiting until just before the game to find out if a pitch was available.

Ten years later, a decision was taken by the Wanderers to become a senior club and within a couple of years they had reached the Buckinghamshire Cup final. The players always looked resplendent in the Oxford and Cambridge blue quartered shirts, and impressed many people as they progressed through the home county leagues. The club even had a spell in the Southern League, but it was from the Spartan League that they eventually joined the Isthmian, the beginning of a long relationship.

Also joining in the same year were Wimbledon, rivals over many years and no doubt everyone associated with the Wanderers relishes the prospect of renewing League battles.

However, back in 1931 it was the Buckinghamshire club who held the upper hand in this their Amateur Cup-winning year. Many of the side including goalkeeper V E Kipping and centre-forward Douglas Vernon had won representative honours, and with the help of a late penalty they overcame Hayes.

The next 20 years were quiet ones for Wycombe so far as honours were concerned, but in the 1950s, still sporting the quartered shirts, they had a side consistently chasing trophies. In fact, all the campaigns ended in glorious failure, but in addition to the many near misses in the Isthmian League, there were two Amateur Cup semis and a second final in 1957, sadly lost to the mighty Bishop Auckland.

The 1960s were times of change, but although there was a new playing outfit of light blue shirts and dark blue shorts, Wanderers avoided the early rush to top semi-professional competition such as the Southern League and remained in Isthmian isolation.

However, during the following period, the Blues regularly won their League championship and this new consistency not only made the football world take more notice, but gave grounds for greater optimism within the club itself. As the non-League pyramid took shape, the Isthmian League eventually became fully committed to integration, and when Wycombe won their seventh championship they were promoted into the GM Vauxhall Alliance. The team were ready for the new challenge and so were the board. Apart from strengthening the playing staff, and having the foresight to employ Martin O'Neill as manager, they overcame the nostalgic pull of Loakes Park, their home for over 90 years, to move to the wonderful new Adams Park.

O'Neill's marvellous squad of players first took the FA Trophy at Wembley in 1991, defeating Kidderminster and then, after a heartbreaking near miss, finally won the Conference to take their place in the Football League. The striking quarters (now returned) and attractive play was to prove a great boost for the senior competition. Wanderers were promoted in their first Football League season and only narrowly missed another twelve months later, before having to settle for later consolidation.

The League was all the richer for the addition of this attractive, enterprising club.

Wycombe (founded 1884) records and strips

1884 to 1939 Southern League, Bucks Contiguous League, Berks and Bucks Senior League, Great Western Suburban League, Spartan League, Isthmian League.

1894-1900

	Division and position		Cup round reached
1946	IL		p
1947	IL		q1

1931

	Division and position		Cup round reached
1948	IL		q2
1949	IL		p
1950	IL		p
1951	IL		q4
1952	IL		q3
1953	IL		q3
1954	IL		p
1955	IL		q2

1957

	Division and position		Cup round reached
1956	IL		1
1957	IL		q4
1958	IL		1
1959	IL		1
1960	IL		2
1961	IL		1
1962	IL		1

1965

	Division and position		Cup round reached
1963	IL		2
1964	IL		q4

1974

	Division and position		Cup round reached
1965	IL		q4
1966	IL		1
1967	IL		1
1968	IL		q4
1969	IL		q1
1970	IL		q4

1981

	Division and position		Cup round reached
1971	IL		1
1972	IL		q1
1973	IL		q3

1993

	Division and position		Cup round reached
1974	IL		2
1975	IL		3
1976	IL		2
1977	IL		2
1978	IL		1
1979	IL		1

1998

	Division and position		Cup round reached
1980	IL		1
1981	IL		1
1982	IL		2
1983	IL		1
1984	IL		1
1985	IL		q4
1986	GMVC		3
1987	IL		q4
1988	GMVC		q1
1989	GMVC		q4
1990	GMVC		q4
1991	GMVC		2
1992	GMVC		1
1993	GMVC		2
1994	N3	4P(pl)	3
1995	N2	6	3
1996	N2	12	1
1997	N2	18	3
1998	N2	14	1

The quartered shirt which has symbolised the Wanderers over the decades.

YORK CITY

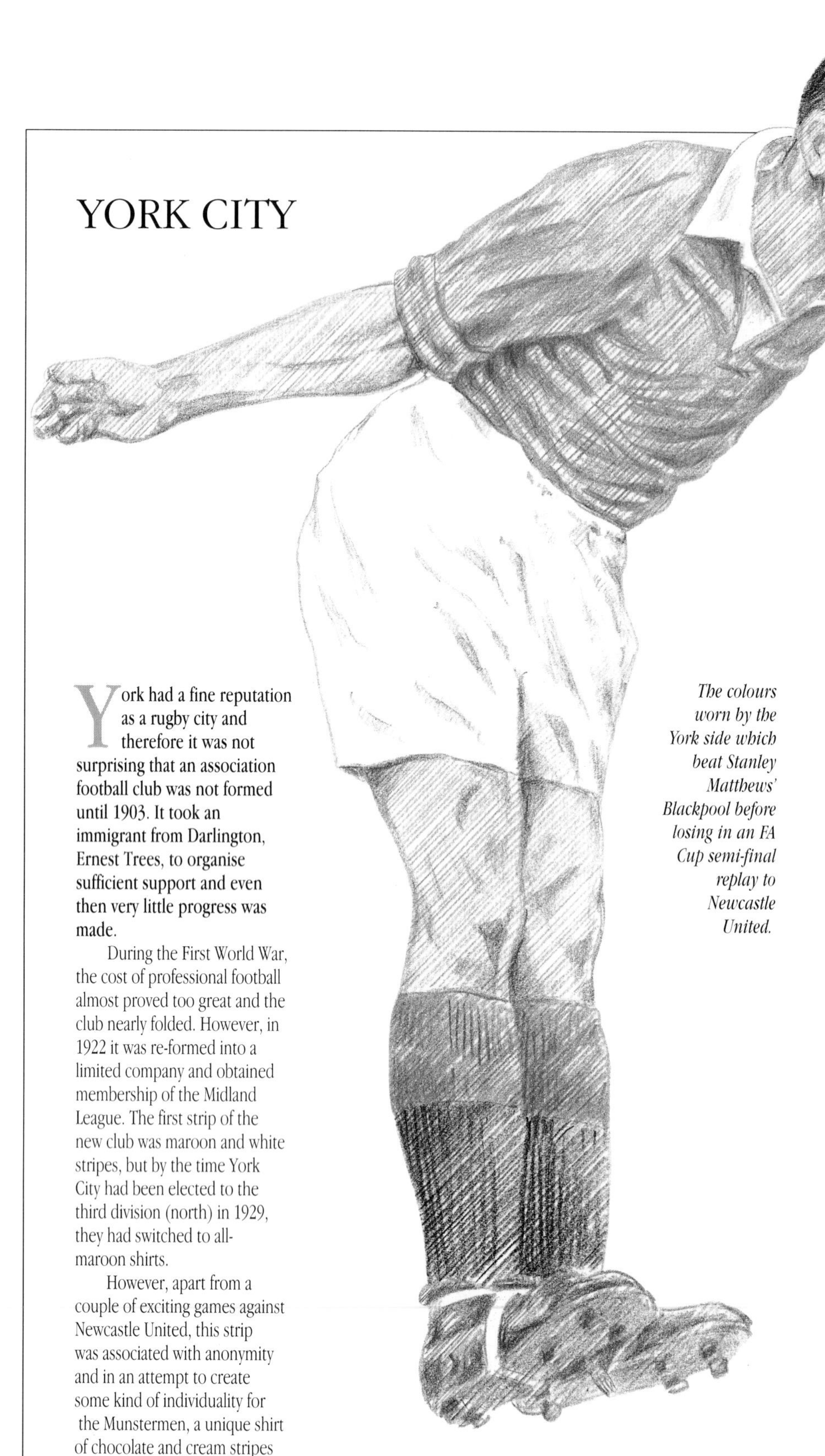

The colours worn by the York side which beat Stanley Matthews' Blackpool before losing in an FA Cup semi-final replay to Newcastle United.

York had a fine reputation as a rugby city and therefore it was not surprising that an association football club was not formed until 1903. It took an immigrant from Darlington, Ernest Trees, to organise sufficient support and even then very little progress was made.

During the First World War, the cost of professional football almost proved too great and the club nearly folded. However, in 1922 it was re-formed into a limited company and obtained membership of the Midland League. The first strip of the new club was maroon and white stripes, but by the time York City had been elected to the third division (north) in 1929, they had switched to all-maroon shirts.

However, apart from a couple of exciting games against Newcastle United, this strip was associated with anonymity and in an attempt to create some kind of individuality for the Munstermen, a unique shirt of chocolate and cream stripes was introduced. The city was associated with the confectionery industry for years, and it was hoped that this association would increase the club's support.

There was no great improvement in the size of the crowds or the points total at the end of each season, so after five years this style was dropped, the official reason being that it clashed too often with opponents shirts! The replacement described as a 'distinctive red' remained unchanged for the next three decades.

It was not until the 1950s that real excitement arrived at Bootham Crescent. With Arthur Bottom and Norman Wilkinson banging in the goals and Tom Forgan saving them at the other end, the City overcame the Blackpool of Matthews and Mortensen, then Spurs, before meeting Newcastle United in the FA Cup semi-final. It took their old Cup adversaries two games to overcome the Munstermen and the loss diminished none of the club's achievements that year. After another exciting knockout run, this time resulting in a quarter-final spot in the League Cup, there was sadly a long spell in the fourth division.

Eventually, when hopes of improvement ran out, the club started experimenting with the strip again. An all-white outfit preceded a return to the all-maroon shirts and the latter version worked a treat. Manager Tom Johnson took his team into the second division in just four seasons and, to celebrate this new-found status, added a large version of the club's initial letter to the shirts.

Thus the famous 'Y-fronts' appeared occasionally on the television as City battled against the likes of Manchester United, Aston Villa, Nottingham Forest and Chelsea. A new shirt, where the colours were reversed, proved a disastrous influence, as in two years York were back in the basement. So, in an effort to exorcise the experience, the deep red returned, this time accompanied by dark blue. This permutation proved inconsistent in its success, but the Munstermen still strived for a chance to take on the big boys again. The 1993 promotion might have been just the beginning.

York (founded 1922) records and strips

Year	Division	Position	Cup round reached
1956	3N	11	4
1957	3N	7	2
1958	3N	13	4
1959	4	3P	1
1960	3	21R	3
1961	4	5	3
1962	4	6	1
1963	4	14	3

1922-1939

1974-1976

1987

Year	Division	Position	Cup round reached
1980	4	17	2
1981	4	24	1
1982	4	17	2
1983	4	7	3

Year	Division	Position	Cup round reached
1989	4	11	1
1990	4	13	1
1991	4	21	2
1992	4	19	2

Year	Division and position		Cup round reached
1930	3N	6	3
1931	3N	12	3
1932	3N	10	1
1933	3N	20	1
1934	3N	12	1
1935	3N	15	3
1936	3N	16	1
1937	3N	12	4
1938	3N	11	qf

Year	Division	Position	Cup round reached
1964	4	22	1
1965	4	3P	2
1966	3	24R	1
1967	4	22	2
1968	4	21	1
1969	4	21	3
1970	4	13	4
1971	4	4P	p
1972	3	19	2
1973	3	18	3

1979-1982

1998

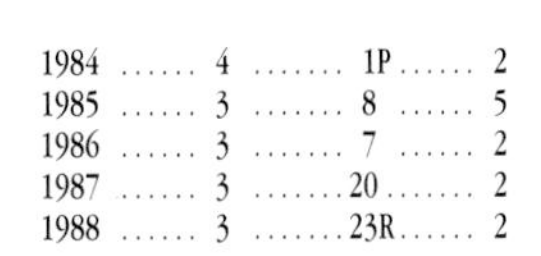

Year	Division	Position	Cup round reached
1984	4	1P	2
1985	3	8	5
1986	3	7	2
1987	3	20	2
1988	3	23R	2

Year	Division	Position	Cup round reached
1993	N3	4P(pl)	1
1994	N2	5	1
1995	N2	9	1
1996	N2	20	1
1997	N2	20	3
1998	N2	16	2

1946-1956

1967-1969

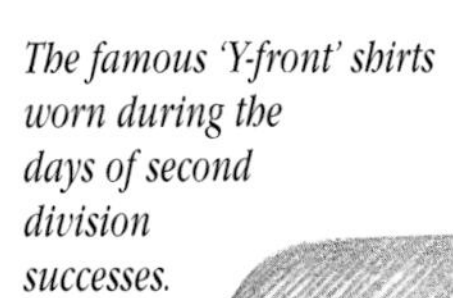

The famous 'Y-front' shirts worn during the days of second division successes.

Year	Division	Position	Cup round reached
1939	3N	20	3
1946			4
1947	3N	15	1
1948	3N	13	1
1949	3N	14	2
1950	3N	22	1
1951	3N	17	3
1952	3N	10	1
1953	3N	4	1
1954	3N	22	1
1955	3N	4	sf

Year	Division	Position	Cup round reached
1974	3	3P	1
1975	2	15	3
1976	2	21R	4
1977	3	24R	2
1978	4	22	1
1979	4	10	4

FAMOUS WINNING 'AWAY' STRIPS

Throughout this book there has been a concentration on the clubs' first-choice strips and the famous occasions on which they were worn. However, there have been many wonderful times, including the highlights of certain clubs' whole histories, when the players have been sporting a change strip.

The law of averages dictates that sometimes a cup final or a championship decider must be played against a team whose colours are the same as your own, and so, over the years, it has often been the alternative away strip which has captured all the glory.

Two rather ordinary all-white outfits take pride of place in the boardrooms of Queen's Park Rangers and Swindon respectively. As two third division clubs on the way up , both defied the odds in beating powerful first division sides in League Cup finals during the 1960s.

White was a popular choice of second shirt in FA Cup finals, too. West Ham United again proved it was a lucky omen versus first division opposition in the win against Arsenal; and who would forget the celebrations of Charlton's Chris Duffy after scoring the winning goal against Burnley in his baggy white shirts and black shorts.

Occasionally, a trophy would be won in colours totally alien to the normal traditional combinations. Any Southampton pictorial history would be awash with red and white stripes, but with the centre-piece starkly contrasting in bright yellow and royal blue, as worn in the 1976 FA Cup upset versus Manchester United. It is interesting to note that Barcelona avoided this problem by changing from their away match strip to their traditional shirts before receiving the European Cup and standing in front of the banks of photographers in 1992.

After three English clubs

QUEENS PARK RANGERS 1967

SOUTHAMPTON 1976

TOTTENHAM HOTSPUR 1982

ASTON VILLA 1982

MANCHESTER CITY 1970

had won that same competition, the same photographers snapped Bobby Charlton of Manchester United, Emlyn Hughes of Liverpool and Dennis Mortimer of Aston Villa holding up the trophy in anything but their traditional shirts. In the Cup Winners' Cup final, Manchester City changed to red and black stripes to avoid clashing with the colours of Gornik Zabrze, even though the Polish miners' club used to wear a different coloured shirt nearly every week anyway!

In contrast, nine out of ten of Tottenham Hotspur's Cup Final appearances have been in their famous lilywhite shirts, the odd one out being the 1982 win over Queen's Park Fangers; their all-yellow kit that day looked as uncharacteristic as the red and black of the Rangers.

In the League, of course, away strips are an important necessity, because of the dominance of shirts in basic colours. Even so, some clubs such as Arsenal take the term 'away strip' literally, often changing even when there is no clash.

It was in their yellow and dark blue strip that Arsenal went to Anfield on that famous night in 1989 and snatched the title away from Liverpool. Even the League officials were not sure what colour ribbons to attach to the trophy on that occasion.

There have, of course, been many other great successes achieved in away strips. The popularity of red and blue shirts will always ensure this, and the memories of most such occasions have been dimmed by history. In the next few seasons there will be others to add to the list. Let's hope these occur on exciting European nights. The European Cup final would do for a start!

HATED 'AWAY' STRIPS

In recent seasons it has become the custom to apply to the away strip all the radical design ideas that traditionalists thought too extreme for the first-choice kits. As a result, most football fans, notoriously conservative in outlook, are inclined to react in extreme terms against these formats.

For example, although Arsenal have worn yellow and dark blue as change strip for over half a century, some Highbury fans and many more around the country have cried out against the multi-patterned version which incorporates the 'A' motif. The chief problem of such designs is the 'dirty' looking effect of the resulting colour mix.

The same can be said about the negative response to Chelsea's diamond patterned shirts, Huddersfield's checks, Everton's zig-zag style and Coventry's bold shoulder stripes. It seems that the very bold combinations really are not appreciated. The ultimate in this category is the famous red and white wiggly lines version, a pattern which traversed both the shirts and shorts of Brighton outfits in 1992. Certainly, such was the strength of the irregular pattern that it was difficult to focus on the shape of the player in action.

Occasionally the colours themselves have been the bone of contention. In the days of Coventry's sky-blue matching shirt and shorts kit, the away strip was a brown and white equivalent. It had been many years since chocolate was a popular colour, and this time, the adverse reaction prompted Jimmy Hill's board to drop it.

When Liverpool introduced a smart green alternative to the broad three-stripe version in 1992, the fans were not impressed. The Anfield faithful had become accustomed to white shirts trimmed with red; and although there had been yellow and then silver versions, they had at least retained the red and white trim.

Many of the problems in this country concerning away strips are due to the fact that most of them are unconnected with the official club colours. In Europe, there is no such problem. There, change strips are often just a reversal of the usual combination but with the emphasis on the second colour. In the east of the continent, there would usually be three

BRIGHTON AND HOVE ALBION
1992

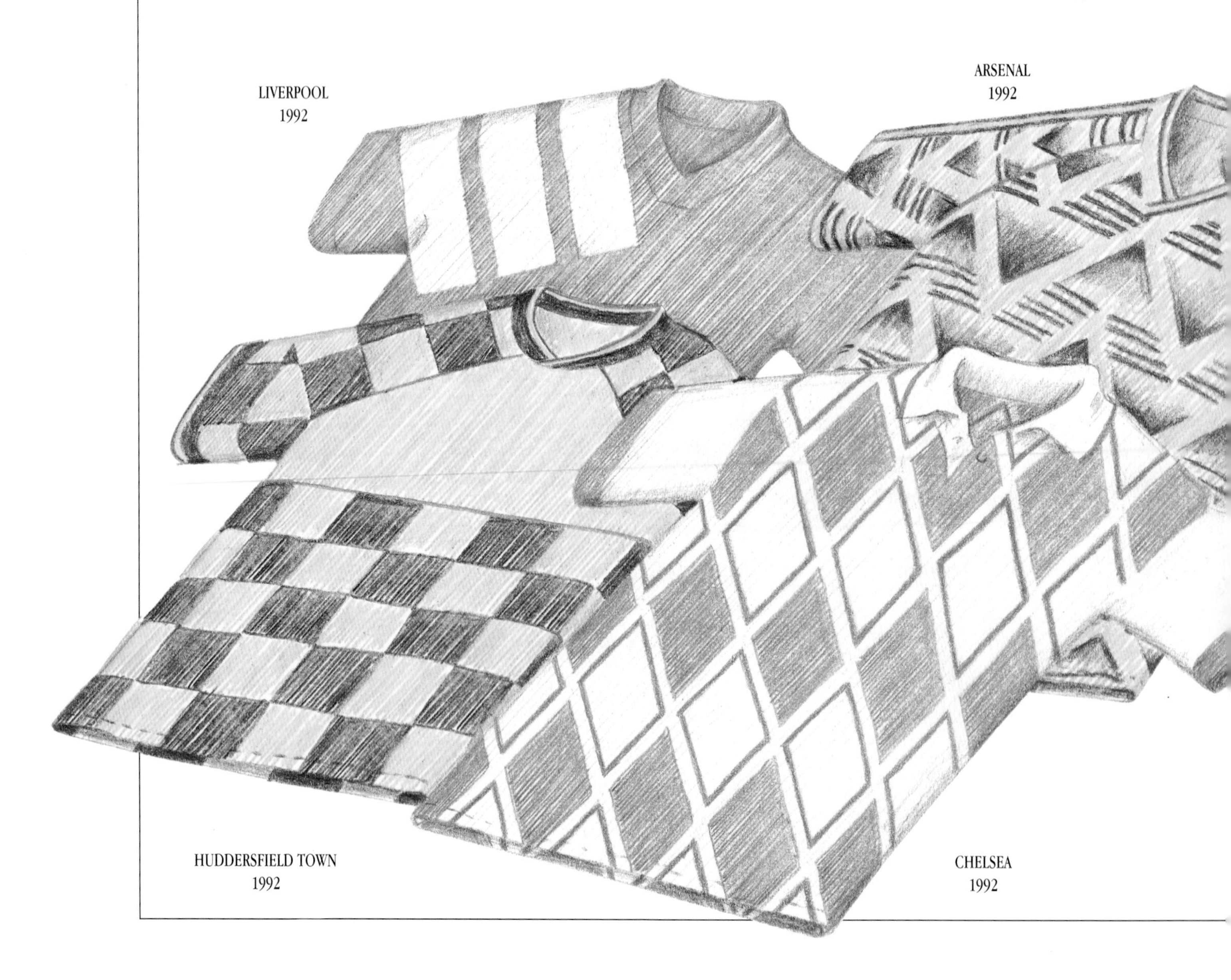

LIVERPOOL
1992

ARSENAL
1992

HUDDERSFIELD TOWN
1992

CHELSEA
1992

COVENTRY CITY
1976

Polish army club, Legia Warzawa wear their colours of red,white, black and green in many combinations.

official club colours and these would be rotated to suit each opposition in turn.

In the Football League, without any official ruling, it is likely that the fans will still be faced with multi-patterned alternatives which are aimed more at the leisure market than the playing field itself.

INFLUENTIAL STRIPS

Over the years, there have been many great occasions or eras which have impressed millions of fans everywhere. The World Cup, European finals or just league competitions have produced wonderful teams which have proved inspirational for many others seeking to emulate them.

By 1960, for example, the whole of Europe recognised Real Madrid as the ultimate masters, on and off the pitch. The Spanish supremos seemed to epitomise all that football should be. The club's all-white strip was neat and simple, its streamlined form devoid of all unnecessary detail and an obvious symbol of the future of successful football.

Don Revie was the first to recognise these qualities and used the all-white image to inspire his own team. The resulting success at Leeds helped to spread the message, so by the end of the decade there were many all-white strips in the Football League and elsewhere.

Earlier, yet another European team had symbolised a change in attitude in British football. In 1953, despite the World Cup hiccup three years earlier, English soccer fans still believed in the infallibility of their own heroes' abilities, but the visit of the Hungarian national team changed that forever. The Magical Magyars, as they became known, thrashed the home side 6-3 (they repeated the dose 7-1 the following year) and for the first time English football leaders started looking abroad for ideas. Billy Wright's team had looked so out of date in their baggy shirts and shorts, and from this time on League clubs began to turn to the Hungarians' style of compact, fitted jerseys and short shorts.

However, it was not only Europe that provided inspiration and a role model for English teams. For example, in the early history of the Football League both yellow and light blue did not feature strongly in the list of club colours. But after the World Cups of the 1970s there began a great re-think. The South American successes of Brazil and Argentina displayed great flair and creativity, the very things that British football was looking for. As a result, the yellow, green and blue of Pele and company became a popular choice for League club change strips, in addition to thousands of 'mini-Brazils' in park football.

Again after the 1978 World Cup there was a sudden rush to

HUNGARY
1953

REAL MADRID
1960

BRAZIL
1958-1970

ARGENTINA
1978

ARSENAL
1933

MANCHESTER UNITED
1957

sport light blue and white stripes as clubs such as Reading, Stockport, Colchester and Halifax sought to persuade their fans that they would soon be treated to football as served up by Kempes, Passarella et al. Spurs' idea of buying Ardiles and Villa, however, proved more practical!

Of course, there have been many strips worn by top English clubs such as Arsenal and Manchester United, which have provided as much or even more influence on Football League outfits, and this is covered further in the section INNOVATORS AND INNOVATIONS.

INNOVATORS AND INNOVATIONS

Manchester United, Arsenal and Liverpool have not only been the leaders of English football on the pitch. Throughout the League's history, their ambitions have put them in the vanguard of new ideas of management and presentation. Even the presentation of the club's colours has often made them innovators and leaders of styles which have been followed by their contemporaries.

It was part of Herbert Chapman's policy of making Arsenal a club apart when he introduced white sleeves and striped stockings. He not only wanted the team to look distinctive, but he also felt the players ought to be able to spot each other more easily on the pitch.

Some of the results of this thinking still remained at Highbury more than 30 years later, when another great manager took charge of a great club, this time at Old Trafford. Matt Busby was already looking towards Europe, and in the aftermath of the Hungarian experience, he began introducing a more streamlined continental strip. United wore the first 'V' collar, short-sleeved shirt and lightweight shorts, and for their continental campaigns, they wore red shorts, a theme taken up permanently by Liverpool later.

It was Manchester United, also, who were responsible for the later introduction of the round collar, before again it was Liverpool who revived the 'V' collar design. These two clubs have been particularly influential in recent decades, but much earlier Aston Villa, a dominant force in their own time, were the club most likely to be the innovator. In the 1920s and 1930s, the Villans wore their famous high-collared jerseys and even 20 years later they, with Don Revie's Manchester City, were responsible for the popularity of pinstriped shirts.

However, although there is no doubting the major influence of these successful clubs, there have also been many other one-off innovations over the years. The north-east provided a few in 1959. Probably inspired by the daring button-down 'V' collar of Gateshead and Crook Town, local 'big boys' Newcastle United normally a traditional club, astounded the football world by turning out their players in shorts with a white trim around the leg, plus stockings with vertical stripes on the turnover.

In the south Millwall, impressed by the Magpies' 'bravery', introduced their own piece of shorts magic with a blue and white candy-stripe special. The resulting wolf-whistles were probably the reason for the 30 year gap before the next innovations in shorts design, when Spurs incorporated the semi-circular trim in their Cup final kit.

Possibly the biggest period of design innovation was the mid-1970s. Admittedly most of the changes were inspired by manufacturers' whims, but these were the days of the Coventry shirt and shorts matching striped kit, West Ham's extended yoke and the famous York City 'Y-fronts'.

Today, most of the changes are superficial, with clubs and manufacturers alike more interested in bizarre printed patterns. Perhaps we will have to wait for another Don Revie, a man always thinking of new ways to develop ideas, before we see the likes of the stocking-tie number-flaps again. Not only was it a great public relations exercise when they were tossed to the fans at the end of every game, but probably was the only new element of kit since numbers were introduced in the late 1930s.

Above right: The Coventry shirts and shorts striped kit with the shorts of Millwall (top), Spurs (middle) and Newcastle (bottom).

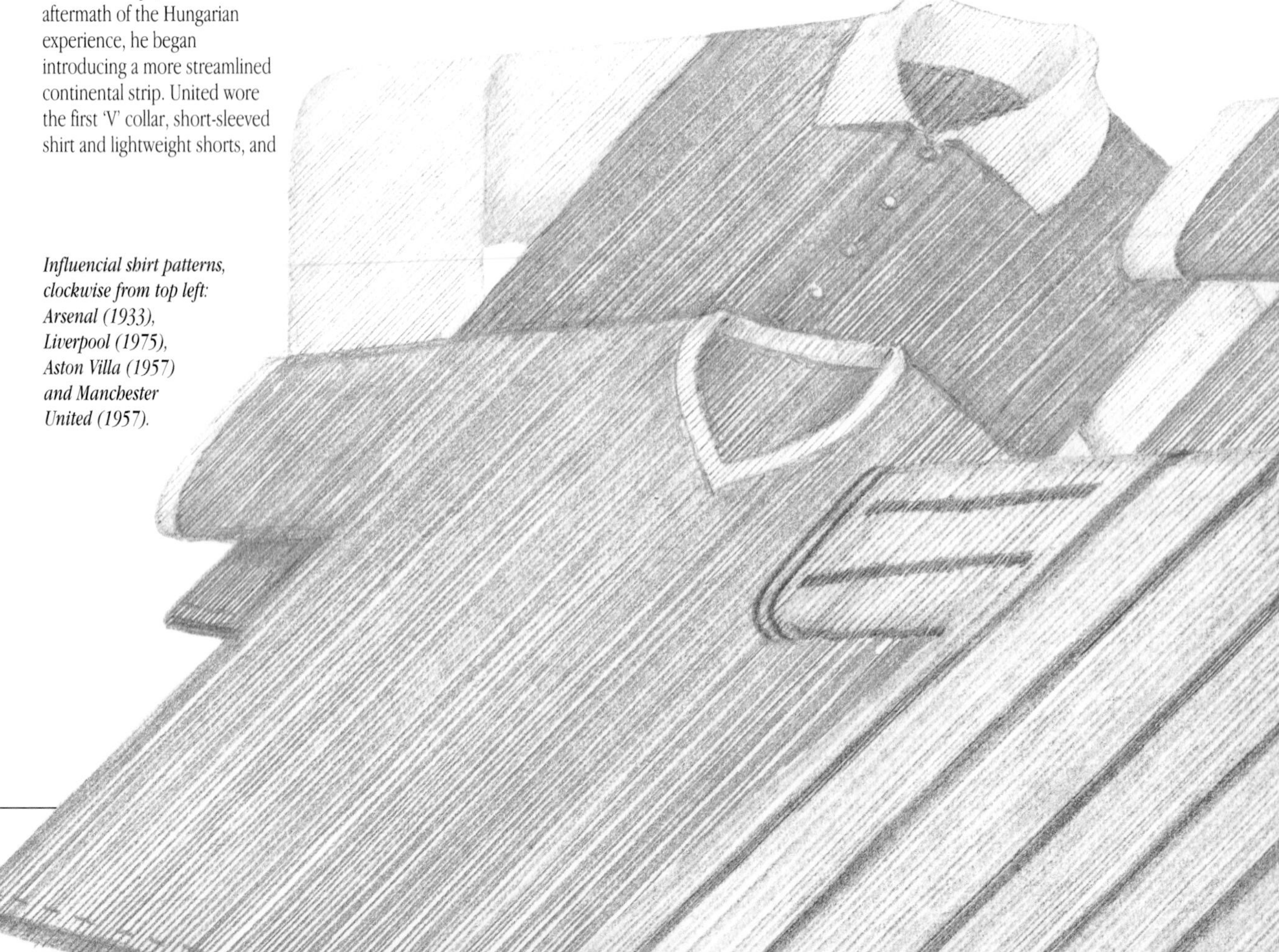

Influencial shirt patterns, clockwise from top left: Arsenal (1933), Liverpool (1975), Aston Villa (1957) and Manchester United (1957).

Below: Innovative stockings worn by Arsenal, Newcastle and Leeds.

REPLICA KITS

There was time not so long ago when if you went to a football match only 20 men would be wearing their team's official shirts. There are times today when it looks as if 20,000 are doing just that! Often on a warm spring or autumn day, a terrace banking can resemble a whole wall of red, blue or whatever the club colours may be. It must be an encouraging sight for the team to see so much obvious support awaiting them.

It is only in recent seasons that the phenomenon of replica shirts has been with us, but already it's not just in the stadia that they appear. At any time of the week, in the shopping arcade, or at night in clubs or bars, you might see a group of Gunners, Wolves or Magpies. It is an extra illustration of bonding, not only with the club, but within the fans themselves.

Even in the close season, the mass showing of shirts is well in evidence throughout the world. Popular parade grounds such as the holiday spots, Majorca, the Canaries or the Spanish mainland see young men wearing opposing club shirts strolling side by side. The only danger is the possible conflict between fans of different countries in these resorts.

Of course, it's not only the fans' local team shirts that might appeal. Such is the influence of fashion demand that the colours of minor Swiss or Brazilian clubs are sported with pride, providing that the design is sufficiently appealing.

But on the whole, it is within the club's immediate environment where most of the merchandising is carried out. The extra revenue for both the club, and indirectly the sponsor, ensures the maximum publicity and outlets. There have been many accusations of 'rip-offs' and general exploitation, particularly in the context of such rapid turn-around of style, but no-one can deny the demand for the latest version at either the beginning of the season or at Christmas.

Other sports have not been slow to spot the potential in terms of income and the encouragement of extra support. The two rugby codes in particular have developed sales on similar lines to soccer; and now the likes of ice hockey, basketball and even, unbelievably, cricket are doing the same. Although blazers will never be replaced in certain parts of Lords, it is quite obvious that on Sundays many grounds around the country will be a sight more colourful.

One final influence resulting from the introduction of replica kits is the effect on park football. Many junior teams in the past had to be satisfied by wearing the nearest equivalent they could find available, when attempting to ape their idols. Nowadays, of course, it is possible to wear exactly the same, and when you don your hero's shirt (with his name on the back if you want), who is to say you are not just as talented as he!

Fans on their way to see their heroes wear their replica kits to add to the impact of face paint and various flags.

ADVERTISING AND SPONSORSHIP

Up to the mid-1980s British football fans used to look at European clubs and despair at the 'advertising hoardings' claiming to be football shirts. In France, Austria and Denmark in particular, advertising and sponsorship panels often covered more surface area than the shirt material itself. Traditionalists in this country insisted that Football League clubs would never stoop to such depths, but as running costs increased and gate revenues could not keep pace, the lure of advertisers' budgets proved irresistible.

Happily, the four British associations decided that discretion would be the order of the day and although all League clubs eventually displayed advertising panels or company logos, the size of the lettering was limited and the number of sponsors was restricted to one per club, thus avoiding the Grand Prix Racing Driver effect which some Austrian club kits have.

As market forces dictated that top clubs were chased by the huge national and international companies, some strange traits developed. It soon became obvious, for example, that advertising was purely for the television coverage. Large hi-tech electronic companies such as JVC, Sharp, NEC and Commodore previously unassociated with fans on the terraces, relished the relatively cheap mass coverage to the consumer audience viewing at home.

As advertising on television increased, so the medium interest in coverage heightened. Independent, cable and satellite companies intensified the fight for air time which would attract further revenue.

Although it was mainly the super clubs that benefited from this change of attitude, at the lower end of the national league system, even the smaller clubs managed to attract sponsors interested in the coverage on possible local television and newspaper sports pages.

With the parallel development of replica strips, there was a further projection of the advertising message. Imagine the sponsor's delight at seeing the company logo being paraded up and down the High Street every day of the week. Obviously, the advertisers would only want to encourage even more changes in the replica offer.

Having become an accepted part of shirt presentation, it now seems only a matter of time before, in these days of leisure wear where designer labels dominate, the advertiser's logo will become all important and a true integral part of the shirt design.

Perhaps the advertisers' aims might be exactly like those of the manufacturers, seeing total domination of visual presentation, and we might just see NEC Everton or Newcastle Breweries United.

Below are examples of shirt advertising in the mid-1990s. All the clubs were successful during this period. Can you recognise their shirts?

A typical example of shirt advertising in Austria. Top Viennese club, FC Austria (seen here in violet and white) display at least four or five different sponsors' names, whilst their opponents, FC Tirol of Innsbruck, have two on the back of their shirts. The shorts are also used for this purpose, and presumably it will not be long before the stockings get into the act.

MANUFACTURERS

Back in the early days of organised football the first kits grew out of random available sportswear, such as rugby shirts, athletic vests and lightweight trousers. Often players would wear ordinary white working shirts before club colours were adopted.

The game at this stage was small scaled and regional, therefore clubs usually contacted the local supplier of sportswear who would even make up individual requests. Manufacturers of the kits themselves were often anonymous, and marketing was very low key.

As interest in football spread and became nationally popular, many of these manufacturers realised the potential of increased sales, but until the Second World War the market was fairly evenly divided.

However, it was during the 1950s that Umbro and Bukta began to dominate the cladding of Football League players, probably because of their location near the big demand from the Lancashire and Yorkshire clubs. The advertising would declare 'as worn by Manchester United, Football League champions' etc, but on the pitch there was no evidence of the visual company promotions which was to come later.

Even at this stage, local suppliers had an important say. Norwich City's silk shirts arrived courtesy of an East Anglian specialist, and Torquay's new blue and gold was a west country original.

But come the late 1960s, Britain's manufacturers slowly became aware of a challenge from afar, as two giants from the continent began their huge international expansion. Puma and Adidas had already made inroads into the English boot market when the latter company revolutionised kit styling by introducing a logo statement on to the kit itself.

In Germany teams had often worn a contrast coloured strip along the sleeves and shorts, but Adidas cleverly incorporated their three stripe motif here, and for the first time observers could see the extent of the popularity of that company's kit. Clever marketing during World Cup periods and the use of major clubs for maximum coverage gave Adidas a big lead in Britain as well as Europe.

Of course other manufacturers were quick to respond and they all in turn had their logos in strips down the sleeves etc. This in turn led to a kind of stalemate and it was the newly formed Admiral in the 1970s who were next to break through. Using a mixture of clever marketing and the first of the tailor-made 'designer kits', it was Admiral who gave us the Coventry matching shirts and shorts set, multi-width stripes

An early suppliers' advertisement.

A smart strip from the 1950s, but the manufacturer was anonymous.

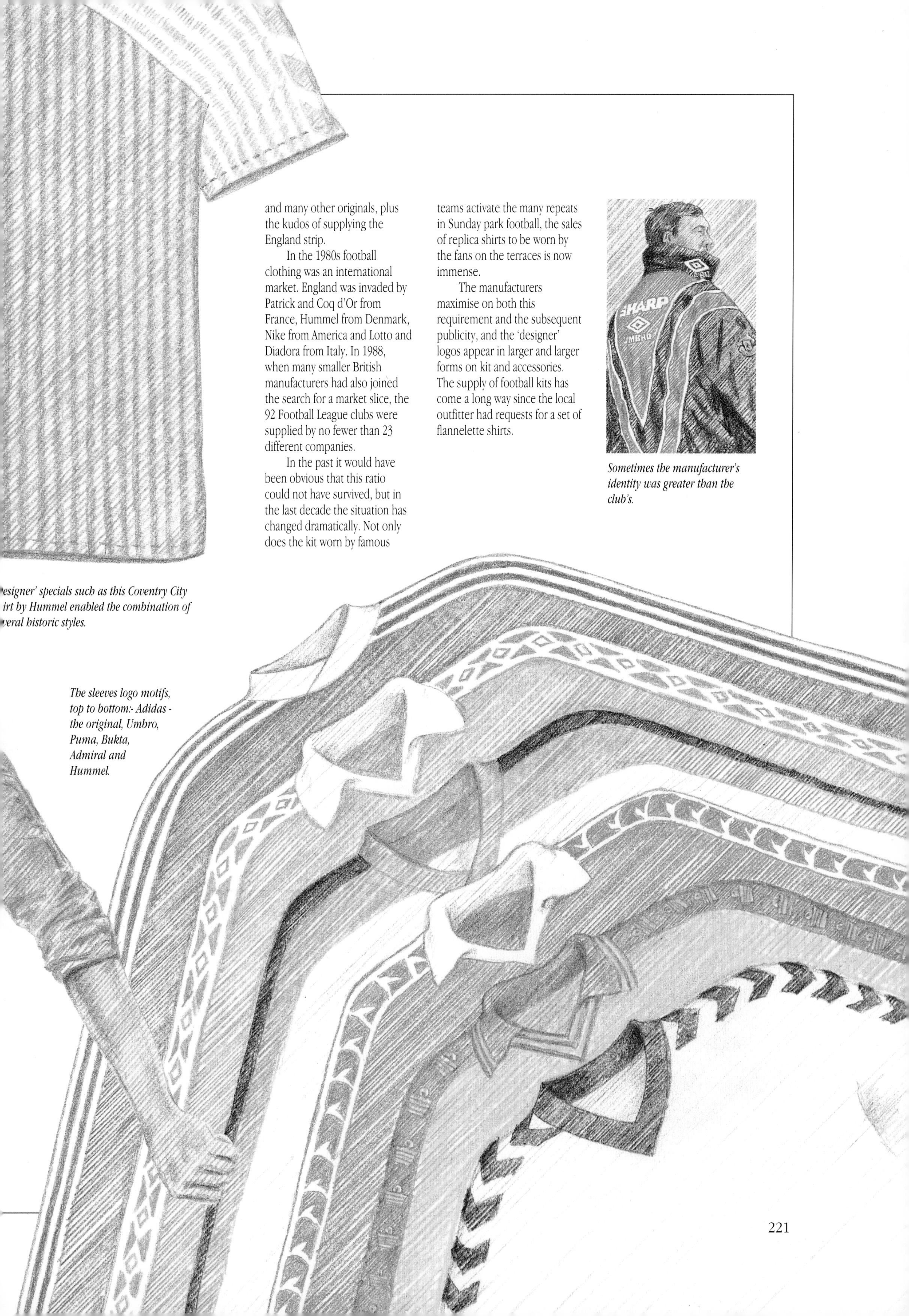

and many other originals, plus the kudos of supplying the England strip.

In the 1980s football clothing was an international market. England was invaded by Patrick and Coq d'Or from France, Hummel from Denmark, Nike from America and Lotto and Diadora from Italy. In 1988, when many smaller British manufacturers had also joined the search for a market slice, the 92 Football League clubs were supplied by no fewer than 23 different companies.

In the past it would have been obvious that this ratio could not have survived, but in the last decade the situation has changed dramatically. Not only does the kit worn by famous teams activate the many repeats in Sunday park football, the sales of replica shirts to be worn by the fans on the terraces is now immense.

The manufacturers maximise on both this requirement and the subsequent publicity, and the 'designer' logos appear in larger and larger forms on kit and accessories. The supply of football kits has come a long way since the local outfitter had requests for a set of flannelette shirts.

Sometimes the manufacturer's identity was greater than the club's.

esigner' specials such as this Coventry City irt by Hummel enabled the combination of veral historic styles.

The sleeves logo motifs, top to bottom:- Adidas - the original, Umbro, Puma, Bukta, Admiral and Hummel.

THE NEXT GENERATION?

This book is devoted to clubs who have played in the Football League at some time in their histories. Many of them have spent the best part of a century in this exalted company, some for just a few seasons, but there are also many other successful clubs who so far have not managed to take that final step.

However, now that many of these 'senior' non-League clubs have updated their ground quality to satisfy Football League standards they have a great opportunity to gain promotion to the national league.

The following clubs are either currently near the top of the GM Vauxhall Conference or have had several seasons challenging for the title.

ALTRINCHAM RUSHDEN & DIAMONDS CHELTENHAM TOWN HEDNESFORD TO

KETTERING TOWN YEOVIL TOWN KIDDERMINSTER HARRIERS

ALTRINCHAM
Although they spent last season in the Unibond Northern Premier, the Robins been on the fringe of Football League recognition for many years, with a long history of successes including FA Trophy wins in 1978 and 1986, Northern Premier Championships and Cheshire League and Cup victories.

CHELTENHAM
The Robins from Gloucestershire were an established GMVC side until losing their way for five years. Now they are back with a vengeance, looking very strong. Manager Steve Cotterill could well create the surprise of 1998.

DAGENHAM & REDBRIDGE
The Daggers slipped away badly in 1997, but no-one would be surprised if they bounced back bigger than ever! The club is used to survival and readjustment. Over the years, Ilford, Leytonstone, Walthamstowe Avenue and Dagenham have merged to form this modern combination. There's still room for another club in East London. We wish them well!

HEDNESFORD
After over a hundred years of playing in minor leagues, the Pitmen have shot through the Southern League system to the upper regionsof the GMVC itself. The proximity of Birmingham no longer seems to be a major deterant. Hednesford have visions of local derbies with Walsall – and maybe others?

KETTERING
The last few years have been disappointing for the Poppies. Until recently there were very few non-League clubs who could claim to be as consistantly strong. Although the club has not won many major honours, it has always looked likely to challenge for a Football League place. Hopefully the current opportunity will not be squandered.

KIDDERMINSTER
The Harriers have been so close to gaining entry to the Football League: denied when the ground wasn't quite ready and pipped by Macclesfield when it was. An uncharacteristally bad start in 1998 will oblige them to wait for at least another season or two. Surely it *is* just a matter of time?

MORECAMBE SLOUGH TOWN DAGENHAM & REDBRIDGE

TELFORD UNITED WOKING STEVENAGE BOROUGH

MORECAMBE
The Shrimps won the FA Trophy in 1974, but then proceeded to underachieve for twenty years. Strange for a club which produced Gordon Milne and Ray Charnley. However, under the management of Jim Harvey, the Lancashire club has recovered much of its former glory, and as the century comes to a close they are again pushing very strongly for promotion.

RUSHDEN & DIAMONDS
Neither Rushden Town or Irthlingborough Diamonds were ever going to frighten anyone, but when the two amalgamated in 1982, backed by the money of Doc Martin, it was a very different matter. The Diamonds swept though the Southern League system, and in their smart new stadium are now challenging strongly for a place in the Football League itself. Ambition at its most efficient.

SLOUGH
The Rebels are not the biggest household name in non-League football, but over the years the club has had significant success in cup and league competitions. It is hoped that recent uncertainty will not undermine any progress.

STEVENAGE
Boro are new town babes – having been formed only in 1976 – but progress has been phenomenal: Chiltern Youth League to the top of the Conference in 19 years. The 1990s are seeing the club as GMVC superstars who are capable of taking on big clubs in knockout competition too. Will the striking red and white strips be seen in the Football League?

TELFORD
The Lilywhites were the first of the 'new town' success stories. Great cup fighters, they have won the FA Trophy three times and been in the FA Cup 5th round, but have not won any major championships. However, they have been an everpresent in the GMVC up to 1998 and despite recent relegation have a strong base for future development.

WOKING
After wiining the Amateur Cup in 1958, the 'Cards' quietly dozed through three decades in the Isthmian League before chairman Phil Ledger and manager Geoff Chapple made them a major power in the land. Three FA Trophy wins in the 1990s accompanied two GMVC runner-up slots. The new leadership faces quite a challenge.

YEOVIL
Yeovil have won no national non-League titles, but lots of Southern and Isthmian championships, particularly from the 1950s to the 1980s. The Glovers really look the part these days with an impressive brand new, 8,700 capacity stadium at Huish Park and a progressive board and management. A new future at a higher level might mean the end of a giant-killing reputation.

THE ALMOST YEARS

Most of the previous pages have been dedicated to the finest moments in each club's history. In most cases, the decision has been an easy one: a League title, a Cup win, a promotion or even just a highest position was an obvious choice. However, for some clubs, there were other moments when an almost equal success was achieved.

Reading's earlier achievements in the second flight have only just been superseded by the latest 'Royals' fantastic push towards the Premier League in 1995. Crewe's equally recent successes have only just put the promotion season of 1963 season in perspective. At the time, it was the Alex's major period of hope for the future.

And how can one ignore the achievements of the Rotherham side that were runners-up in the inaugural season of the League Cup. That side, which was only one goal away from a major trophy, certainly pushed the 1955 version all the way.

These three examples illustrate most of what football clubs thrive upon, great memories, near things and the hope for an even greater future.

CREWE ALEXANDRA
1963

ROTHERHAM UNITED
1961

READING
1987